BEST-LOVED
HOLIDAY
RECIPES

Quick and Easy Holiday Cooking

Meredith Corporation
Des Moines, Iowa

BEST-LOVED
HOLIDAY
RECIPES

Meredith Corporation Print Advantage
Vice President, Production: Bruce Heston
National Sales Director: Linda Hyden
Associate Director: Doug Johnston

Waterbury Publications, Inc.
Editorial Director: Lisa Kingsley
Associate Editor: Tricia Laning
Creative Director: Ken Carlson
Associate Design Director: Doug Samuelson
Graphic Designer: Kim Hopkins
Graphic Designer: Mindy Samuelson

Meredith Publishing Group
President: Jack Griffin
Executive Vice President: Andy Sareyan
Vice President, Manufacturing: Bruce Heston

Meredith Corporation
Chairman of the Board: William T. Kerr
President and Chief Executive Officer: Stephen M. Lacy

In Memoriam: E. T. Meredith III (1933-2003)

All of us at Meredith Print Advantage are dedicated to providing you with information
and ideas to enhance your home. We welcome your comments and suggestions. Write to
us at: MeredithPrint Advantage, 1716 Locust St., Des Moines, IA 50309-3023.

Cover Photograph: Festive Red Velvet Cake, page 72;
Back Cover Photograph: Turkey with Raspberry Sauce, page 14

Table of Contents

Festive Red Velvet Cake, page 72

Introduction 4

Christmas Feasts in a Flash 6

Easy-Does-It Appetizers 28

Snappy Breakfasts and Brunches . . 44

Holiday Breads in a Hurry 56

Desserts on the Double 68

Simplified Sweets 82

Save-the-Day Slow Cooker 102

"Gingerbread" Houses
   without the Gingerbread 112

Edible Gifts in a Jiff 118

Busy-Day Dinners for December . . 130

Fast and Fancy
   New Year's Celebration 140

Emergency Substitutions 156

Index 157

Plump Apple Dumplings with
Caramel Sauce, page 79

This collection of quick and easy recipes will make your holiday season the best you've ever had!

Open your homes and your hearts to a special type of Christmas this year: one spent with your family rather than with the kitchen utensils and stove. From appetizers to desserts, and everything in between, these reliable recipes will keep your dinner guests satisfied, while allowing you plenty of time to join in the holiday fun.

Best-Loved Holiday Recipes features recipes that cut preparation times drastically without compromising the flavor and appeal of home cooking. By using convenience products, smaller portions of food, and that good old slow cooker, you can be in and out of the kitchen in no time—even after baking cookies, preparing appetizers, and laying out a complete Christmas feast.

A chapter is dedicated to freeing the stove and oven by cooking foods in the beloved slow cooker. Pull that old friend out of the cupboard and let it take care of at least one holiday dish for you. Whether you're looking for a main dish, side dish, or dessert that requires little preparation and even less attention, you'll find the perfect recipe for that portable cooking invention.

And don't fret: The hectic month of December is not overlooked! With Christmas shopping, holiday visiting, card writing, and package wrapping—not to mention the parties and pageants to attend—this month is definitely the busiest time of year. Who wants to cook dinner after all that hustle and bustle? With a few common ingredients (many in your cupboard already) and a few extra minutes, you can whip up a dinner that will calm and satisfy any hungry family.

So who's ready for the holiday goodies? Well, start reading and planning! The Christmas season is a glorious time to indulge in a sampling of foods, from the special cookies to the holiday ham; but it's an even better time to relish the company of loved ones. So rather than spending too much time hovering over pots on the stove, peruse these holiday recipes to find the perfect feasts and sweets to fit into your Christmas schedule.

Easy Cranberry-Orange Ring, page 122

Christmas Feasts in a Flash

WHETHER YOU'RE LOOKING FOR AN ENTIRE MENU on which to base your Christmas feast, or just searching for one last side dish to round out a meal, this chapter caters to the needs of every home cook. With actual hands-on preparation times at 30 minutes or less, these recipes will be finished—or at least in the oven or on the stove—before you know it. Spending less time in the kitchen doesn't mean you have to sacrifice that gourmet touch. From Holiday Beef Tenderloin to Quick Bread Salad, this chapter provides all the flavor of a traditional Christmas feast with less time spent in the kitchen.

Holiday Beef Tenderloin, page 1

Potato and Leek Soup

Resembling a giant scallion (green onion) in appearance, leeks are favored for their mellow flavor. To clean, remove wilted outer leaves, slice the leek lengthwise in half, and rinse it thoroughly under cold running water. Cut off the root and green tops and use only the remaining white section.

Prep: 20 minutes **Cook:** 30 minutes
Makes: 8 servings

6	cups cubed, peeled russet or Idaho potatoes (2 pounds)
2	14-ounce cans chicken broth
2	cups sliced celery (4 stalks)
⅔	cup thinly sliced leek (2 medium)
¼	cup butter or margarine
4	cups cubed, peeled sweet potatoes (1½ pounds)
½	teaspoon black pepper
½	teaspoon ground nutmeg
3	cups milk
1	teaspoon salt
	Salt and black pepper

1. In a 4-quart Dutch oven or large saucepan combine russet potatoes and 2 cups of the broth. Bring to boiling; reduce heat. Cover and simmer about 10 minutes or until potatoes are tender; do not drain. Cool slightly.

2. Transfer the potato mixture to a blender or food processor. Cover and blend until smooth; set aside.

3. In a large saucepan cook celery and leek in hot butter for 3 to 4 minutes or until tender. Add sweet potatoes, the remaining broth, the ½ teaspoon pepper, and nutmeg. Bring to boiling; reduce heat. Cover and simmer for 10 minutes. Stir in pureed potato mixture, milk, and the 1 teaspoon salt. Cook and stir about 5 minutes more or until thickened. Season to taste with additional salt and pepper.

Nutrition Facts per serving: 255 cal., 8 g total fat (4 g sat. fat), 24 mg chol., 822 mg sodium, 39 g carbo., 4 g fiber, 8 g pro.
Daily Values: 177% vit. A, 29% vit. C, 15% calcium, 9% iron

Creamy Wild Rice, Mushroom, and Spinach Soup

Many versions of creamy wild rice soup circulate through the culinary world at one time or another, but this one—featuring fresh spinach and wild mushrooms—takes the prize. Flavored with bacon, shallots, and sherry, this soup will start the Christmas meal in style.

Prep: 20 minutes **Cook:** 50 minutes
Makes: 8 side-dish servings

3	slices bacon
⅓	cup finely chopped shallots
⅓	cup finely chopped carrot
2	cloves garlic, minced
3	cups chicken broth
⅓	cup wild rice, rinsed and drained
2	cups sliced fresh cremini, shiitake, and/or button mushrooms

Healthful Soup Thickeners Ever have a vegetable cream soup that tasted more like butter or cream than vegetables? Most likely such a soup relied on cream, cornstarch, and/or a mixture of butter and flour to thicken the soup. Such thickening agents work fine in some recipes but can mask the delicate flavors of certain vegetable-based soups. The thickening agent used for Potato and Leek Soup (recipe, above) is made by first cooking potato in chicken stock, then pureeing or finely mashing the mixture. The resulting puree is naturally thickened by the starch in the potato, and requires no further additions to aid in consistency. What's more, the puree allows the full flavors of the vegetables to come through, and reduces unnecessary calories from cream, butter, and/or flour.

Potato and Leek Soup

Creamy Wild Rice, Mushroom, and Spinach Soup

2   tablespoons butter, softened
2   tablespoons all-purpose flour
¼   teaspoon salt
⅛   teaspoon black pepper
2   cups whipping cream, half-and-half,
      or light cream
4   cups chopped fresh spinach
1   tablespoon dry sherry (optional)

1. In a large saucepan cook bacon over medium heat until crisp, turning occasionally. Remove bacon from saucepan and drain on paper towels; reserve 1 tablespoon drippings in saucepan. Crumble bacon and set aside.

2. Add shallots, carrot, and garlic to drippings in the saucepan. Cook and stir over medium heat about 4 minutes or until tender. Add broth and wild rice.

Bring to boiling; reduce heat. Cover and simmer for 35 minutes. Add mushrooms; simmer, covered, for 5 to 10 minutes more until rice is tender.

3. In a small bowl stir together butter, flour, salt, and pepper to make a paste. Stir the flour mixture into the rice mixture in saucepan. Cook and stir until slightly thickened and bubbly. Cook and stir for 1 minute more. Add whipping cream. Cook and stir over medium heat until heated through (do not boil). Stir in spinach and sherry, if desired. Ladle soup into bowls. Sprinkle with crumbled bacon.

Nutrition Facts per serving: 320 cal., 29 g total fat (17 g sat. fat), 95 mg chol., 550 mg sodium, 12 g carbo., 1 g fiber, 6 g pro.
Daily Values: 61% vit. A, 10% vit. C, 6% calcium, 5% iron

Asparagus and Squash Soup

Brimming with fresh vegetables and garnished with lemon slices, this smooth creamy soup is a snap to make. When the lush green of late spring returns, this dish is also perfect to serve at supper on the porch.

Start to Finish: 30 minutes
Makes: 8 side-dish servings

1	cup chopped carrots (4 medium)
⅔	cup finely chopped shallots
2	tablespoons butter or olive oil
3	14-ounce cans chicken broth
1	teaspoon dried thyme or tarragon, crushed
¼	teaspoon freshly ground black pepper
1	pound asparagus, trimmed and cut into ½-inch pieces
2	small yellow summer squash, quartered and thinly sliced (about 2 cups)
1	cup whipping cream
8	thin lemon slices
½	cup chopped, seeded, and peeled tomato (1 medium)

1. In a large saucepan cook carrots and shallots in hot butter over medium heat about 5 minutes or until nearly tender, stirring occasionally.

2. Add broth, thyme, and pepper. Bring just to boiling; add asparagus and squash. Reduce heat; simmer, uncovered, for 3 to 5 minutes or until tender. Stir in whipping cream and heat through. Ladle soup into bowls. Top each serving with a lemon slice and chopped tomato.

Nutrition Facts per serving: 171 cal., 15 g total fat (8 g sat. fat), 51 mg chol., 655 mg sodium, 8 g carbo., 2 g fiber, 3 g pro.
Daily Values: 55% vit. A, 19% vit. C, 5% calcium, 6% iron

Cauliflower-Crab Chowder

This creamy seafood chowder will whet the appetites of your Christmas guests and prepare them for the meal ahead. With only 15 minutes of prep, this chowder frees you to take care of more important holiday tasks.

Prep: 15 minutes **Cook:** 20 minutes
Makes: 6 appetizer servings

2	cups loose-pack frozen cauliflower
½	cup water
3	tablespoons butter
3	tablespoons all-purpose flour
1	14-ounce can vegetable or chicken broth
1¼	cups milk
1	3-ounce package cream cheese, cubed
2	tablespoons chopped pimiento or roasted red sweet pepper
2	teaspoons dried parsley
1	teaspoon dried chives
¼	teaspoon salt
1	6-ounce package frozen crabmeat, thawed and drained
¼	cup dry white wine or dry sherry

1. In a medium saucepan combine cauliflower and water. Bring to boiling; reduce heat. Cover and simmer about 4 minutes or until crisp-tender. Do not drain. Cut large pieces of cauliflower; set aside.

2. Meanwhile, in a large saucepan melt butter. Stir in flour. Add broth and milk. Cook and stir over medium heat until slightly thickened and bubbly.

3. Stir in the undrained cauliflower, the cream cheese, pimiento, parsley, chives, and salt. Cook and stir over low heat until cheese melts. Stir in crab; heat through. Stir in wine. Serve immediately.

Nutrition Facts per serving: 195 cal., 13 g total fat (7 g sat. fat), 64 mg chol., 564 mg sodium, 9 g carbo., 1 g fiber, 10 g pro.
Daily Values: 13% vit. A, 34% vit. C, 11% calcium, 6% iron

Golden Fruit Holiday Salad

Fresh Calimyrna figs are sold in most supermarkets around the holiday season. If you happen to find them in your area, substitute them for the dried version.

Start to Finish: 30 minutes
Makes: 8 side-dish servings

10	cups mesclun or other spring salad greens (two 5-ounce packages)
1	medium pear, cored and thinly sliced
12	dried Calimyrna (light) figs, quartered
⅓	cup golden raisins
½	cup mayonnaise or salad dressing
3	tablespoons milk
2	tablespoons chutney, snipped
½	to 1 teaspoon curry powder
⅛	teaspoon salt
⅓	cup sliced almonds, toasted
¼	cup sliced green onions (2)

1. Divide greens, pear slices, figs, and raisins evenly among 8 salad plates.

2. For the dressing, in a small bowl stir together mayonnaise, milk, chutney, curry powder, and salt.

3. Spoon the dressing over each salad. Sprinkle with almonds and green onions. Serve immediately.

Nutrition Facts per serving: 253 cal., 14 g total fat (2 g sat. fat), 10 mg chol., 145 mg sodium, 32 g carbo., 5 g fiber, 3 g pro.
Daily Values: 6% vit. A, 9% vit. C, 9% calcium, 8% iron

Quick Bread Salad

In Italy, day-old bread is put to good use as a replacement for croutons. The much larger pieces hold the dressing better and impart exceptional flavor in every bite. If you like, skip making the homemade dressing and replace it with a purchased vinaigrette.

Start to Finish: 20 minutes **Makes:** 8 to 10 servings

⅓	cup olive oil
¼	cup red wine vinegar
1	teaspoon sugar
1	teaspoon dried oregano, crushed
½	teaspoon salt
½	teaspoon black pepper
8	ounces whole wheat sourdough or other country-style bread, cut into 1½-inch cubes
1	10-ounce package Italian blend salad greens
1	large tomato, cut into thin wedges
½	cup halved yellow cherry tomatoes or yellow sweet pepper cut into ½-inch pieces
¾	cup pitted Greek black olives or other ripe olives

1. For dressing, in a screw-top jar combine oil, vinegar, sugar, oregano, salt, and black pepper. Cover and shake well.

2. In a large salad bowl combine bread cubes, greens, tomato wedges, yellow cherry tomatoes, and olives. Drizzle with the dressing; toss gently to coat. Serve immediately.

Nutrition Facts per serving: 183 cal., 11 g total fat (2 g sat. fat), 0 mg chol., 433 mg sodium, 18 g carbo., 2 g fiber, 3 g pro.
Daily Values: 9% vit. A, 9% vit. C, 5% calcium, 9% iron

Quick Bread Salad

Christmas Chutney

This cranberry condiment pairs beautifully with meat and poultry, and is also tasty with crackers and cheese.

Prep: 15 minutes **Cook:** 15 minutes
Cool: 30 minutes **Makes:** 2½ cups

1	cup dried **Mission figs,** coarsely snipped
2	cups fresh cranberries
1	medium orange, peeled and coarsely chopped
1½	cups sugar
⅓	cup cider vinegar
¼	cup dry sherry or orange juice
½	teaspoon curry powder
½	teaspoon ground cinnamon
¼	teaspoon ground ginger
⅛	teaspoon ground allspice

1. In a large saucepan combine all ingredients; bring to boiling. Reduce heat and boil gently, uncovered, for 12 to 15 minutes or until mixture is thick and liquid is syrupy. Cool.

2. Transfer chutney to a covered container and store in the refrigerator for up to 1 week.

Nutrition Facts per 2 tablespoons chutney: 94 cal., 0 g total fat (0 g sat. fat), 0 mg chol., 1 mg sodium, 23 g carbo., 2 g fiber, 0 g pro.
Daily Values: 8% vit. C, 2% calcium, 2% iron

Spinach Salad with Apples and Pecans

Tender baby spinach, endive, apple, and toasted nuts are tossed with creamy blue cheese and a light vinaigrette dressing for a deliciously different appetizer salad. If desired, the endive can be eliminated from the recipe and replaced with extra spinach.

Start to Finish: 20 minutes **Makes:** 8 servings

1	small shallot, minced
2	tablespoons sherry vinegar
1	tablespoon red wine vinegar
2	teaspoons Dijon-style mustard
⅓	cup olive oil
¼	teaspoon salt
	Dash black pepper
1	6- or 7-ounce package fresh baby spinach

Christmas Chutney

1 **large Belgian endive, cut into thin
   strips (5 ounces)**
1 **large apple or pear, cored, quartered,
   and sliced**
2 **ounces Stilton or blue cheese,
   crumbled**
½ **cup pecan or walnut halves, toasted**

1. For dressing, in a small bowl whisk together shallot, sherry vinegar, red wine vinegar, and mustard. Gradually whisk in oil, salt, and pepper until combined. Set aside.

2. In a large bowl combine spinach, endive, and apple. Drizzle with dressing; toss to coat. Divide salad among 8 plates. Sprinkle each serving with cheese and pecans.

Nutrition Facts per serving: 170 cal., 16 g total fat (3 g sat. fat), 5 mg chol., 220 mg sodium, 5 g carbo., 2 g fiber, 3 g pro.
Daily Values: 42% vit. A, 15% vit. C, 7% calcium, 6% iron

Cranberry-Pear Sauce

Made with ruby port, crystallized ginger, and pears, this cranberry sauce barely resembles the holiday dish your grandma used to make. Serve it with roasted turkey and chicken, or pair it with roasted pork as a sensational sauce.

Start to Finish: 30 minutes **Makes:** about 3 cups

1 **medium tangerine or orange**
1 **12-ounce package fresh cranberries**
1 **medium pear, peeled, cored, and
   diced (1 cup)**
¾ **cup sugar**
½ **cup ruby port**
2 **tablespoons crystallized ginger,
   chopped**
   **Tangerine or orange peel strips
   (optional)**

1. Finely shred the peel from the tangerine and squeeze the juice into a bowl.

2. In a 2-quart saucepan combine shredded peel and juice, the cranberries, pear, sugar, and port. Bring to boiling; reduce heat. Boil gently, uncovered, for 10 to 15 minutes or until the cranberries pop but still have some shape and the

sauce thickens. Stir in crystallized ginger. If desired, garnish with additional tangerine or orange peel. Serve warm or chilled with roasted turkey, chicken, or pork. Store leftovers in a tightly covered container in the refrigerator for up to 1 week.

Nutrition Facts per ¼ cup: 92 cal., 0 g total fat (0 g sat. fat), 0 mg chol., 2 mg sodium, 21 g carbo., 2 g fiber, 0 g pro.
Daily Values: 1% vit. A, 11% vit. C, 1% calcium, 2% iron

Herb Gravy

If you're planning to serve the traditional roasted poultry for Christmas dinner, this brandy-herb gravy is a quick and flavorful necessity. Dried herbs can be substituted for fresh to save both time and money.

Start to Finish: 20 minutes **Makes:** about 2¼ cups

   **Pan drippings from roasted turkey,
   goose, or chicken**
   Chicken broth
¼ **cup all-purpose flour**
2 **tablespoons apple brandy or brandy**
1 **tablespoon snipped fresh thyme or
   1 teaspoon dried thyme, crushed**
1 **tablespoon snipped fresh sage or
   1 teaspoon dried sage, crushed**
   Salt and black pepper
   Fresh sprig of thyme (optional)

1. Pour pan drippings into a fat separator or into a large glass measuring cup. If using a fat separator, pour off the fat into a glass measuring cup. If using a large measuring cup, use a spoon to skim fat from the drippings. Pour ¼ cup of the fat into a medium saucepan; discard remaining fat.

2. Add enough chicken broth to the drippings in the measuring cup to equal 2 cups. Stir flour into fat in the saucepan. Add drippings mixture all at once to flour mixture in saucepan. Stir in brandy, thyme, and sage. Cook and stir over medium heat until slightly thickened and bubbly. Cook and stir for 1 minute more. Season gravy to taste with salt and pepper. Pour gravy into a gravy boat or bowl. If desired, garnish with a fresh sprig of thyme.

Nutrition Facts per ¼ cup: 79 cal., 6 g total fat (2 g sat. fat), 5 mg chol., 255 mg sodium, 3 g carbo., 0 g fiber, 1 g pro.
Daily Values: 1% vit. C, 1% iron

Christmas Countdown Not all of the tasks on your dinner to-do list have to wait until the last minute. Plenty of chores can be accomplished prior to the big day.

Two weeks ahead

- Confirm the number of dinner guests planning to attend your feast. If any guests are unsure of their plans, assume they're coming. Too much food is better than not enough.
- Plan the menu for each course of the meal. When picking each menu item, be sure not to select too many dishes that need to be in the oven or on the stove at the same time.
- Write your shopping list, including all the ingredients you'll need for Christmas dinner.
- Decide when the best time to shop is. Do you have enough space in the refrigerator for all the groceries?
- Think about cookware, dishes, glassware, etc. Do you have everything you'll need, or is there something that you need to borrow or purchase?

One week ahead

- Make cranberry sauces or chutneys you plan to serve. These items will keep well in the refrigerator.
- Will you make homemade rolls, cookies, cakes, or pies? If possible, bake these items ahead and freeze until the day before the dinner.

Two to three days ahead

- Depending on the weight of the turkey (if using), remove it from the freezer and place it in the refrigerator to thaw (see Turkey Thaw on page 16).

The day before

- Set the table.
- Assemble all of the serving dishes and utensils for the meal.
- Thaw any frozen baked desserts you plan to serve.
- Prepare any recipe that can be stored in the refrigerator and reheated the next day.

Turkey with Raspberry Sauce

To satisfy that holiday turkey craving without roasting an entire bird, try this simple recipe using turkey tenderloins. If you prefer your poultry without a fruity sauce, prepare the meat as directed and serve it with a purchased gravy.

Prep: 15 minutes **Cook:** 20 minutes
Makes: 4 servings

1	teaspoon dried thyme, crushed
1	teaspoon dried sage, crushed
1	teaspoon salt
½	teaspoon black pepper
4	turkey tenderloins (about 2 pounds)
2	tablespoons olive oil or cooking oil
½	cup seedless raspberry jam
¼	cup orange juice
¼	cup red wine vinegar

1. In a small bowl combine thyme, sage, salt, and pepper; rub evenly over turkey tenderloins.

2. In an extra-large skillet cook turkey in hot oil over medium heat for 18 to 20 minutes or until turkey is no longer pink (170°F), turning once. Remove turkey from skillet; cover it with foil to keep warm.

3. For raspberry sauce, stir together jam, orange juice, and vinegar; carefully add to skillet. Bring to boiling; reduce heat. Boil gently, uncovered, about 2 minutes or until sauce is desired consistency. Bias-cut tenderloins into ½-inch slices. Arrange turkey on 4 dinner plates. Drizzle with the raspberry sauce.

Nutrition Facts per serving: 221 cal., 5 g total fat (1 g sat. fat), 68 mg chol., 206 mg sodium, 15 g carbo., 0 g fiber, 27 g pro.
Daily Values: 1% vit. A, 9% vit. C, 3% calcium, 9% iron

Turkey with Raspberry Sauce

Spicy Glazed Turkey Breast

If your family doesn't like dark meat, a whole turkey breast is probably a more economical choice for the holiday feast.

Prep: 20 minutes **Roast:** 2 hours **Stand:** 10 minutes
Oven: 325°F **Makes:** 8 servings

1	10-ounce jar jalapeño pepper jelly
2	tablespoons lime juice
1	clove garlic, minced
¾	teaspoon salt
¾	teaspoon black pepper
1	6- to 6 ½-pound whole turkey breast
	Salt and black pepper
	Jalapeño pepper jelly (optional)

1. For glaze, in a small saucepan stir together jalapeño pepper jelly, lime juice, garlic, the ¾ teaspoon salt, and the ¾ teaspoon pepper. Cook and stir over medium heat until jelly is melted. Remove from heat and set aside.

2. Sprinkle turkey with additional salt and pepper. Place turkey, skin side up, on a rack in a shallow roasting pan. Insert an oven-safe meat thermometer into the thickest part of the breast, not touching bone. Roast, uncovered, in a 325° oven for 2 to 2¾ hours, or until juices run clear and thermometer registers 170°F, generously brushing with glaze 2 or 3 times during the last 30 minutes of roasting.

3. Transfer turkey to a cutting board; cover loosely with foil and let stand 10 to 15 minutes before carving. If desired, pass additional jalapeño jelly with carved turkey.

Nutrition Facts per serving: 564 cal., 20 g total fat (5 g sat. fat), 197 mg chol., 401 mg sodium, 25 g carbo., 0 g fiber, 67 g pro.
Daily Values: 3% vit. C, 6% calcium, 20% iron

Dijon-Rosemary Roast Leg of Lamb

This leg of lamb recipe makes more than you might need for your holiday dinner or party, so save the leftovers for delicious sandwich options.

Prep: 15 minutes **Roast:** 2¼ hours
Stand: 15 minutes **Oven:** 325°F
Makes: 12 to 16 servings

3	tablespoons Dijon-style mustard
1	tablespoon finely chopped shallot
1	tablespoon lemon juice
1	tablespoon olive oil
½	teaspoon dried rosemary, crushed
½	teaspoon salt
½	teaspoon black pepper
2	large cloves garlic, minced
1	6-pound leg of lamb, hip bone removed, shank intact

1. In a small bowl whisk together mustard, shallot, lemon juice, oil, rosemary, salt, pepper, and garlic; set aside. Trim fat from lamb. (If necessary, use toothpicks to connect the flaps of meat where the hip bone was removed.) Spread mustard mixture over lamb leg.

2. Place lamb, fat side up, on a rack in a shallow roasting pan. Insert an oven-safe meat thermometer into thickest part of meat. The thermometer should not touch bone. Roast in a 325° oven until desired doneness. (Allow 2¼ to 2¾ hours for medium doneness [155°F].) Cover lamb loosely with foil and let stand for 15 minutes before carving. (The meat's temperature will rise 5°F during standing.) Remove toothpicks before serving.

Nutrition Facts per serving: 207 cal., 7 g total fat (2 g sat. fat), 100 mg chol., 259 mg sodium, 1 g carbo., 0 g fiber, 33 g pro.
Daily Values: 1% vit. C, 2% calcium, 17% iron

Turkey Thaw The safest place to thaw the turkey is in the refrigerator. Place the package-wrapped bird breast side up in a shallow pan to catch the juices as the turkey defrosts, and allow 1 day for each 4 pounds of meat to thaw. Meat also can be thawed in the sink under cold running water, which typically takes 30 minutes per pound. Place the packaged bird breast side down in a sink filled with cold (never warm or hot) water, ensuring the entire turkey is covered. Change the water in the sink every 30 minutes to keep the surface of the meat cold to prevent growth of bacteria. A thawed turkey can be stored for up to 4 days in the refrigerator.

Apricot-Glazed Spiced Pork Roast

During the last 15 minutes of cooking, the roast is finished with several applications of apricot glaze.

Prep: 20 minutes **Roast:** 1 hour
Stand: 15 minutes **Chill:** 1 hour **Oven:** 325°F
Makes: 8 servings

1½	teaspoons ground cumin
½	teaspoon garlic salt
½	teaspoon ground cinnamon
½	teaspoon ground ginger
¼	teaspoon ground cloves
1	2½- to 3-pound boneless pork top loin roast (single loin)
1	cup apricot preserves
2	to 3 tablespoons white wine vinegar

1. For rub, in a small bowl stir together cumin, garlic salt, cinnamon, ginger, and cloves. Sprinkle rub mixture evenly over roast and rub it in. Wrap roast in plastic film and chill for 1 to 2 hours.

2. Unwrap roast and discard plastic film. Place roast on a rack in a shallow roasting pan. Insert an oven-safe meat thermometer into center of roast. Roast in a 325° oven for 1 to 1½ hours or until meat thermometer registers 135°F.

3. Meanwhile, for glaze, in a small saucepan cook and stir apricot preserves and vinegar over medium heat until preserves are melted. Remove from heat. Brush roast generously with the glaze. Roast for 15 minutes more or until meat thermometer registers 150°F, brushing 2 or 3 times with glaze.

4. Remove roast from oven; cover loosely with foil. Let stand for 15 minutes. The temperature of the roast after standing should be 160°F. Reheat remaining glaze and serve with roast.

Nutrition Facts per serving: 326 cal., 9 g total fat (3 g sat. fat), 77 mg chol., 125 mg sodium, 28 g carbo., 1 g fiber, 31 g pro.
Daily Values: 7% vit. C, 2% calcium, 8% iron

Apricot-Glazed Spiced Pork Roast

Fruited Baked Ham

Ham can be purchased in three ways: cooked, partially cooked, and uncooked. Make sure the one you purchase for this recipe is fully cooked.

Prep: 10 minutes **Roast:** 1½ hours **Oven:** 325°F
Makes: 12 to 16 servings

1	3- to 4-pound boneless cooked smoked ham
1½	cups cherry preserves
¾	cup apricot preserves
3	tablespoons orange juice

1. Line a shallow roasting pan with foil. If desired, score top of ham in a diamond pattern by making shallow diagonal cuts at 1-inch intervals. Place ham in prepared pan. Insert an oven-safe meat thermometer into center of ham. Roast, uncovered, in 325° oven for 1½ to 1¾ hours or until thermometer registers 140°F.

2. Meanwhile, for sauce, in a medium saucepan combine cherry and apricot preserves and orange juice. Heat through. Spoon about ½ cup of the sauce mixture over the ham for the last 20 minutes of baking. Slice ham and serve with the remaining sauce.

Nutrition Facts per serving: 347 cal., 6 g total fat (2 g sat. fat), 62 mg chol., 1,524 mg sodium, 42 g carbo., 1 g fiber, 29 g pro.
Daily Values: 12% vit. C, 2% calcium, 8% iron

Holiday Beef Tenderloin

If your family doesn't polish off the meat during Christmas dinner, leftovers of both the tenderloin and jam will liven up lunchtime sandwiches the next day.

Prep: 15 minutes **Roast:** 45 minutes
Stand: 15 minutes **Oven:** 425°F **Makes:** 8 servings

1	medium onion, cut into 1-inch wedges
3	cloves garlic, peeled
2	tablespoons olive oil
2	14½-ounce cans diced fire-roasted tomatoes, drained
½	teaspoon kosher salt
½	teaspoon sugar

Holiday Beef Tenderloin

18

½ teaspoon finely shredded orange peel
1 2½-pound center-cut beef
    tenderloin roast
1 tablespoon olive oil
1 teaspoon kosher salt
1 teaspoon freshly ground black pepper
    Orange peel strips (optional)

1. For tomato jam, in a shallow baking pan arrange onion and garlic in a single layer. Drizzle with the 2 tablespoons oil; toss to coat. Roast, uncovered, in a 425° oven for 15 minutes. Remove garlic with a slotted spoon; set aside. Roast about 10 minutes more or until onion starts to brown. Transfer onion and garlic to a cutting board; cool slightly. Coarsely chop onion and garlic. In a medium bowl stir together the roasted onion and garlic, the drained tomatoes, ½ teaspoon kosher salt, the sugar, and ½ teaspoon finely shredded orange peel. Set aside.

2. Brush tenderloin with the 1 tablespoon oil; sprinkle all sides with the 1 teaspoon each of kosher salt and pepper. Place roast on a rack in a shallow roasting pan.

3. Roast, uncovered, in the 425° oven until tenderloin reaches desired doneness. (Allow 35 to 40 minutes for medium-rare doneness [135°F] or 45 to 50 minutes for medium doneness [150°F].) Cover loosely with foil; let stand for 15 minutes. (The temperature will rise 10°F during standing.)

4. To serve, cut beef into ½-inch slices; serve with tomato jam. If desired, garnish with orange peel strips. Refrigerate any leftover tomato jam and use within 3 days.

Nutrition Facts per serving: 308 cal., 17 g total fat (5 g sat. fat), 87 mg chol., 657 mg sodium, 7 g carbo., 0 g fiber, 30 g pro.
Daily Values: 8% vit. A, 22% vit. C, 3% calcium, 25% iron

Glazed Sweet Potatoes

Glazed Sweet Potatoes

Just like other potatoes, sweet potatoes can be baked, mashed, or hashed, but are sweetly sublime when sautéed with onions and brown sugar, as in this recipe.

Start to Finish: 25 minutes **Makes:** 8 servings

3 pounds sweet potatoes, peeled and
    cut into ½-inch slices
2 cups coarsely chopped onions
    (2 large)
½ teaspoon dried rosemary, crushed
⅓ cup butter or margarine
⅓ cup packed brown sugar
¼ cup chopped pecans,
    toasted (optional)

1. In a large saucepan or 4-quart Dutch oven cook sweet potatoes, covered, in enough lightly salted boiling water to cover for 10 to 12 minutes or until tender. Drain and set aside.

2. Meanwhile, in a large skillet cook onions and rosemary in hot butter over medium heat for 8 to 10 minutes or until onions are tender; stirring frequently. Add brown sugar, stirring to dissolve. Add sweet potatoes. Stir gently to combine. Cook, uncovered, for 5 to 8 minutes or until potatoes are glazed, stirring gently once or twice. Transfer to a serving dish. If desired, sprinkle with pecans.

Nutrition Facts per serving: 239 cal., 11 g total fat (4 g sat. fat), 21 mg chol., 77 mg sodium, 35 g carbo., 5 g fiber, 3 g pro.
Daily Values: 308% vit. A, 38% vit. C, 6% calcium, 6% iron

Lemony Asparagus and New Potatoes

2. In a 2-quart saucepan cook potatoes, covered, in a small amount of lightly salted boiling water for 12 minutes. Add asparagus. Cook, covered, about 4 minutes more or until asparagus is crisp-tender and potatoes are tender; drain. Transfer potatoes and asparagus to a serving bowl.

3. Meanwhile, for dressing, in a small bowl whisk together oil, lemon peel, salt, and thyme. Add to the vegetables; toss gently to coat. If desired, garnish with fresh thyme. Serve warm.

Nutrition Facts per serving: 98 cal., 3 g total fat (0 g sat. fat), 0 mg chol., 156 mg sodium, 16 g carbo., 2 g fiber, 3g pro.
Daily Values: 21% vit. C, 1% calcium, 7% iron

Savory Mashed Potatoes

Although many types of potatoes can be used for mashing, Yukon gold is ideal because of its flavorfully moist, gold-colored flesh. In a pinch, substitute refrigerated mashed potatoes and add all of the extra ingredients after the potatoes are reheated.

Prep: 20 minutes **Cook:** 20 minutes
Makes: 8 servings

3	pounds Yukon gold potatoes, peeled and cut into 2-inch cubes
4	ounces bacon, finely chopped
1	tablespoon olive oil
½	cup minced shallots
1	cup soft bread crumbs
2	teaspoons dried parsley
6	tablespoons butter or margarine, softened
1	teaspoon salt
¾	cup milk, warmed

1. In a 4-quart Dutch oven cook potatoes, covered, in enough boiling water to cover about 15 minutes or until tender.

2. Meanwhile, in a small skillet cook bacon until crisp. Remove bacon with a slotted spoon and drain on paper towels. Add oil and shallots to drippings in skillet; cook for 2 minutes. Add bread crumbs; cook until golden. Remove skillet from heat. Stir in parsley and bacon.

Lemony Asparagus and New Potatoes

If your diet restricts you from indulging too heavily in holiday goodies, this may be the perfect side dish for Christmas dinner. Flavored with lemon and thyme, this light potato-asparagus combo serves as both the vegetable and starch portion of the meal.

Prep: 15 minutes **Cook:** 16 minutes
Makes: 8 servings

1½	pounds fresh asparagus spears
16	tiny new potatoes, unpeeled and cut into quarters
4	teaspoons olive oil
1	teaspoon finely shredded lemon peel
½	teaspoon salt
½	teaspoon dried thyme, crushed

1. Snap off and discard woody bases from the asparagus spears. If desired, scrape off scales. Cut into 2-inch pieces. Set aside.

3. Drain potatoes and return to Dutch oven. Mash with a potato masher or beat with an electric mixer on low speed. Add butter and salt. Gradually beat in warmed milk until desired consistency. Transfer to serving bowl; top with crumb mixture.

Nutrition Facts per serving: 337 cal., 18 g total fat (8 g sat. fat), 36 mg chol., 522 mg sodium, 36 g carbo., 3 g fiber, 7 g pro.
Daily Values: 9% vit. A, 42% vit. C, 5% calcium, 10% iron

Easy Roasted Potatoes

These basic seasoned potatoes are the perfect way to round out any holiday menu. Tailor-make the potatoes to complement the Christmas meat by replacing the rosemary with your favorite dried herbs, such as thyme, basil, or dill.

Prep: 10 minutes **Bake:** 55 minutes **Oven:** 325°F
Makes: 8 servings

6	medium round red or white potatoes (2 pounds), quartered, or 2 pounds tiny new potatoes, halved
¼	cup olive oil or melted butter
1	teaspoon dried rosemary, crushed
½	teaspoon onion powder
¼	teaspoon garlic salt
¼	teaspoon black pepper
⅛	teaspoon paprika

1. Place potatoes in a greased 13×9×2-inch baking pan. In a small bowl combine oil, rosemary, onion powder, garlic salt, pepper, and paprika; drizzle over potatoes, tossing to coat.

2. Bake in a 325° oven for 45 minutes. Stir potatoes; bake 10 to 20 minutes more or until potatoes are tender and edges are brown.

Nutrition Facts per serving: 124 cal., 7 g total fat (1 g sat. fat), 0 mg chol., 36 mg sodium, 14 g carbo., 2 g fiber, 2 g pro.
Daily Values: 21% vit. C, 1% calcium, 7% iron

Parsley-Herb Rice

The starch portion of a meal comes in a variety of ways. For Christmas, the most popular are stuffing and sweet or regular potatoes. For a less traditional, but just as delicious dish, try this lightly buttered, basil and parsley rice recipe.

Prep: 15 minutes **Cook:** 15 minutes
Stand: 5 minutes **Makes:** 8 servings

2⅔	cups water
1⅓	cups uncooked white long grain or regular brown rice
¼	cup butter or margarine
1½	teaspoons dried basil, crushed, or 2 tablespoons snipped fresh basil
¾	teaspoon salt or 1 tablespoon instant chicken bouillon granules
½	cup dried cranberries
½	cup snipped fresh parsley
½	cup chopped walnuts

1. In a medium saucepan combine the water, rice, butter, dried basil (if using), and salt. Bring to boiling; reduce heat. Cover and simmer about 15 minutes for long grain rice (about 40 minutes for brown rice) or until rice is tender and liquid is absorbed. Remove from heat. Stir in cranberries. Let stand, covered, for 5 minutes.

2. Stir fresh basil (if using), parsley, and walnuts into the cooked rice just before serving.

Nutrition Facts per serving: 240 cal., 11 g total fat (4 g sat. fat), 16 mg chol., 267 mg sodium, 32 g carbo., 2 g fiber, 4 g pro.
Daily Values: 11% vit. A, 9% vit. C, 3% calcium, 11% iron

Parsley-Herb Rice

Walnut-Sage Potatoes

The rich, nutty essence of Gruyère cheese paired with lightly toasted walnuts is the perfect way to enhance the mellow flavors of potatoes. A snippet of fresh sage completes this side-dish delight.

Prep: 30 minutes **Bake:** 1¼ hours
Stand: 10 minutes **Oven:** 325°F **Makes:** 8 servings

6	medium potatoes (2 pounds)
½	cup chopped onion (1 medium)
2	cloves garlic, minced
2	tablespoons walnut oil or cooking oil
3	tablespoons all-purpose flour
¾	teaspoon salt
¼	teaspoon black pepper
2½	cups milk
3	tablespoons snipped fresh sage
1	cup shredded Gruyère cheese (4 ounces)
⅓	cup broken walnut pieces, toasted Fresh sage leaves (optional)

1. Peel potatoes, if desired, and thinly slice (there should be 6 cups). Place potatoes in a colander. Rinse with cold water; set aside to drain.

2. For sauce, in a medium saucepan cook onion and garlic in hot oil over medium heat until tender but not brown. Stir in flour, salt, and pepper. Add milk all at once. Cook and stir over medium heat until thickened and bubbly. Remove from heat; stir in the 3 tablespoons snipped fresh sage.

3. Grease a 2-quart round glass casserole with glass cover. Layer half of potatoes in casserole. Cover with half of the sauce. Sprinkle with half of the cheese. Repeat layering with the potatoes and sauce. (Cover and chill remaining Gruyère cheese until needed.)

4. Bake casserole, covered, in a 350° oven for 45 minutes. Uncover; bake 25 to 30 minutes more or until potatoes are just tender. (Or, bake in 325°F oven, covered, for 1 hour. Uncover; bake 25 to 30 minutes more.) Sprinkle the remaining cheese and the walnuts over top. Let stand 10 minutes before serving. If desired, garnish with fresh sage leaves.

Make Ahead Tip: Peel potatoes for Walnut-Sage Potatoes, if desired, and thinly slice (there should be 6 cups). Cook potatoes in boiling, salted water for 5 minutes; drain. Continue as directed through step 3. Cover and chill in the refrigerator up to 24 hours. To serve, bake as directed.

Nutrition Facts per serving: 285 cal., 13 g total fat (4 g sat. fat), 21 mg chol., 310 mg sodium, 33 g carbo., 2 g fiber, 10 g pro.
Daily Values: 7% vit. A, 28% vit. C, 26% calcium, 4% iron

Wild Rice and Spinach Skillet

Instead of the same old foods for every Christmas feast, try some new dishes! When combined with spinach and cream cheese, wild rice is not only nutritious, but supremely delicious as well.

Start to Finish: 35 minutes **Makes:** 8 servings

1	6-ounce package long grain and wild rice mix
1	10-ounce can condensed beef broth
1	pound mushrooms, thinly sliced (6 cups)
2	tablespoons butter
1	10-ounce package frozen chopped spinach, thawed and well-drained
1	8-ounce package cream cheese, cut up

1. Cook rice mix according to package directions except use the broth for part of the liquid.

2. Meanwhile, in a large skillet cook mushrooms in hot butter until tender. Add spinach and cream cheese, stirring to combine and melt cheese. Stir in rice. Heat through.

Make Ahead Tip: Prepare as above. Spread in a 2-quart rectangular baking dish. Cover and chill overnight. To reheat, bake, covered, in a 350°F oven for 40 to 45 minutes or until heated through, stirring once. (Or bake, covered, in a 425°F oven for 20 to 25 minutes or until heated through, stirring once.)

Nutrition Facts per serving: 231 cal., 14 g total fat (8 g sat. fat), 39 mg chol., 620 mg sodium, 20 g carbo., 2 g fiber, 9 g pro.
Daily Values: 65% vit. A, 16% vit. C, 9% calcium, 10% iron

Walnut-Sage Potatoes

The Dig on Potatoes Potatoes generally fit into three categories: mealy, waxy, or all-purpose, which is determined by the tuber's texture after cooking. Mealy potatoes, such as the russet, are somewhat crumbly after cooking, and perform well when mashed or baked. Other potatoes, such as the long white potato, red potato, and the yellow varieties (Yukon gold, Finnish Yellow, and Yellow Rose) are considered all-purpose and are excellent in most dishes, including mashed, boiled, or fried. Waxy potatoes, such as any variety of new (young) potato, have thin skins and a crisp texture that helps them retain their shape. New potatoes are ideal for potato salad because of their shape-holding trait, but also are used for boiling and roasting.

Apricot, Spinach, and Couscous Dressing

Couscous is quite popular in North Africa, where it is an important dietary staple. Made from granular semolina, which is coarsely ground durum wheat, couscous can be served as a porridge with milk, sweetened and served with fruit, or mixed with savory ingredients in a salad or dressing.

Prep: 25 minutes **Cook:** 10 minutes
Stand: 5 minutes **Makes:** 6 servings

1¼	cups reduced-sodium chicken broth
1	cup couscous
2	slices bacon
1	clove garlic, minced
½	cup thinly sliced celery (1 stalk)
⅓	cup finely chopped onion (1 small)
⅓	cup dried apricots, snipped
½	teaspoon dried thyme, crushed
½	teaspoon finely shredded lemon peel
⅛	teaspoon salt
⅛	teaspoon black pepper
1	cup baby spinach leaves
¼	cup pine nuts or chopped almonds, toasted
¼	to ½ cup apricot nectar

1. In a medium saucepan bring the broth to boiling; stir in couscous. Remove from heat. Cover and let stand for 5 minutes. Fluff couscous with a fork. Cover and set aside.

2. Meanwhile, in a large skillet cook bacon until crisp. Drain bacon on paper towels, reserving 1 tablespoon bacon drippings in the skillet. Cook garlic in bacon drippings over medium heat for 30 seconds. Add celery and onion; cook about 4 minutes or until vegetables are tender, stirring occasionally. Stir in apricots, thyme, lemon peel, salt, and pepper. Cook and stir for 1 minute more.

3. In a large bowl toss together the vegetable mixture and couscous. Crumble bacon; add bacon, spinach, and pine nuts to couscous mixture. Stir in just enough of the apricot nectar to moisten the couscous. Serve immediately.

Nutrition Facts per serving: 219 cal., 7 g total fat (2 g sat. fat), 4 mg chol., 226 mg sodium, 33 g carbo., 3 g fiber, 7 g pro.
Daily Values: 19% vit. A, 4% vit. C, 3% calcium, 8% iron

Ginger-Honey Glazed Carrots

Fast and flavorful, these glazed carrots are the ideal accompaniment to more time-consuming main dishes. Just cook, glaze, and serve.

Start to Finish: 20 minutes **Makes:** 8 servings

4	cups water
1	teaspoon salt
2	pounds packaged peeled baby carrots
2	tablespoons butter or margarine
2	tablespoons honey
1½	teaspoons ground ginger

1. In a 12-inch heavy skillet combine water and salt. Bring to boiling. Add carrots. Return to boiling; reduce heat. Cover and simmer for 10 to 12 minutes or until carrots are tender. Drain carrots; set aside.

2. In the same heavy skillet combine butter, honey, and ginger. Stir constantly over medium heat until butter is melted. Carefully add the carrots. Toss gently for 2 to 3 minutes or until carrots are thoroughly coated and heated through.

Nutrition Facts per serving: 91 cal., 3 g total fat (2 g sat. fat), 8 mg chol., 169 mg sodium, 15 g carbo., 3 g fiber, 1 g pro.
Daily Values: 248% vit. A, 7% vit. C, 4% calcium, 2% iron

Almond Broccoli

Dressed with a light butter and orange juice glaze, and garnished with toasted almonds, this vitamin-rich vegetable will disappear as quickly as the meat and mashed potatoes. Cut the broccoli to fit your family's size preferences—big or small, the broccoli pieces will still be delicious!

Start to Finish: 30 minutes **Makes:** 8 servings

2	pounds broccoli, trimmed and cut into 2-inch pieces
1/3	cup butter
1/4	cup fresh orange juice
1	teaspoon finely shredded orange peel
1/2	teaspoon salt
1/3	cup sliced almonds, toasted
	Orange wedges (optional)

1. Place a large steamer basket in a 4-quart Dutch oven. Add water to reach just below the bottom of the basket. Bring to boiling. Add broccoli to steamer basket. Cover and reduce heat. Steam for 8 to 10 minutes or just until stems are tender. Transfer broccoli to a serving dish. Cover with foil.

2. Meanwhile, in large skillet melt butter over medium-high heat; cook and stir for 3 to 4 minutes or until medium brown in color. Add orange juice and cook for 10 seconds. Remove from heat; stir in orange peel and salt. Pour over broccoli; sprinkle with almonds and garnish with orange wedges.

Nutrition Facts per serving: 130 cal., 11 g total fat (4 g sat. fat), 21 mg chol., 225 mg sodium, 7 g carbo., 2 g fiber, 3 g pro.
Daily Values: 14% vit. A, 94% vit. C, 5% calcium, 4% iron

Almond Broccoli

Maple-Glazed Brussels Sprouts and Onions

Maple-Glazed Brussels Sprouts and Onions

Brussels sprouts look like miniature heads of cabbage and are thought to have been first grown in Belgium several hundred years ago. If you choose to buy this vegetable fresh, look for light green sprouts with tight compact heads.

Start to Finish: 25 minutes **Makes:** 8 servings

3	tablespoons butter
2	10-ounce packages frozen Brussels sprouts
1	10-ounce package frozen whole small onions
⅓	cup pure maple syrup
	Salt and black pepper
¼	cup chopped walnuts, toasted

1. In a large skillet melt butter over medium heat. Add frozen Brussels sprouts and onions. Cook, covered, about 10 minutes or until vegetables are nearly tender, stirring occasionally.

2. Drizzle vegetables with maple syrup. Cook, uncovered, for 1 to 2 minutes more or until vegetables are tender, stirring occasionally. Season to taste with salt and pepper. Transfer vegetables to a serving bowl. Sprinkle with walnuts.

Nutrition Facts per serving: 139 cal., 7 g total fat (3 g sat. fat), 12 mg chol., 83 mg sodium, 18 g carbo., 4 g fiber, 4 g pro.
Daily Values: 12% vit. A, 90% vit. C, 7% calcium, 5% iron

Scalloped Corn

This deliciously thick dish can be served as either a vegetable or a starch side dish. If your cooking time is limited, it could be used as both—just be sure to make extra!

Prep: 20 minutes **Bake:** 35 minutes
Stand: 10 minutes **Oven:** 325°F
Makes: 6 to 8 servings

1	10-ounce package frozen whole kernel corn
½	cup chopped onion (1 medium)
½	cup chopped green or red sweet pepper (optional)
¼	cup water
¼	teaspoon salt
2	eggs, slightly beaten
1	14¾- or 16-ounce can cream-style corn
1	cup milk
1	cup coarsely crushed saltine crackers (about 20 crackers)
½	cup coarsely crushed saltine crackers (about 10 crackers)
2	tablespoons butter or margarine, melted
¼	cup shredded cheddar cheese (1 ounce) (optional)

1. In a medium saucepan combine frozen corn, onion, green sweet pepper (if desired), water, and salt. Bring to boiling; reduce heat. Cover and simmer about 5 minutes or until vegetables are crisp-tender. Drain thoroughly.

2. Meanwhile, in a large bowl stir together eggs, cream-style corn, milk, and the 1 cup crushed crackers. Stir in the cooked vegetables. Transfer mixture to a greased 2-quart square baking dish. In a small bowl combine the ½ cup crushed crackers and the melted butter; sprinkle over corn mixture.

3. Bake in a 325° oven for 35 to 40 minutes or until a knife inserted near the center comes out clean. If desired, sprinkle with cheese. Let stand for 10 minutes before serving.

Nutrition Facts per serving: 243 cal., 9 g total fat (4 g sat. fat), 85 mg chol., 531 mg sodium, 37 g carbo., 2 g fiber, 8 g pro.
Daily Values: 8% vit. A, 9% vit. C, 8% calcium, 8% iron

Sautéed Peas and Celery

Turn plain frozen peas into a gourmet treat worthy of second helpings. The simplicity of this dish makes it a perfect accompaniment to everything from holiday roasts on Christmas to baked fish on a busy evening.

Start to Finish: 20 minutes **Makes:** 8 servings

1	tablespoon olive oil
½	cup chopped red onion (1 medium)
½	cup chopped celery (1 stalk)
2	10-ounce packages frozen peas, thawed
¼	cup chopped celery leaves
½	teaspoon salt
¼	teaspoon freshly ground black pepper

1. In a large skillet heat oil over medium heat. Add onion and cook about 5 minutes or until tender. Add celery and cook about 3 minutes or until tender.

2. Increase heat to medium high. Add peas and cook for 3 to 5 minutes more or until peas are heated through. Remove from heat. Stir in celery leaves, salt, and pepper. Serve immediately.

Nutrition Facts per serving: 82 cal., 2 g total fat (0 g sat. fat), 0 mg chol., 221 mg sodium, 12 g carbo., 5 g fiber, 4 g pro.
Daily Values: 13% vit. A, 19% vit. C, 3% calcium, 8% iron

Helping Hands Save Time When guests or family members offer to help, give them easy tasks that will make them feel useful and save you some time.
- Set the table.
- Fill glasses with ice and water.
- Uncork and pour the wine.
- Reheat vegetables in the microwave.
- Carve the meat.
- Carry food to the table.
- Gather diners for the meal.
- Offer a toast at the meal.

Easy-Does-It Appetizers

FROM SIMPLE TO IMPRESSIVE, THESE QUICK NIBBLES deserve the appreciative murmur they receive at your next cocktail party. Anyone who has put together a full spread of hors d'oeuvres for a gathering—casual or elegant—knows that time is of the essence when preparing several recipes for one occasion. Some appetizers must be impressive and awe-inspiring, while others must be prepared quickly. With a full of array of choices for any celebration, the goodies for a fancy party can be as easily assembled as the snacks for a casual gathering with friends. For even quicker ideas to increase any appetizer spread, check out the tipbox ideas on pages 34 and 37.

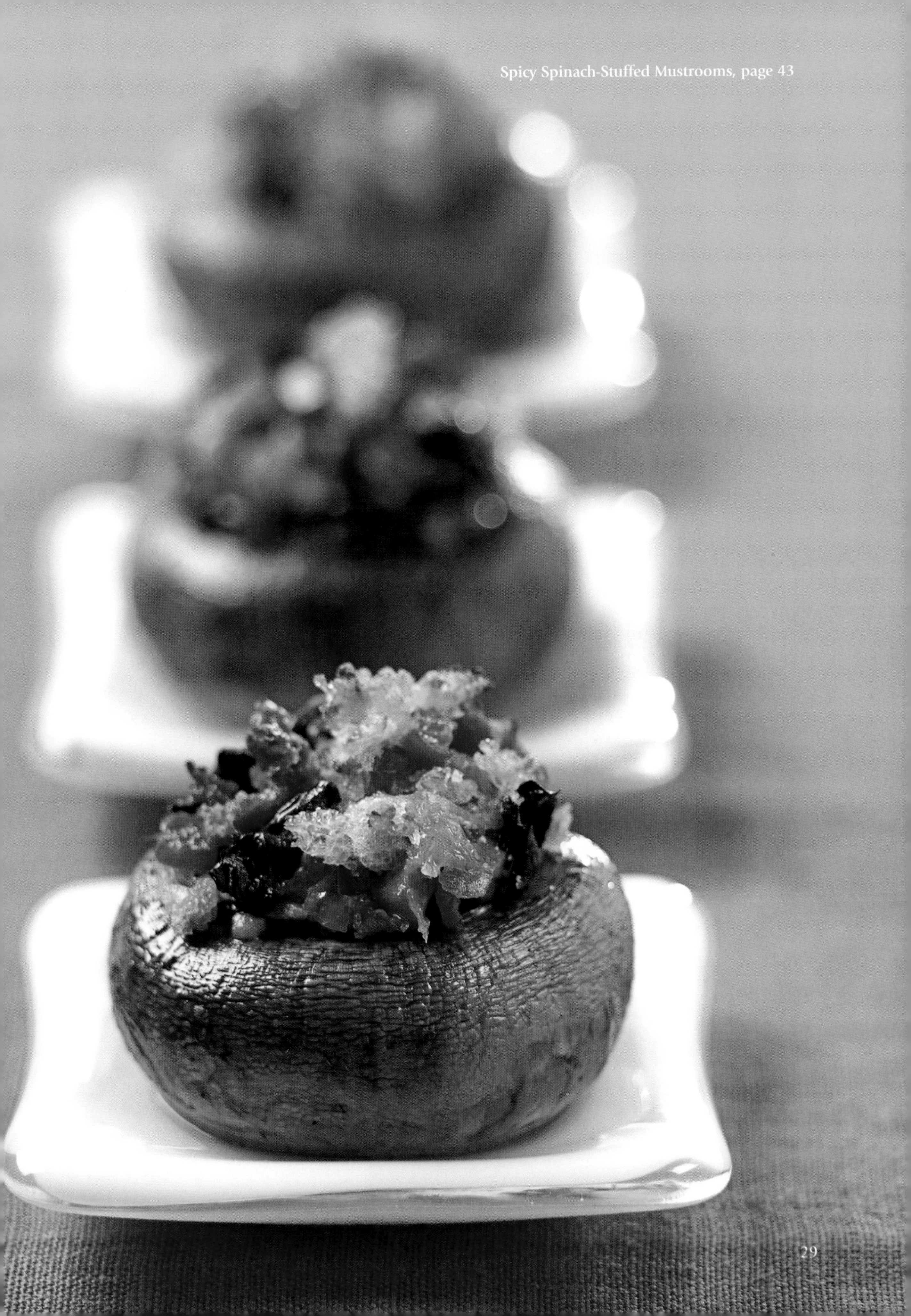

Spicy Spinach-Stuffed Mustrooms, page 43

Spicy-Savory Snack Mix

Sweet, hot, and crunchy. No wonder these herb-coated almonds disappear quickly. Make a bowl—maybe two—especially if you plan to serve a selection of cocktails at your holiday parties.

Start to Finish: 25 minutes **Oven:** 375°F
Makes: 3 cups

1	cup whole almonds or peanuts
¾	cup pecan halves
¼	cup hazelnuts (filberts)

1	tablespoon butter
1	tablespoon finely snipped fresh rosemary or 1 teaspoon dried rosemary, crushed
1	tablespoon brown sugar
2	teaspoons soy sauce
½	teaspoon crushed red pepper
1	cup pretzel nuggets

1. Spread almonds, pecan halves, and hazelnuts in a single layer in a 15×10×1-inch baking pan. Bake about 8 minutes or until nuts are lightly toasted, stirring once or twice.

2. Meanwhile, in a large saucepan melt butter over medium heat. Remove from heat. Stir in rosemary, brown sugar, soy sauce, and crushed red pepper. Add the nuts and pretzels to butter mixture; toss to coat. Turn out onto a baking sheet; cool. Store in a tightly covered container in the refrigerator up to 1 month or in the freezer up to 3 months.

Nutrition Facts per ¼ cup: 161 cal., 14 g total fat (2 g sat. fat), 3 mg chol., 122 mg sodium, 8 g carbo., 2 g fiber, 4 g pro.
Daily Values: 1% vit. A, 1% vit. C, 4% calcium, 5% iron

Holiday Nibblers

White yogurt-covered pretzels, green pistachios, and red dried cranberries create a festive color combination for the holidays. For Christmas gifts, fill decorative see-through bags with this colorful mix.

Start to Finish: 5 minutes **Makes:** 4 cups

2	cups vanilla-flavored yogurt-covered pretzels
1	cup roasted, salted shelled pistachio nuts
1	cup dried cranberries or cherries

1. In a medium bowl combine pretzels, pistachio nuts, and cranberries. Store in a tightly covered container at room temperature up to 1 month.

Nutrition Facts per ¼ cup: 114 cal., 6 g total fat (2 g sat. fat), 0 mg chol., 82 mg sodium, 15 g carbo., 1 g fiber, 2 g pro.
Daily Values: 1% vit. A, 3% calcium, 3% iron

Holiday Nibblers

Fruity Holiday Punch

Whether or not you choose to add liquor to this yuletide drink, the full fruit flavors alone will keep your guests coming back for more.

Start to Finish: 10 minutes
Makes: 30 (4-ounce) servings

1	12-ounce can frozen lemonade concentrate
1	10-ounce package frozen strawberries in syrup
1	8-ounce can crushed pineapple (juice pack), undrained
3	1-liter bottles ginger ale, chilled
1	cup rum or vodka (optional)

1. In a blender combine frozen lemonade concentrate, frozen strawberries with the syrup, and undrained pineapple. Cover and blend until smooth. If desired, pour strawberry mixture into a covered container and chill for up to 24 hours.

2. To serve, pour strawberry mixture into a large punch bowl. Slowly pour ginger ale down side of bowl. If desired, stir in rum.

Nutrition Facts per serving: 69 cal., 0 g total fat (0 g sat. fat),
0 mg chol., 8 mg sodium, 18 g carbo., 0 g fiber, 0 g pro.
Daily Values: 11% vit. C, 1% calcium, 2% iron

Tomato Sipper

This slow-cooked party beverage can simmer in the crockery cooker for hours while you prepare the rest of the holiday spread.

Prep: 10 minutes
Cook: 4 to 5 hours (low-heat setting) or
2 to 2½ hours (high-heat setting)
Makes: 8 (6-ounce) servings

1	46-ounce can vegetable juice
1	stalk celery, halved crosswise
2	tablespoons brown sugar
2	tablespoons lemon juice
2	teaspoons Worcestershire sauce

1. In a 3½- to 4-quart slow cooker combine vegetable juice, celery stalk, brown sugar, lemon juice, and Worcestershire sauce.

2. Cover and cook on low-heat setting for 4 to 5 hours or on high-heat setting for 2 to 2½ hours. Discard celery. Ladle into heatproof cups.

Nutrition Facts per serving: 50 cal., 0 g total fat (0 g sat. fat),
0 mg chol., 443 mg sodium, 11 g carbo., 1 g fiber, 1 g pro.
Daily Values: 27% vit. A, 71% vit. C, 3% calcium, 5% iron

Easy Eggnog Fix-Ups

Add spice to your holidays with these delicious and satisfying eggnog variations.

Makes: 8 to 10 servings

1	quart purchased eggnog

1. Mocha Eggnog: Combine eggnog, 1 cup strong coffee, and ¼- to ½-cup chocolate-flavored syrup. Serve warm or chilled topped with whipped cream and chocolate shavings.

Nutrition Facts per serving: 239 cal., 14 g total fat (4 g sat. fat),
21 mg chol., 95 mg sodium, 23 g carbo., 0 g fiber, 4 g pro.
Daily Values: 4% vit. A, 9% calcium, 1% iron

2. Minty White Chocolate Eggnog: In a medium saucepan combine eggnog, 1 cup white baking pieces, and ⅓ cup crushed peppermint candy. Heat and stir over low heat until white chocolate pieces are melted and mixture is heated through. Serve warm topped with whipped cream and sprinkled with additional crushed peppermint candy or with a candy cane as a stirrer.

Nutrition Facts per serving: 406 cal., 23 g total fat (11 g sat. fat),
21 mg chol., 128 mg sodium, 43 g carbo., 0 g fiber, 3 g pro.
Daily Values: 4% vit. A, 9% calcium

3. Hazelnut Eggnog: Combine eggnog and ¼ cup hazelnut-flavored liqueur. Serve warm or chilled topped with whipped cream and sprinkled with finely chopped hazelnuts.

Nutrition Facts per serving: 264 cal., 17 g total fat (4 g sat. fat),
21 mg chol., 86 mg sodium, 21 g carbo., 0 g fiber, 4 g pro.
Daily Values: 4% vit. A, 2% vit. C, 9% calcium, 1% iron

Shrimp Salad Toasts

To toast party bread, arrange bread slices in a single layer on a baking sheet. Bake in a 350°F oven for 5 to 10 minutes or until toasted, turning once.

Start to Finish: 25 minutes **Makes:** 28 appetizers

2	4-ounce cans small shrimp, drained
1/3	cup mayonnaise or salad dressing
1	tablespoon lemon juice
1/4	teaspoon salt
1/4	teaspoon black pepper
28	slices party pumpernickel bread, toasted
1	lemon
	Fresh dill sprigs (optional)

1. For shrimp salad, in a small bowl combine shrimp, mayonnaise, lemon juice, salt, and pepper. Spoon shrimp salad evenly onto toasted bread slices.

2. Cut lemon into very thin slices; remove seeds. Halve slices. Top each shrimp salad with a lemon slice and, if desired, fresh dill sprig.

Nutrition Facts per serving: 49 cal., 2 g total fat (0 g sat. fat), 16 mg chol., 104 mg sodium, 4 g carbo., 1 g fiber, 3 g pro.
Daily Values: 2% vit. C, 1% calcium, 3% iron

Oriental Shrimp Kabobs

This simple, yet elegant recipe turns a few common ingredients into a remarkable display piece for the appetizer table. For an even classier presentation, use longer fancy metal skewers, then place several in an attractive cup, jar, or vase.

Prep: 20 minutes **Marinate:** 1 hour
Makes: 16 appetizers

2	tablespoons rice vinegar
2	tablespoons Worcestershire sauce for chicken
1/4	teaspoon toasted sesame oil
16	extra-large peeled and deveined cooked shrimp (about 1 pound)
1/2	of 1 medium cucumber
16	pieces pickled sushi ginger (1/4 cup)
16	4-inch wooden cocktail picks or 6-inch wooden skewers

1. In a medium bowl stir together rice vinegar, Worcestershire sauce, and sesame oil. Remove tails from shrimp, if present. Add shrimp to vinegar mixture; toss to coat. Cover and marinate in the refrigerator for 1 to 2 hours, stirring occasionally. Drain shrimp; discard marinade.

2. If desired, peel cucumber. Halve cucumber lengthwise and cut into 1/2-inch slices. Thread shrimp, cucumber, and ginger onto cocktail picks.

Nutrition Facts per serving: 35 cal., 0 g total fat (0 g sat. fat), 55 mg chol., 90 mg sodium, 1 g carbo., 0 g fiber, 6 g pro.
Daily Values: 1% vit. A, 1% vit. C, 1% calcium, 6% iron

Shrimp Crostini

Crostini means "little toasts," which is a fairly accurate description of the broiled, oil-brushed baguette slices used as a base for this classy appetizer.

Start to Finish: 20 minutes **Makes:** 16 crostini

16	large peeled and deveined cooked shrimp (about 8 ounces)
1/3	cup shredded fresh basil
1	tablespoon olive oil
2	teaspoons white wine vinegar
1/4	teaspoon salt
1/4	teaspoon freshly ground pepper
16	slices baguette-style French bread
2	large cloves garlic, halved
4	teaspoons olive oil

1. In a medium bowl combine shrimp, basil, the 1 tablespoon olive oil, the vinegar, salt, and pepper; set aside.

2. Arrange bread slices on a baking sheet. Broil 3 to 4 inches from heat about 1 minute or until lightly toasted. Turn and broil remaining sides until toasted. Rub toasts with cut sides of garlic cloves; brush with the 4 teaspoons olive oil. Arrange toasts on serving platter.

3. Using a slotted spoon, place 1 shrimp on each crostini. Serve immediately.

Nutrition Facts per serving: 52 cal., 2 g total fat (0 g sat. fat), 28 mg chol., 112 mg sodium, 4 g carbo., 0 g fiber, 4 g pro.
Daily Values: 2% vit. A, 1% vit. C, 1% calcium, 4% iron

Shrimp Crostini

Coconut Shrimp with Mango-Ginger Dip

Seafood lovers everywhere will sing the praises of this simple version of coconut shrimp, rounded out with a fruity three-ingredient dipping sauce. This recipe yields only 10 servings, so either make extra for the buffet table or use it as the appetizer course for a small sit-down dinner.

Prep: 15 minutes **Bake:** 10 minutes **Oven:** 400°F
Makes: 10 appetizer servings

1	pound fresh or frozen peeled, deveined shrimp
1	cup flaked coconut, toasted and chopped
½	cup seasoned fine dry bread crumbs
¾	teaspoon curry powder
2	egg whites, slightly beaten
	Nonstick cooking spray
½	cup mango chutney
¼	cup orange juice
¼	teaspoon ground ginger

1. Thaw shrimp, if frozen. Rinse shrimp; pat dry with paper towels.

2. Generously grease a 15×10×1-inch baking pan; set aside. In a shallow bowl combine coconut, bread crumbs, and curry powder. Place egg whites in another small shallow bowl. Dip shrimp into the egg whites; then dip into the coconut mixture, pressing it firmly onto the shrimp. Place on prepared baking pan. Coat shrimp with nonstick cooking spray.

3. Bake in a 400° oven about 10 minutes or until shrimp is opaque. Meanwhile, for dip, in a small bowl combine mango chutney, orange juice, and ginger. Serve with the shrimp.

Nutrition Facts per serving: 154 cal., 5 g total fat (4 g sat. fat), 69 mg chol., 307 mg sodium, 16 g carbo., 1 g fiber, 12 g pro.
Daily Values: 3% vit. A, 12% vit. C, 4% calcium, 8% iron

Asian Shrimp Dip

Featuring shrimp as the main ingredient, this creamy appetizer gets its Asian flair from soy sauce, water chestnuts, and ginger. Garnish with chopped green onions or criss-cross with two strips of red pepper.

Prep: 15 minutes **Chill:** 2 hours **Makes:** 2 cups

1	8-ounce carton dairy sour cream
1	4- to 4¼-ounce can tiny shrimp, drained
½	cup finely chopped water chestnuts (about ½ of one 8-ounce can)
¼	cup finely chopped green onions (2)
2	tablespoons milk
1	tablespoon soy sauce
½	teaspoon ground ginger
¼	teaspoon garlic powder
	Sliced green onion or sweet pepper strips
	Vegetable dippers such as sugar snap peas, celery sticks, and/or sweet pepper strips

1. In a medium bowl combine sour cream, shrimp, water chestnuts, the ¼ cup green onion, milk, soy sauce, ginger, and garlic powder; mix well. Cover and chill for 2 to 24 hours.

Last Minute Fix-Ups

• **Antipasto Kabobs:** Marinate cooked cheese-filled tortellini, quartered artichoke hearts, cherry tomatoes, green olives, and whole pickled banana peppers in bottled Italian dressing for 2 to 24 hours. Thread 1 of each of the ingredients onto 6-inch skewers, adding a thin roll of salami, if desired.

• **Fruit Kabobs:** Thread star fruit (carambola) slices, kiwifruit slices, mandarin orange wedges, papaya wedges, and pineapple cubes onto 6-inch skewers. If desired, add different kinds of fruit.

• **Cheese-Filled Veggies:** Pipe or spoon flavored cream cheese onto chunks of red or green pepper, slices of cucumber, or into hollowed cherry tomatoes.

• **Pinwheels:** Layer tortillas with flavored cream cheese, turkey or beef, spinach leaves, and slices of your favorite cheese. Roll up tightly, seal the sides with cream cheese, and refrigerate until the rolls are firm. Cut rolls into ½- to 1-inch slices and place on an attractive platter.

2. Before serving, stir dip and transfer to a serving bowl. Garnish with sliced green onions. Serve with vegetable dippers.

Nutrition Facts per 1 tablespoon dip: 25 cal., 2 g total fat (1 g sat. fat), 9 mg chol., 40 mg sodium, 1 g carbo., 0 g fiber, 1 g pro.
Daily Values: 1% vit. A, 1% vit. C, 2% calcium, 1% iron

Asparagus with Dijon-Horseradish Dip

Why relegate tender asparagus to the side? Here it stars as a fresh and light starter with a tasty horseradish dipping sauce.

Start to Finish: 25 minutes
Makes: 12 appetizer servings

- 1½   pounds medium asparagus spears
- 12   ounces sugar snap peas
- 1   cup mayonnaise or salad dressing
- 2   to 3 tablespoons prepared horseradish
- 2   tablespoons honey dijon-style mustard
- ½   teaspoon freshly ground black pepper
- ⅛   teaspoon salt

1. Snap off and discard woody bases from asparagus. If desired, remove tips and strings from sugar snap peas. In a large deep skillet bring 1 inch of salted water to boiling. Add asparagus to skillet. Return to boiling; reduce heat. Simmer, uncovered, for 2 minutes. Add sugar snap peas and cook, uncovered, about 2 minutes more or until vegetables are crisp-tender. Drain and transfer to a bowl of ice water until cooled. Drain and set aside. (Or, cover tightly and chill up to 4 hours.)

2. Meanwhile, for dip, in a small bowl combine mayonnaise, horseradish, mustard, pepper, and salt; mix well. Serve immediately or cover and chill up to 4 hours. Serve the vegetables with dip.

Nutrition Facts per serving: 163 cal., 15 g total fat (2 g sat. fat), 13 mg chol., 180 mg sodium, 6 g carbo., 2 g fiber, 2 g pro.
Daily Values: 4% vit. A, 13% vit. C, 2% calcium, 6% iron

Southwest Cheese Fondue

The pungent kick of cumin powder puts the Southwest in this fondue, while colorful flashes of red and green sweet pepper add visual (and flavor) appeal. Keep some milk on hand to thin the fondue if it becomes too thick during the evening.

Start to Finish: 15 minutes Makes: about 14 servings

- 2   10 ¾-ounce cans condensed cream of potato soup
- 2   cups shredded process American cheese (8 ounces)
- ½   cup finely chopped red and/or green sweet pepper
- ⅓   cup milk
- ½   teaspoon ground cumin
       Crusty bread cubes, corn chips, and/or vegetable dippers
       Milk (optional)

1. Place soup in a medium saucepan. Mash any pieces of potato in the soup. Stir in cheese, sweet pepper, the ⅓ cup milk, and the cumin. Cook over medium heat until cheese is melted and mixture is heated through, stirring occasionally until smooth.

2. Transfer mixture to a fondue pot. Keep mixture warm over a fondue burner. Serve with crusty bread cubes, corn chips, and/or vegetable dippers. If mixture becomes too thick, stir in additional milk.

Nutrition Facts per serving (fondue only): 97 cal., 6 g total fat (4 g sat. fat), 19 mg chol., 553 mg sodium, 6 g carbo., 0 g fiber, 5 g pro.
Daily Values: 7% vit. A, 17% vit. C, 10% calcium, 1% iron

Asparagus with Dijon-Horseradish Dip

Feta-Walnut Dip

1. In a food processor combine cheese, walnuts, milk, parsley, garlic, dried oregano, and crushed red pepper. Cover and process until smooth, scraping sides of bowl as necessary. Spoon dip into a serving bowl. If desired, garnish with fresh oregano leaves. Serve with bagel chips and/or fresh vegetables.

Nutrition Facts per 2 tablespoons dip: 86 cal., 7 g total fat (3 g sat. fat), 17 mg chol., 212 mg sodium, 2 g carbo., 0 g fiber, 4 g pro. **Daily Values:** 4% vit. A, 3% vit. C, 11% calcium, 2% iron

Monterey Jack Fondue

Although long a favorite in California, Monterey Jack cheese didn't hit the national scene until the late 1960s. Just about then, Better Homes and Gardens® featured the trendy cheese in this time-honored fondue. The recipe once again has been resurrected for its wonderful ease and tantalizing flavors.

Start to Finish: 15 minutes
Makes: 8 appetizer servings

3	tablespoons butter
1	clove garlic, minced
3	tablespoons all-purpose flour
⅛	teaspoon cayenne pepper
¾	cup chicken broth
1	5-ounce can (⅔ cup) evaporated milk
1¼	cups shredded Monterey Jack cheese (5 ounces)
	French bread cubes and/or sweet pepper strips

1. In a 1½-quart saucepan melt butter over medium heat. Add garlic; cook and stir for 30 seconds. Stir in flour and cayenne pepper. Stir in broth and evaporated milk all at once. Cook and stir until thickened and bubbly. Gradually add cheese, stirring until cheese is melted. Transfer to a fondue pot placed over fondue burner.

2. Serve with bread cubes and sweet pepper strips. (Stir in additional chicken broth, as necessary, for desired consistency.)

Nutrition Facts per ¼-cup fondue: 141 cal., 11 g total fat (7 g sat. fat), 33 mg chol., 237 mg sodium, 4 g carbo., 1 g fiber, 6 g pro.
Daily Values: 7% vit. A, 1% vit. C, 18% calcium, 2% iron

Feta-Walnut Dip

Sometimes referred to as pickled cheese because it is packaged in a salty whey brine, feta is a Greek-style cheese traditionally made from sheep or goat's milk. However, these days commercial producers often use cow's milk to produce this rich, tangy cheese.

Start to Finish: 15 minutes Makes: 1½ cups

2	cups crumbled feta cheese (8 ounces)
½	cup walnut pieces, toasted
¼	cup milk
¼	cup packed fresh flat-leaf parsley or curly parsley
1	clove garlic, minced
½	teaspoon dried oregano, crushed
¼	to ½ teaspoon crushed red pepper
	Bagel chips and/or vegetable dippers such as red pepper strips, baby carrots, or celery

Blue Cheese Ball

It just wouldn't be a holiday party without some version of a cheese ball. This recipe features blue cheese for a quick gourmet kick. Enhance the nutty flavor of the walnuts by lightly toasting them prior to chopping.

Prep: 20 minutes **Chill:** 4 hours
Makes: 2½ cups spread

- 2   8-ounce packages cream cheese, softened
- 1   4-ounce package crumbled blue cheese (1 cup)
- 1   teaspoon garlic powder
- ¼   teaspoon Worcestershire sauce for chicken
      Dash bottled hot pepper sauce
- ½   cup chopped walnuts, toasted
      Assorted crackers

1. In a large bowl beat together cream cheese, blue cheese, garlic powder, Worcestershire sauce, and hot pepper sauce with an electric mixer on low to medium speed until combined. Cover and chill about 4 hours or until firm enough to handle.

2. Shape the cheese mixture into a ball or log. Roll in walnuts to coat. Serve immediately or store, covered, in the refrigerator up to 24 hours. Serve with crackers.

Nutrition Facts per 2 tablespoons spread: 118 cal., 11 g total fat (6 g sat. fat), 29 mg chol., 147 mg sodium, 1 g carbo., 0 g fiber, 3 g pro.
Daily Values: 7% vit. A, 5% calcium, 2% iron

Quick Chile Con Queso Dip

This reliable party dip is so easy it only takes 10 minutes to make in the microwave. Who knew a combo of salsa and cheese soup could be a star snack?

Start to Finish: 10 minutes **Makes:** about 3 cups dip

- 1   16-ounce jar salsa (1¾ cups)
- 1   11-ounce can condensed nacho cheese soup
- ½   cup chopped green sweet pepper
      Tortilla chips
      Milk (optional)

1. Place salsa in a medium microwave-safe bowl; cover with vented plastic film. Cook on 100% (high) power for 1 to 3 minutes or until salsa is hot, stirring once.

2. Stir in soup. Cover with vented plastic film. Microwave on high for 1 to 2 minutes more or until soup is combined with the salsa and mixture is heated through, stirring once. Stir in sweet pepper.

3. Serve dip with tortilla chips. (If mixture becomes too thick, stir in a small amount of milk.)

Nutrition Facts per ¼-cup dip: 39 cal., 2 g total fat (1 g sat. fat), 3 mg chol., 330 mg sodium, 5 g carbo., 1 g fiber, 1 g pro.
Daily Values: 10% vit. A, 17% vit. C, 3% calcium, 2% iron

Saucepan method: In a medium saucepan heat salsa until very hot. Reduce heat to low. Add soup. Cook and stir until mixture is smooth. Stir in sweet pepper. Serve as directed in step 3.

Relish the Ease Relish trays are a simple way to add a gourmet flair to your holiday appetizers! Select an elegant platter, purchase a few of your favorite goodies, and create sections or rows of each. Tasty options available at most supermarkets include:

- Roasted red peppers
- Green, black, gourmet, and specialty stuffed olives
- Cheese cubes: alone or wrapped in strips of deli meat such as prosciutto or salami
- Marinated artichoke hearts
- Smoked, sliced salmon lox
- Marinated or fresh vegetables
- Pickled peppers

Another option is to present a platter of crackers, toasted pita wedges, or crostini (toasted baguette slices) surrounding a bowl of purchased olive tapenade, hummus, or tomato pesto in the center of the platter. Provide spreading knives or spoons.

Brie en Croûte

The fancy French name for this appetizer translates as Brie cheese wrapped in a crust. What a treat it is with jalapeño pepper jelly smeared on top. If spicy heat isn't your idea of a palate-pleaser, use a bottled fruit chutney instead of the jalapeño jelly.

Prep: 30 minutes **Bake:** 20 minutes
Stand: 10 minutes **Oven:** 400°F
Makes: 2 rounds (12 appetizer servings)

½	of a 17.3-ounce package frozen puff pastry, thawed (1 sheet)
2	tablespoons jalapeño pepper jelly
2	4½-ounce rounds Brie or Camembert cheese
2	tablespoons chopped nuts, toasted
1	egg, slightly beaten
	Apple and/or pear slices

1. Unfold pastry on a lightly floured surface; roll into a 16×10-inch rectangle. Cut into two 8-inch circles; reserve trimmings. Spread jelly over top of each cheese round. Sprinkle with nuts; press nuts into jelly. Combine egg and 1 tablespoon water; set mixture aside.

2. Place pastry circles over cheese rounds. Invert cheese and pastry. Brush pastry edges with a little egg mixture. Bring edges of pastry up and over cheese rounds, pleating and pinching edges to cover and seal. Trim any excess pastry. Place rounds, smooth sides up, on a greased baking sheet. Brush egg mixture over tops and sides. Cut small slits in the pastry for steam to escape. Using hors d'oeuvre cutters, cut shapes from reserved pastry. Brush shapes with egg mixture; place on cheese rounds.

3. Bake in a 400° oven for 20 to 25 minutes or until pastry is deep golden brown. Let stand for 10 to 20 minutes before serving. Serve with apple and/or pear slices.

Nutrition Facts per serving: 183 cal., 13 g total fat (4 g sat. fat), 39 mg chol., 215 mg sodium, 10 g carbo., 0 g fiber, 6 g pro.
Daily Values: 3% vit. A, 4% calcium, 1% iron

Pesto Brie

Sandwiched between two layers of Brie cheese, the herbed tang of pesto mingles perfectly with the rich flavors of the cheese. Rather than make your own basil pesto, this recipe can be simplified by using ½ cup purchased pesto. For a festive garnish, top with small basil leaves and a tiny cluster of cranberries.

Prep: 25 minutes **Chill:** overnight
Makes: 32 appetizer servings

2	cups loosely packed fresh basil leaves
3	tablespoons pine nuts, toasted
1	tablespoon olive oil
½	teaspoon black pepper
¼	teaspoon salt
2	cloves garlic, minced
1	2-pound round of Brie cheese, chilled
	Crackers

1. In a food processor combine basil, pine nuts, oil, pepper, and salt. Cover and process until smooth. Stir in garlic.

2. Slice chilled Brie in half horizontally. Spread basil mixture evenly over bottom half. Replace top half of cheese. Wrap in plastic film and refrigerate overnight. Serve at room temperature with crackers.

Nutrition Facts per serving: 103 cal., 9 g total fat (5 g sat. fat), 28 mg chol., 194 mg sodium, 0 g carbo., 0 g fiber, 6 g pro.
Daily Values: 6% vit. A, 1% vit. C, 6% calcium, 2% iron

Brie en Croûte

Chile and Chorizo Cheese Dip

Chile and Chorizo Cheese Dip

Packed full of cheese, green chiles, and seasoned sausage, this appetizer will be the talk of the party. The dip can't be transferred to a serving plate after baking, so depending on how you want to serve it, you may want to bake it in an attractive au gratin dish rather than a skillet.

Prep: 20 minutes **Bake:** 10 minutes **Oven:** 375°F
Makes: 10 to 12 servings

8	ounces uncooked chorizo sausage
1/3	cup thinly sliced onion (1 small)
1	4½-ounce can diced green chile peppers, drained
1/4	cup bottled roasted red sweet peppers, drained and sliced
1	pound Monterey Jack cheese, cut into ½-inch cubes
	Tortilla chips or warm flour tortillas

1. In a 10-inch cast-iron skillet* cook sausage over medium heat until cooked through. Remove sausage from skillet; drain off fat. In the same skillet cook onion over medium heat until tender, stirring frequently. Stir in chile peppers and roasted sweet peppers; cook until heated through. Remove onion mixture from skillet.

2. Divide meat mixture between two 1-quart au gratin dishes. Sprinkle pepper mixture and cheese over chorizo. Or arrange cheese in an even layer in the hot skillet. Top with onion mixture. Sprinkle cooked chorizo over all.

3. Bake in a 375° oven for 10 to 15 minutes or until cheese is melted. Serve with tortilla chips or spoon dip into flour tortillas and roll up.

*Note: If you do not have a cast-iron skillet, prepare as above through step 1 using a large skillet. Arrange cheese in a 2-quart au gratin dish. Top with onion mixture; sprinkle cooked chorizo over all. Bake in a 375° oven for 20 minutes or until cheese is melted. Serve as directed above.

Nutrition Facts per serving: 276 cal., 22 g total fat (12 g sat. fat), 60 mg chol., 552 mg sodium, 2 g carbo., 0 g fiber, 17 g pro.
Daily Values: 7% vit. A, 24% vit. C, 35% calcium, 4% iron

Artichoke-Chèvre Pastry Bites

In French, chèvre literally means "goat," but also refers to the cheese made from the animal's milk. Pure-white in color, goat-milk cheese has a pleasing tart flavor that is unique.

Prep: 20 minutes **Bake:** 20 minutes **Oven:** 400°F
Makes: about 30 appetizers

½   of a 17.3-ounce package (1 sheet)
    frozen puff pastry, thawed
1   6-ounce jar marinated artichoke
    hearts, drained and chopped
3   ounces goat cheese (soft chèvre)
¼   to ½ teaspoon crushed red pepper
1   egg, beaten (optional)
    Sesame seeds (optional)

1. Carefully unfold thawed pastry. Cut along the folds to make 3 rectangles; set aside.

2. For filling, in a small bowl combine artichoke hearts, goat cheese, and crushed red pepper. Spread ⅓ of the filling lengthwise along half of a pastry rectangle to within ½ inch of a long edge. Fold the other long side of pastry over filling; pinch edges to seal. Cut crosswise into 1-inch slices. Place on an ungreased baking sheet. Repeat 2 times with remaining pastry and filling. If desired, brush pastries with egg and sprinkle with sesame seeds.

3. Bake in a 400° oven for 18 to 20 minutes or until golden brown. Serve warm.

Nutrition Facts per serving: 48 cal., 3 g total fat (0 g sat. fat),
0 mg chol., 59 mg sodium, 3 g carbo., 0 g fiber, 1 g pro.
Daily Values: 2% vit. C, 1% calcium, 1% iron

Blue Cheese-Pecan Phyllo Bites

You don't have to be a baking expert to indulge in the delights of leaf-thin crispy phyllo dough. Now it comes in pre-formed miniature shells. All you have to do is spoon in the filling and artfully arrange them on a decorative platter.

Start to Finish: 30 minutes **Makes:** 30 appetizers

1   8-ounce package cream cheese,
    softened
2   2.1-ounce packages baked miniature
    phyllo dough shells (30 total)
4   ounces blue cheese, crumbled
⅓   cup dried tart cherries, snipped
1   recipe Sugared Pecans

1. In a small bowl stir the cream cheese until smooth. Spoon it into the bottom of the dough shells. Top with blue cheese and cherries. Sprinkle with Sugared Pecans.

Sugared Pecans: Spread ⅓ cup chopped pecans in a medium skillet. Sprinkle with 1 tablespoon sugar and ¼ teaspoon salt. Heat, without stirring, over medium heat. When sugar begins to melt, turn heat to medium-low. Gently stir pecans until all of the sugar is melted and pecans are lightly coated. Transfer pecans to a foil-lined baking sheet; cool. To serve, break apart.

Make-Ahead Tip: Prepare as directed above. Store in a tightly covered container in the refrigerator up to 24 hours.

Nutrition Facts per serving: 77 cal., 6 g total fat (2 g sat. fat),
11 mg chol., 104 mg sodium, 4 g carbo., 0 g fiber, 2 g pro.
Daily Values: 3% vit. A, 3% calcium, 2% iron

Knowing the Blues Blue-veined cheese is turned into this special delicacy when it is sprayed with mold spores (such as Penicillium roqueforti), and sometimes dotted with holes so the mold can penetrate. The result of this time-consuming process is bluish green veins throughout the cheese, which impart its classical appearance, aroma, and flavor. Common varieties of blue cheese include Gorgonzola, Roquefort, Danablu, and Stilton. Blue cheese is often sold crumbled in containers, which saves a step in recipes.

Blue Cheese-Pecan Phyllo Bites

Prosciutto-Wrapped Dates

Prosciutto is the Italian word for "ham," that is, seasoned and salt-cured meat. However, rather than being smoked, it is air-dried and pressed so the texture is firm and dense. Commonly used to wrap appetizers—such as cooked shrimp, melon balls, and pears—it is sold thinly sliced for easy folding.

Prep: 20 minutes **Makes:** about 36 appetizers

1	8-ounce package whole pitted dates
35	to 40 whole smoked almonds (about 1¼ ounces)
3	ounces prosciutto, cut into ½-inch strips
	Cracked black pepper

1. Stuff each date with a smoked almond. Wrap a strip of prosciutto around each date. Grind freshly cracked pepper over dates. Serve immediately or cover and chill up to 4 hours.

Nutrition Facts per serving: 29 cal., 1 g total fat (0 g sat. fat), 2 mg chol., 70 mg sodium, 5 g carbo., 1 g fiber, 1 g pro.
Daily Values: 1% calcium, 1% iron

Salami Cone Skewers

With only four ingredients, these cheese-filled salami pieces couldn't be easier to prepare. If you don't have a pastry bag, use a self-sealing plastic bag with a small hole cut out of one corner. Seal the bag prior to squeezing out the cheese.

Start to Finish: 15 minutes **Makes:** 22 appetizers

1	5.2-ounce package Boursin cheese
1	tablespoon milk
4	ounces hard salami slices
4	whole pepperoncini, coarsely chopped

1. In a small bowl stir together cheese and milk. Place cheese mixture in a pastry bag fitted with a large star tip.

2. Cut salami slices in half. Twist each slice to form a cone. Insert a wooden toothpick through each cone to hold its shape. Pipe cheese mixture into salami cones. Sprinkle each cone with chopped pepperoncini. Serve immediately or chill up to 4 hours before serving.

Nutrition Facts per serving: 48 cal., 5 g total fat (3 g sat. fat), 4 mg chol., 197 mg sodium, 0 g carbo., 0 g fiber, 2 g pro.

Stuffed Jalapeños

Satisfy the cravings of the daredevil heat-seekers on your Christmas party list with these quick tear-jerking appetizers. If jalapeños are too hot for your palate, give the milder Anaheim peppers a try.

Prep: 20 minutes **Bake:** 15 minutes **Oven:** 350°F
Makes: 24 appetizers

½	of one 8-ounce tub cream cheese
2	tablespoons finely chopped green onion (1)
2	tablespoons chopped bottled roasted red sweet pepper
1	clove garlic, minced
12	fresh jalapeño peppers or 2 to 3 fresh Anaheim peppers, halved lengthwise and seeded*

Stuffed Jalapeños

1. In a small bowl stir together cream cheese, green onion, roasted red sweet pepper, and garlic. Spoon the cheese mixture into the jalapeño or Anaheim pepper halves. Place stuffed peppers on a 15×105×1-inch baking pan.

2. Bake in a 350° oven about 15 minutes or until peppers are slightly softer. If using Anaheim peppers, cut each into 2-inch bite-size pieces.

***Note:** When working with chile peppers, wear plastic or rubber gloves. If your bare hands do touch the chile peppers, wash your hands well.

Nutrition Facts per serving: 19 cal., 2 g total fat (1 g sat. fat), 5 mg chol., 14 mg sodium, 1 g carbo., 0 g fiber, 0 g pro.
Daily Values: 2% vit. A, 9% vit. C, 1% calcium, 1% iron

Spicy Spinach-Stuffed Mushrooms

Heaped with a savory filling of Italian sausage, fresh spinach leaves, and Parmesan cheese, these sensational appetizers take stuffed mushrooms to a new level.

Prep: 30 minutes **Bake:** 10 minutes **Oven:** 425°F
Makes: 24 appetizers

24	large fresh mushrooms, 1½- to 2-inches in diameter
2	tablespoons olive oil
	Salt and pepper
8	ounces spicy bulk Italian sausage
¼	cup finely chopped onion
¼	cup finely chopped red sweet pepper
1	clove garlic, minced
1	cup fresh spinach, chopped
¼	cup finely shredded Parmesan cheese
¼	cup fine dry bread crumbs

1. Rinse and drain mushrooms. Remove stems; set aside. Brush mushroom caps with olive oil. Sprinkle with salt and pepper. Set aside.

2. In a large skillet cook chopped stems, sausage, onion, sweet pepper, and garlic over medium heat until sausage is brown. Stir in spinach; cook until

Spicy Spinach-Stuffed Mushrooms

wilted. Stir in Parmesan cheese and bread crumbs. Remove from heat. Spoon sausage mixture into mushroom caps. Place on a greased baking sheet.

3. Bake in a 425° oven about 10 minutes or until stuffing is brown and mushrooms are tender.

Nutrition Facts per serving: 57 cal., 5 g total fat (1 g sat. fat), 8 mg chol., 127 mg sodium, 2 g carbo., 0 g fiber, 2 g pro.
Daily Values: 3% vit. A, 6% vit. C, 2% calcium, 2% iron

Snappy Breakfasts and Brunches

DINNER MAY BE THE PRIMARY MEAL ON CHRISTMAS DAY, but that doesn't mean family members and guests are willing to go hungry until supper time. Start the day off right with stratas, frittatas, pancakes, and more. Whether you're looking for a quick pick-me-up of oatmeal before the gift giving begins or a sit-down spread that rivals the afternoon feast, you'll find a little of everything in this chapter.

Waking up early on Christmas morning to cook breakfast may not be your idea of a good time, so do most of the preparations weeks before with Cream-Cheese Stuffed French Toast or the night before with Baked Denver Strata. Or how about an easy way to enhance pancake mix? Depending on the ingredients you have on hand and your family's preferences, choose between holiday-inspired Gingerbread Pancakes and warm and comforting Banana Pancakes. From fruit to omelets, skillet dishes to oatmeal, a simple morning meal is only a page or two away.

Baked Denver Strata, page 49

Autumn Frittata

The centerpiece of an autumn brunch should be this delicious dish infused with the seasonal flavors of fennel and sweet potatoes. Although bearing a somewhat sweeter taste, a 16-ounce can of sweet potatoes can be substituted for fresh if you're running short on time.

Prep: 25 minutes **Bake:** 20 minutes **Oven:** 350°F
Makes: 4 to 6 servings

2	medium sweet potatoes (1 pound)
6	eggs
1	tablespoon snipped fresh parsley
1	teaspoon dried thyme, crushed
½	teaspoon salt
1	medium fennel bulb, trimmed, cored, and thinly sliced (about 1 cup)
½	cup thinly sliced red onion (1 medium)
2	tablespoons olive oil
¼	cup finely shredded Parmesan cheese

1. In a medium saucepan cook sweet potatoes, covered, in enough boiling water to cover, for 25 to 35 minutes or until tender. Drain; cool slightly. Peel and slice sweet potatoes; set aside.

2. In a medium bowl beat together eggs, parsley, thyme, and salt with a rotary beater or whisk.

3. In a large nonstick ovenproof skillet cook and stir fennel and onion in hot oil for 5 to 7 minutes or until tender. Remove from heat. Layer sliced sweet potatoes on top of fennel and onion in skillet. Pour the egg mixture over sweet potatoes.

4. Bake in a 350° oven about 20 minutes or until a knife inserted near the center comes out clean. Sprinkle top with Parmesan cheese.

Nutrition Facts per serving: 411 cal., 23 g total fat (9 g sat. fat), 341 mg chol., 988 mg sodium, 25 g carbo., 4 g fiber, 24 g pro.
Daily Values: 312% vit. A, 42% vit. C, 51% calcium, 15% iron

Tortilla Skillet

If you like, top this breakfast skillet with sour cream, sliced black olives, and additional salsa.

Prep: 25 minutes **Bake:** 10 minutes **Oven:** 350°F
Makes: 4 servings

6	6-inch corn tortillas
4	eggs, slightly beaten
1	tablespoon cooking oil
1	16-ounce jar salsa
1	cup chopped cooked ham or chicken
½	cup frozen whole kernel corn
1½	cups shredded Monterey Jack cheese (6 ounces)
¼	cup finely chopped red onion
	Bias-sliced green onions (optional)

1. Tear tortillas into 1½-inch pieces. Place on an ungreased baking sheet. Bake in a 350° oven for 10 to 12 minutes or until crisp and light brown.

2. In a large bowl combine beaten eggs and the tortilla pieces. In a large skillet heat oil over medium heat; add egg mixture. Cook, without stirring, just until mixture begins to set on the bottom. With a spatula, lift and fold egg mixture until egg is cooked but still moist and tortillas are coated. Stir in salsa, ham, corn, and 1 cup of the cheese. Heat through, stirring gently.

3. Transfer to a serving dish. Top with remaining ½ cup cheese and chopped onion. If desired, sprinkle with sliced green onions.

Nutrition Facts per serving: 473 cal., 26 g total fat (11 g sat. fat), 268 mg chol., 1,231 mg sodium, 36 g carbo., 5 g fiber, 27 g pro.
Daily Values: 27% vit. A, 32% vit. C, 43% calcium, 27% iron

Fennel 101 The large, bulbous base of fennel has a sweet, delicate flavor somewhat similar to licorice. Treated like a vegetable, the base is the most common part to be used, but the stems can be eaten raw or cooked, and the feathery foliage can be snipped and used as a garnish. Follow these tips for selection and preparation.

• Look for fennel that is firm and free of cracks or brown spots, with bright green, unwilted foliage and crisp stalks.

• Prior to use, rinse well and pat dry.

• Cut off a thin piece at the stem end to remove the tough brown area.

• Chop off the stalks and foliage.

• Halve the bulb lengthwise, and cut out the hard center core if the bulb is large.

• Thinly slice each half of the fennel bulb.

Hash Brown Omelet

Hash Brown Omelet

Bacon, hash brown potatoes, eggs, and cheese are breakfast favorites in many houses across the county, but until you taste them combined into one hearty skillet, you won't know breakfast bliss. If you like, add black olives and mushrooms with the green pepper.

Start to Finish: 15 minutes **Makes:** 4 servings

4	slices bacon
2	cups refrigerated shredded hash brown potatoes (about half of a 20-ounce package)
¼	cup chopped onion
¼	cup chopped green sweet pepper
4	eggs
¼	cup milk
½	teaspoon salt
	Dash black pepper
1	cup shredded cheddar cheese (4 ounces)
	Bias-sliced green onions (optional)

1. In a large skillet cook bacon until crisp. Drain bacon on paper towels, reserving 2 tablespoons of the drippings in skillet. Crumble bacon; set aside.

2. In a large bowl stir together potatoes, chopped onion, and sweet pepper. Pat potato mixture evenly into the skillet. Cook, uncovered, over low heat about 7 minutes or until crisp, turning once.

3. Meanwhile, in a small bowl beat together eggs, milk, salt, and black pepper with a wire whisk or rotary beater. Pour egg mixture over potato mixture. Sprinkle with cheddar cheese and bacon. Cook, covered, over low heat for 5 to 7 minutes or until egg mixture is set. Loosen omelet; fold in half. Turn out of skillet onto a serving plate. Cut into wedges to serve. If desired, garnish with green onions.

Nutrition Facts per serving: 382 cal., 25 g total fat (12 g sat. fat), 256 mg chol., 729 mg sodium, 20 g carbo., 1 g fiber, 19 g pro.
Daily Values: 12% vit. A, 20% vit. C, 27% calcium, 7% iron

Turkey-Asparagus Brunch Bake

If you have turkey left over from Christmas dinner, chop it and add it instead of the uncooked ground turkey in this recipe. Depending on which vegetable you prefer (or what you have on hand), you can use frozen asparagus or broccoli for this colorful morning meal.

Prep: 30 minutes **Bake:** 20 minutes **Oven:** 425°F
Makes: 8 servings

1	10-ounce package frozen cut asparagus or cut broccoli
1	pound uncooked ground turkey
1	cup chopped onion (1 large)
½	cup chopped red sweet pepper
1	6-ounce package seasoned croutons (about 2 ½ cups)
2	cups milk
3	eggs
1	cup all-purpose flour
¼	cup grated Parmesan cheese
1	teaspoon lemon-pepper seasoning
¼	teaspoon salt
1	cup shredded Swiss cheese (4 ounces)

1. Grease a 3-quart rectangular baking dish; set aside. Cook asparagus according to package directions. Drain and set aside.

2. In a large skillet cook turkey, onion, and sweet pepper over medium heat until no pink remains in turkey and vegetables are tender. Remove from heat. Drain off fat. Arrange croutons in prepared baking dish; top with cooked turkey mixture and asparagus.

3. In a large bowl combine milk, eggs, flour, Parmesan cheese, lemon-pepper seasoning, and salt. Beat until smooth with a wire whisk or rotary beater. (Or, combine these ingredients in a blender. Cover and blend for 20 seconds.)

4. Pour egg mixture evenly over layers in baking dish. Bake, uncovered, in a 425° oven about 20 minutes or until a knife inserted near center comes out clean. Sprinkle with Swiss cheese. Bake about 5 minutes more or until cheese melts.

Make-Ahead Tip: Prepare casserole as directed through Step 3. Pour egg mixture into a bowl or pitcher; cover and chill up to 24 hours. Cover and chill turkey and asparagus in the baking dish up to 24 hours. To bake, stir egg mixture well and pour it over turkey mixture. Bake, uncovered, in a 425° oven about 30 minutes or until a knife inserted near the center comes out clean. Continue as directed in the recipe.

Nutrition Facts per serving: 326 cal., 16 g total fat (7 g sat. fat), 146 mg chol., 635 mg sodium, 21 g carbo., 2 g fiber, 23 g pro.
Daily Values: 19% vit. A, 46% vit. C, 26% calcium, 12% iron

Egg Dish Trivia

What is it: a strata, an omelet, a frittata, a quiche, a soufflé, or just a breakfast casserole? Actually, whoever creates the dish has free reign over the name, but there are a few technical definitions to consider when making that choice.

Strata: A layered, baked casserole dish composed of beaten eggs and milk, bread cubes, and a variety of meats, cheeses, and/or vegetables.

Omelet: Beaten eggs cooked in a frying pan until firm, then folded over a savory filling of meat, cheese, and/or vegetables. Alternately, a sweet filling can be used and the omelet dusted with powdered sugar.

Frittata: An Italian omelet with the filling ingredients and the eggs combined before cooking.

Quiche: A savory, custardlike filling of eggs, cream, vegetables, meat, and/or cheese baked in a pastry shell. Resembles a pie.

Soufflé: A sweet or savory combination of egg yolks, beaten egg whites, and other ingredients, typically baked in a round dish with high sides. The hot air inside of baked soufflés rises and causes them to be extremely fragile. The delicate soufflé begins to deflate as soon as it is removed from the oven, so it must be served immediately.

Baked Denver Strata

An old favorite, the Denver omelet, is revitalized in this trendy one-dish meal. Complete with veggies, cheese, meat, and eggs, this new version adds English muffins to the mix.

Prep: 25 minutes **Bake:** 35 minutes
Stand: 10 minutes **Oven:** 350°F
Makes: 10 to 12 servings

6	English muffins, split and quartered
9	eggs
1	cup milk
1	4½-ounce can diced green chile peppers, drained
¼	teaspoon salt
¼	teaspoon black pepper
1	cup diced cooked ham
½	cup finely chopped green onions (4)
1	2½-ounce can sliced pitted ripe olives, drained
1	7-ounce jar roasted red sweet peppers, drained and cut into strips
1½	cups shredded provolone cheese (6 ounces)
½	cup shredded cheddar cheese (2 ounces)

1. Arrange English muffin quarters in a single layer in a greased 3-quart rectangular baking dish. Set aside.

2. In a large bowl beat together eggs, milk, chile peppers, salt, and black pepper with a wire whisk or rotary beater. Pour egg mixture over muffin quarters; sprinkle with ham, green onions, olives, roasted sweet peppers, provolone cheese, and cheddar cheese. If desired, cover and chill for 2 to 24 hours until ready to bake.

3. Bake, uncovered, in a 350° oven about 35 minutes (45 minutes, if chilled) or until a knife inserted near the center comes out clean. Let stand for 10 minutes before serving.

Nutrition Facts per serving: 279 cal., 14 g total fat (6 g sat. fat), 218 mg chol., 744 mg sodium, 20 g carbo., 2 g fiber, 18 g pro.
Daily Values: 11% vit. A, 77% vit. C, 31% calcium, 14% iron

Cheesy Ham Quiche

Cheesy Ham Quiche

With all the usual ingredients of a regular egg dish—milk, cheese, eggs, and meat—this tasty version adds a pie shell to the mix.

Prep: 20 minutes **Bake:** 45 minutes
Stand: 15 minutes **Oven:** 350°F **Makes:** 6 servings

½	of one 15-ounce package rolled refrigerated unbaked pie crust (1 crust)
4	eggs, slightly beaten
1	cup half-and-half, light cream, or milk
1	cup finely chopped cooked ham
½	cup shredded cheddar cheese (2 ounces)
½	cup shredded mozzarella cheese (2 ounces)
½	teaspoon black pepper
⅛	teaspoon ground red pepper

1. Roll out pie crust according to package directions. Transfer pastry to a 9-inch pie plate. Trim pastry to ½ inch beyond edge of plate. Fold under extra pastry. Crimp edges as desired.

2. In a medium bowl whisk together eggs and half-and-half. Stir in ham, cheddar cheese, mozzarella cheese, black pepper, and ground red pepper.

3. Pour egg mixture into the prepared pastry shell. Bake in a 350° oven 45 to 50 minutes or until a knife inserted near the center comes out clean. Let stand 15 minutes before serving.

Nutrition Facts per serving: 357 cal., 24 g total fat (11 g sat. fat), 191 mg chol., 604 mg sodium, 20 g carbo., 0 g fiber, 14 g pro.
Daily Values: 9% vit. A, 2% vit. C, 21% calcium, 6% iron

Gingerbread Pancakes

This recipe doesn't use the gingerbread to form little people or houses, but it certainly brings home that spicy holiday taste. For an extra special treat, warm some purchased lemon curd and drizzle it over the pancakes before serving.

Prep: 20 minutes **Cook:** 3 minutes per batch
Makes: 9 to 10 pancakes

2	**cups packaged buttermilk complete pancake mix**
1	**teaspoon ground cinnamon**
1	**teaspoon ground ginger**
1	**teaspoon ground nutmeg**
2	**eggs, slightly beaten**
²⁄₃	**cup milk**
¹⁄₃	**cup molasses**
¹⁄₃	**cup strong coffee**
3	**tablespoons cooking oil**
	Butter, maple syrup, or lemon curd

1. In a large bowl combine pancake mix, cinnamon, ginger, and nutmeg. In a medium bowl combine eggs, milk, molasses, coffee, and oil. Add egg mixture to dry pancake mixture all at once. Stir just until moistened (batter should be lumpy).

2. Heat a lightly greased griddle or heavy skillet over medium heat until a few drops of water sizzle on the surface. For each pancake, pour about ¼ cup of the batter onto the hot griddle. Spread batter into a circle about 4 inches in diameter.

3. Cook over medium heat for 1 to 2 minutes on each side or until pancakes are golden brown, turning to cook second sides when pancakes have bubbly surfaces and edges are slightly dry (watch carefully so pancakes do not overbrown). Keep warm in a covered ovenproof dish in a 300°F oven. Serve with butter, maple syrup, or lemon curd.

Nutrition Facts per serving: 210 cal., 8 g total fat (2 g sat. fat), 55 mg chol., 338 mg sodium, 31 g carbo., 1 g fiber, 5 g pro.
Daily Values: 2% vit. A, 16% calcium, 12% iron

Gingerbread Pancakes

Banana Pancakes

All you have to do for this recipe is add the extra ingredients to a pancake mix. Then serve these oh-so-easy flapjacks with flavored yogurt or fresh fruit for a scrumptious early-morning treat.

Prep: 15 minutes **Cook:** 2 minutes per batch
Makes: 20 pancakes

> 1¾ **cups packaged buttermilk pancake mix**
> ¼ **teaspoon ground cinnamon**
> 2 **cups milk**
> 2 **ripe medium bananas, mashed (about ¾ cup)**
> 2 **eggs, slightly beaten**
> 3 **tablespoons butter, melted, or cooking oil**
> ⅓ **cup finely chopped walnuts or pecans, toasted**
>   **Cinnamon sugar (optional)**

1. In a large bowl combine pancake mix and cinnamon; set aside. In a medium bowl whisk together milk, bananas, eggs, and melted butter. Add milk mixture to the dry pancake mixture all at once. Stir just until moistened (batter should be lumpy). Stir in nuts.

2. Heat a lightly greased griddle or heavy skillet over medium heat until a few drops of water sizzle on the surface. For each pancake, pour about ¼ cup of batter onto the hot griddle.

3. Cook over medium heat for 1 to 2 minutes on each side or until pancakes are golden brown, turning to second sides when pancakes have bubbly surfaces and edges are slightly dry. Serve immediately or keep warm in a loosely covered ovenproof dish in a 300°F oven. If desired, sprinkle with cinnamon sugar.

Nutrition Facts per serving: 94 cal., 4 g total fat (1 g sat. fat), 28 mg chol., 161 mg sodium, 11 g carbo., 1 g fiber, 3 g pro.
Daily Values: 3% vit. A, 2% vit. C, 7% calcium, 3% iron

Maple-Bacon Oven Pancake

Maple-Bacon Oven Pancake

Sweet and savory, this pancake features a delicious combo of bacon, cheese, and maple-flavored syrup. Pair this tasty treat with a salad composed of your favorite fresh fruit.

Prep: 15 minutes **Bake:** 10 minutes **Oven:** 425°F
Makes: 12 servings

> 1½ **cups packaged biscuit mix**
> 1 **cup shredded cheddar cheese (4 ounces)**
> 2 **eggs**
> ¾ **cup milk**
> ¼ **cup maple-flavored syrup**
> 5 **slices bacon, crisp-cooked, drained, and crumbled**
>   **Maple-flavored syrup (optional)**

1. Grease and flour a 13×9×2-inch baking pan; set aside. In a medium bowl combine biscuit mix, half of the cheddar cheese, the eggs, milk, and the ¼ cup syrup; beat until nearly smooth. Spread batter in prepared baking pan.

2. Bake in a 425° oven for 10 to 12 minutes or until a toothpick inserted near center comes out clean. Sprinkle with remaining cheddar cheese and the bacon; bake for 3 minutes more. Cut into squares. If desired, serve with additional syrup.

Nutrition Facts per serving: 156 cal., 8 g total fat (4 g sat. fat), 49 mg chol., 323 mg sodium, 15 g carbo., 0 g fiber, 6 g pro.
Daily Values: 3% vit. A, 11% calcium, 4% iron

Cream Cheese-Filled French Toast

With a rich creamy filling, this version of French toast will be an instant hit. The make-ahead directions allow to you save some time on the morning of a brunch by preparing the toast up to three months in advance.

Prep: 20 minutes **Cook:** 4 minutes per batch
Makes: 9 servings

1	recipe Cream Cheese Filling
1	8-ounce French bread baguette
1	5-ounce can (⅔ cup) evaporated milk
⅓	cup milk
¼	cup butter or margarine
3	eggs
¾	cup sugar
1	teaspoon vanilla
2	tablespoons cooking oil
	Maple-flavored or fruit-flavored syrup

1. Prepare Cream Cheese Filling; set aside. Cut bread into ¾-inch slices; set aside.

2. In a small saucepan combine evaporated milk, milk, and butter; heat just until butter melts. In a medium bowl beat eggs with a fork; stir in sugar, vanilla, and warm milk mixture. Pour egg mixture into a shallow baking dish. Place bread slices in egg mixture, turning to coat both sides. Let bread slices stand in egg mixture for 5 minutes to soak bread.

3. In a large skillet heat oil over medium heat. Add several bread slices; cook for 2 to 3 minutes on each side or until golden. If desired, keep warm in a 300°F oven. Repeat with remaining bread, adding more oil if necessary.

4. Working with half of the slices of toast, spread about 1 heaping tablespoon of the Cream Cheese Filling onto each slice; top with remaining slices. Serve with desired syrup.

Cream Cheese Filling: In a food processor or large mixing bowl combine one 8-ounce package cream cheese, softened; ¼ of an 8-ounce container frozen whipped dessert topping, thawed; 2 tablespoons sugar; and 2 tablespoons dairy sour cream. Cover and process until smooth or beat with an electric mixer on low to medium speed until smooth.

Make-Ahead Tip: Prepare as directed through step 3. Place the cooked slices of toast on a baking sheet and freeze just until firm. Place in freezer container. Seal, label, and freeze for up to 3 months. To reheat, place frozen slices in a single layer on an ungreased baking sheet. Bake, uncovered, in a 400°F oven for 10 to 12 minutes or until heated through. Meanwhile, prepare Cream Cheese Filling. Fill and serve as directed in step 4.

Nutrition Facts per serving: 379 cal., 23 g total fat (12 g sat. fat), 119 mg chol., 312 mg sodium, 36 g carbo., 1 g fiber, 8 g pro.
Daily Values: 13% vit. A, 4% vit. C, 10% calcium, 7% iron

Name It After the French Many popular dishes and foods bear the name of the French, including french fries, French bread, French toast, French onion soup, French dressing, and french beans. Although some of these names actually refer to frenching food by cutting it into thin, lengthwise slices—as in french fries or french beans—others imply that the food originated in France.

In the case of French toast, the French actually call their version of this dish *pain perdu*, meaning "lost bread." They came up with this name because the fried egg-covered toast was a popular way to salvage dry bread that was a day or two old.

Little to no evidence exists on the actual origins of American French toast, although some say it was named after a man named Mr. French, and others say it was named German toast until World War II. Possibly it was just named French toast because of its similarity to the French version, *pain perdu*. In any case, it doesn't seem to matter where the popular breakfast dish was named; French toast is here to stay!

Oatmeal with Fruit and Nuts

Christmas Morning French Toast

Although this recipe is the perfect way to use up leftover raisin bread, it is just as delicious with fresh bread. Real maple syrup brings out the luscious flavor of this breakfast masterpiece.

Start to Finish: 25 minutes **Makes:** 4 to 5 servings

1	16-ounce loaf raisin bread (unsliced)
3	eggs, beaten
¾	cup half-and-half, light cream, or milk
2	teaspoons granulated sugar
1	teaspoon vanilla
2	tablespoons butter
	Sifted powdered sugar
	Maple syrup

1. Trim ends from bread. Slice the loaf of bread into 8 to 10 slices.

2. In a shallow bowl or 9-inch pie plate whisk together eggs, half-and-half, sugar, and vanilla. Dip bread slices into egg mixture, coating both sides.

3. In a 12-inch nonstick skillet or on a griddle melt 1 tablespoon of the butter over medium heat; add half of the bread slices and cook for 2 to 3 minutes on each side or until golden brown. Repeat with remaining bread and butter. Sprinkle French toast with powdered sugar and serve with maple syrup.

Nutrition Facts per serving: 517 cal., 17 g total fat (7 g sat. fat), 183 mg chol., 537 mg sodium, 78 g carbo., 5 g fiber, 15 g pro.
Daily Values: 9% vit. A, 1% vit. C, 16% calcium, 17% iron

Oatmeal with Fruit and Nuts

Turn that bland bowl of oatmeal into a taste extravaganza with quick and easy additions. If desired, substitute different ingredients for the fruit and nuts, such as dried cherries, prunes, pecans, or walnuts.

Prep: 20 minutes **Cook:** 5 minutes **Makes:** 4 servings

3	cups water
½	teaspoon ground cinnamon
¼	teaspoon salt (optional)
1⅓	cups regular rolled oats
1	small apple or pear, chopped
¼	cup snipped, pitted dates
2	tablespoons sliced almonds, toasted
1	tablespoon brown sugar
	Milk, warmed (optional)

1. In a medium saucepan combine water, cinnamon, and, if desired, salt. Bring to boiling; stir in oats. Cook for 5 minutes, stirring occasionally. Let stand, covered, until oatmeal thickens.

2. Divide oatmeal mixture among 4 serving bowls. Top with apple, dates, almonds, and brown sugar. If desired, serve with warm milk.

Nutrition Facts per serving: 214 cal., 4 g total fat (1 g sat. fat), 0 mg chol., 7 mg sodium, 40 g carbo., 6 g fiber, 6 g pro.
Daily Values: 3% vit. C, 4% calcium, 10% iron

Baked Fruit Ambrosia

When you're having friends or extended family in for breakfast or brunch, start the meal with this easily prepared cinnamon-spiced fruit combo.

Prep: 10 minutes **Bake:** 15 minutes **Oven:** 350°F
Makes: 4 servings

- 2 **medium oranges**
- 1 **8-ounce can pineapple tidbits (juice pack), drained**
- ½ **teaspoon finely shredded orange peel**
- ¼ **teaspoon ground cinnamon**
- 2 **tablespoons shredded coconut**
  Fresh raspberries (optional)

1. Peel and section oranges; cut into bite-size pieces. Divide orange pieces and pineapple among four 6-ounce custard cups. Sprinkle with orange peel and cinnamon. Top with coconut.

2. Bake in a 350° about 15 minutes or until fruit is heated through and coconut is golden. If desired, garnish with fresh raspberries. Serve warm.

Nutrition Facts per serving: 66 cal., 1 g total fat (1 g sat. fat), 0 mg chol., 12 mg sodium, 14 g carbo., 2 g fiber, 1 g pro.
Daily Values: 2% vit. A, 36% vit. C, 2% calcium, 1% iron

Christmas Fruit Medley

Once upon a time, fresh fruit was a rarity on a snowy winter morning in most of the country. Thanks to improved transportation from the southern states, every home can now enjoy juicy fruit any time of the year.

Start to Finish: 25 minutes **Makes:** 8 to 10 servings

- ½ **cup dried tart cherries**
- ¼ **cup honey**
- ½ **teaspoon finely shredded lime peel**
- 1 **to 2 tablespoons lime juice**
- 1 **cup seedless green grapes, halved**
- 1 **cup seedless red grapes, halved**
- 1 **Granny Smith apple, cored and cut into bite-size pieces**
- 1 **Red Delicious apple, cored and cut into bite-size pieces**
- 2 **fresh kiwifruit, peeled and cut into wedges**

1. Place dried cherries in a small bowl; add enough boiling water to cover cherries. Let stand about 15 minutes or until cherries are plump. Drain.

2. Meanwhile, in a large bowl combine honey, lime peel, and lime juice. Stir in green and red grapes, Granny Smith and Red Delicious apples, kiwifruit, and the cherries. Serve immediately or cover and chill up to 2 hours before serving.

Nutrition Facts per serving: 116 cal., 0 g total fat (0 g sat. fat), 0 mg chol., 2 mg sodium, 30 g carbo., 2 g fiber, 1 g pro.
Daily Values: 1% vit. A, 42% vit. C, 1% calcium, 2% iron

Baked Fruit Ambrosia

Christmas Fruit Medley

Holiday Breads in a Hurry

SWEET OR SAVORY, SNACK OR SIDE DISH, these breads will add cheer to any table or gathering. Refrigerated convenience products assume new life when embellished with extra ingredients for that homemade touch. Cinnamon roll dough is enhanced with blueberries and pecans; breadstick dough awakens anew when covered with Italian seasoning and Parmesan cheese; and purchased biscuit dough tickles the taste buds when oozing with sugar and orange juice. For those who still like to mix the ingredients by hand, be assured that made-from-scratch doesn't have to mean all day in the kitchen. Prepare a batch of buttermilk biscuits or mushroom popovers just minutes before dinner is ready, and before you know it, your Christmas clan will mop up the gravy with fresh-from-the-oven bread.

Savory Holiday Bread, page 62

Sweet Pretzel Snowflakes

Even though these winter-themed goodies start with frozen sweet roll dough, they require a little extra time to prepare on the morning of a brunch. Best when served warm from the oven, these cookie-shaped breads are exceptional when smeared with a bit of lemon curd or jam.

Prep: 40 minutes **Rise:** 5 minutes **Bake:** 8 minutes per batch **Oven:** 400°F **Makes:** 24 to 36 pretzels

- 1   **16-ounce loaf frozen sweet roll dough, thawed**
- 1   **egg white, slightly beaten**
- 1   **tablespoon water**
      Pearl sugar or colored coarse sugar

1. Lightly grease 3 large baking sheets; set aside.

2. On a lightly floured surface roll thawed dough into a 16-inch square (about ¼-inch thickness), occasionally stopping and letting dough rest, if necessary. Using a 2½- to 3-inch snowflake-shape cookie cutter, cut dough, dipping cutter into flour between cuts. Arrange snowflake cutouts, about 2 inches apart, on prepared baking sheets. Let rise about 5 minutes before baking. Gather dough scraps and gently shape into a ball. Cover and let rest for 5 minutes. Roll out dough to ¼-inch thickness and cut out additional snowflakes.

3. In a small bowl stir together egg white and water. Brush cutouts with some of the egg white mixture. Sprinkle with some of the sugar.

4. Bake in a 400° oven about 8 minutes or until light golden brown. Transfer to wire racks and cool.

Nutrition Facts per serving: 57 cal., 1 g total fat (1 g sat. fat), 11 mg chol., 36 mg sodium, 10 g carbo., 0 g fiber, 2 g pro.
Daily Values: 1% calcium, 3% iron

Cheddar Spoon Bread

To add a peppery punch of flavor to this soft, fluffy bread, substitute Monterey Jack cheese with jalapeño peppers for the more basic cheddar. Moist enough to serve with a spoon, this hearty side dish is a tasty replacement or addition to potato and rice dishes.

Prep: 25 minutes **Bake:** 45 minutes **Oven:** 325°F **Makes:** 8 servings

- 1½   **cups milk**
- ½   **cup cornmeal**
- 2   **cups shredded cheddar cheese or Monterey Jack cheese (8 ounces)**
- 1   **tablespoon butter or margarine**
- 1½   **teaspoons baking powder**
- 1   **teaspoon sugar**
- ¼   **teaspoon salt**
- 4   **eggs**

1. In a large saucepan stir together milk and cornmeal. Cook over medium-high heat, stirring constantly until mixture is thickened and bubbly; remove from heat. Add cheese, butter, baking powder, sugar, and salt; stir until cheese melts.

2. Separate eggs. Add yolks, one at a time, to cornmeal mixture, stirring after each addition just until combined (mixture will be thick).

3. In a large mixing bowl beat egg whites with an electric mixer on high speed until stiff peaks form (tips stand straight). Stir about ⅓ of the beaten egg whites into the cornmeal mixture. Gently fold remaining beaten egg whites into the cornmeal mixture until combined. Spoon into an ungreased 2-quart casserole or soufflé dish.

4. Bake in a 325° oven for 45 to 50 minutes or until a knife inserted near the center comes out clean. Serve immediately.

Nutrition Facts per serving: 221 cal., 14 g total fat (8 g sat. fat), 143 mg chol., 393 mg sodium, 10 g carbo., 1 g fiber, 12 g pro.
Daily Values: 13% vit. A, 1% vit. C, 32% calcium, 5% iron

Mostly Mushrooms Popovers

Careful planning is essential for dinner popovers, as these puffy delights become soggy if not served promptly. If more than six people come to dinner, make several batches so each guest can relish a popover.

Prep: 15 minutes **Bake:** 35 minutes
Stand: 5 minutes **Oven:** 400°F **Makes:** 6 popovers

Mostly Mushrooms Popovers

3	teaspoons shortening or nonstick cooking spray
⅓	cup dried mushrooms, such as shiitake or porcini
½	teaspoon salt
¼	teaspoon dried thyme, crushed
⅛	teaspoon black pepper
1	cup milk
2	eggs, beaten
1	tablespoon cooking oil
1	cup all-purpose flour

1. Using ½ teaspoon shortening for each cup, grease the bottoms and sides of the cups of a popover pan or six 6-ounce custard cups. (Or, lightly coat cups with cooking spray.) Place the custard cups on a 1×5×10×1-inch baking pan; set aside. In a small bowl pour boiling water over dried mushrooms to cover; let stand for 5 minutes. Drain, pressing out the liquid. Finely chop mushrooms.

2. In a medium bowl stir together mushrooms, salt, thyme, and pepper. Add milk, eggs, and oil. Using a rotary beater, beat until mixed. Add flour and beat just until mixture is smooth. Spoon batter into prepared cups, filling each half full.

3. Bake in a 400° oven for 35 to 40 minutes or until firm. Remove from oven. Immediately prick each popover with a fork to let steam escape. (For crisper popovers, turn off the oven and return popovers to oven for 5 minutes or until desired crispness is reached.) Loosen edges. Remove popovers from cups. Serve immediately.

Nutrition Facts per serving: 156 cal., 7 g total fat (2 g sat. fat), 74 mg chol., 237 mg sodium, 17 g carbo., 1 g fiber, 5 g pro.
Daily Values: 3% vit. A, 6% calcium, 7% iron

Bacon-Cheddar Loaves

Bacon and cheddar are a tempting combo no matter what the recipe, but when swirled together in bread batter, the results are amazing.

Prep: 20 minutes **Bake:** 60 minutes **Cool:** 10 minutes
Oven: 350°F **Makes:** 2 loaves (28 servings)

4	cups all-purpose flour
1	tablespoon baking powder
¾	teaspoon salt
¼	teaspoon cayenne pepper
2	eggs, beaten
2¼	cups milk
½	cup butter, melted
6	slices bacon, crisp-cooked, drained, and crumbled
1	cup shredded cheddar cheese (4 ounces)

1. Grease two 8×4×2-inch loaf pans; set pans aside. In a large bowl combine flour, baking powder, salt, and cayenne pepper. In a medium bowl combine eggs, milk, and butter; add all at once to flour mixture. Stir just until moistened (batter should be lumpy). Fold in bacon and cheese. Divide batter evenly between the prepared pans.

2. Bake in a 350° oven for 60 to 65 minutes or until brown and a toothpick inserted near the center of loaves comes out clean. Cool in pans on wire racks for 10 minutes. Remove from pans. Cool completely on wire racks. If desired, wrap and store overnight in refrigerator. Let stand at room temperature 30 minutes before slicing.

Nutrition Facts per serving: 132 cal., 7 g total fat (3 g sat. fat), 32 mg chol., 180 mg sodium, 14 g carbo., 0 g fiber, 4 g pro.
Daily Values: 4% vit. A, 7% calcium, 5% iron

Buttermilk Biscuits

These irresistible biscuits are great for dipping into a creamy chowder or mopping up the last of the gravy. If you have any left over at the end of dinner, they also make a delectable breakfast treat when smeared with honey or jam. In fact, you may want to set aside a couple before dinner, just so you'll be sure to have some the next morning.

Prep: 10 minutes **Bake:** 12 minutes **Oven:** 425°F
Makes: 8 biscuits

2	cups all-purpose flour
2	teaspoons baking powder
1	teaspoon sugar
½	teaspoon baking soda
½	teaspoon salt
6	tablespoons butter, cut up
¾	cup buttermilk

1. In a large bowl stir together flour, baking powder, sugar, baking soda, and salt. Using a pastry blender, cut in butter until mixture resembles coarse crumbs. Make a well in the center of the flour mixture. Add buttermilk all at once. Using a fork, stir just until moistened.

2. Turn dough out onto a lightly floured surface. Knead dough by folding and gently pressing for 3 or 4 strokes until smooth. Roll dough ¾-inch thickness. Cut with a floured 2½-inch biscuit cutter. If necessary, re-roll the scraps and cut. Place biscuits, 1 inch apart, on an ungreased baking sheet.

3. Bake for 12 to 14 minutes or until golden. Remove biscuits from baking sheet and serve warm.

Nutrition Facts per serving: 196 cal., 10 g total fat (5 g sat. fat), 25 mg chol., 373 mg sodium, 24 g carbo., 1 g fiber, 4 g pro.
Daily Values: 6% vit. A, 5% calcium, 7% iron

Parmesan Rosettes

With a distinctly Italian flavor, these dinner rolls pair perfectly with soup and salad for a quick and easy winter meal.

Prep: 15 minutes **Bake:** 15 minutes **Oven:** 375°F
Makes: 12 rosettes

1	11-ounce package refrigerated breadsticks (12)
3	tablespoons grated Parmesan cheese
1	teaspoon sesame seeds

Parmesan Rosettes

How to shape Parmesan Rosettes

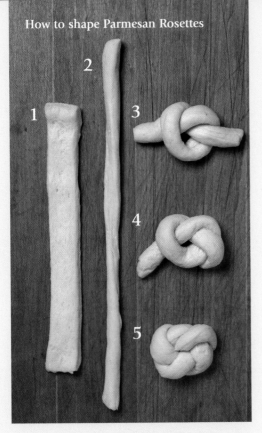

Peppery Cheese Bread

Spicy brown mustard, plenty of pepper, cheddar cheese, and yogurt provide luscious contrasts in this loaf.

Prep: 15 minutes **Bake:** 45 minutes
Cool: 1 hour 10 minutes **Oven:** 350°F
Makes: 1 loaf (16 servings)

2½   cups all-purpose flour
1   tablespoon sugar
1½   to 2 teaspoons cracked black pepper
1   teaspoon baking powder
¾   teaspoon salt
½   teaspoon baking soda
2   eggs, beaten
1   8-ounce carton plain low-fat yogurt
½   cup cooking oil
¼   cup milk
1   tablespoon spicy brown mustard
1   cup shredded cheddar cheese
     (4 ounces)
¼   cup thinly sliced green onions (2)

½   teaspoon dried Italian seasoning, crushed
¼   teaspoon garlic powder
2   tablespoons butter, melted

1. Separate breadsticks into individual pieces (Step 1 of picture, above). On a lightly floured surface roll each piece into a 12-inch rope (Step 2).

2. Tie each rope in a loose knot, leaving 2 long ends (Step 3). Tuck the top end of the rope under roll (Step 4). Bring bottom end up and tuck into center of roll (Step 5).

3. In a shallow dish combine cheese, sesame seeds, Italian seasoning, and garlic powder. Brush the top and sides of each rosette with melted butter. Carefully dip the top and sides of each rosette into the cheese mixture.

4. Place rosettes, 2 to 3 inches apart, on an ungreased baking sheet. Bake in a 375°F oven about 15 minutes or until golden. Serve warm.

Nutrition Facts per serving: 135 cal., 5 g total fat (2 g sat. fat), 6 mg chol., 324 mg sodium, 18 g carbo., 1 g fiber, 4 g pro.
Daily Values: 1% vit. A, 2% calcium, 6% iron

1. Grease bottom and ½ inch up the sides of an 8×4×2-inch loaf pan; set aside. In a large bowl stir together flour, sugar, pepper, baking powder, salt, and baking soda. Make a well in center of flour mixture; set aside.

2. In a medium bowl stir together eggs, yogurt, oil, milk, and mustard. Add egg mixture all at once to flour mixture. Add cheddar cheese and green onions. Stir just until moistened (batter should be lumpy). Spoon batter into prepared pan, spreading evenly with a spatula.

3. Bake in a 350° oven for 45 to 50 minutes or until a wooden toothpick inserted near center comes out clean. Cool in pan on a wire rack for 10 minutes. Remove bread from pan. Cool for 1 hour on a wire rack. Serve warm. Wrap any leftovers and store in refrigerator for up to 3 days.

Nutrition Facts per serving: 179 cal., 10 g total fat (3 g sat. fat), 35 mg chol., 239 mg sodium, 16 g carbo., 1 g fiber, 5 g pro.
Daily Values: 4% vit. A, 1% vit. C, 9% calcium, 7% iron

Savory Holiday Bread

This cheesy bread obtains its festive colors from the incorporation of dried tomatoes and green onions.

Prep: 25 minutes **Bake:** 40 minutes **Oven:** 350°F
Makes: 1 loaf (18 servings)

3	cups all-purpose flour
2	cups shredded Italian-style cheese blend (8 ounces)
2	teaspoons baking powder
1	teaspoon salt
½	teaspoon garlic powder
3	eggs, beaten
1	5-ounce can (⅔ cup) evaporated milk
⅓	cup thinly sliced green onion
¼	cup butter, melted
¼	cup oil-packed dried tomatoes, drained and finely chopped
1	egg yolk
1	tablespoon water

1. In a large bowl combine flour, cheese, baking powder, salt, and garlic powder. Add eggs, milk, green onions, melted butter, and dried tomatoes. Stir until combined.

2. Turn dough out onto a lightly floured surface. Knead dough by folding and gently pressing dough for 10 to 12 strokes or until it holds together. Divide dough into 3 equal pieces. Roll each piece into a 14-inch rope. Place ropes 1-inch apart on a greased baking sheet; braid ropes, pinching ends to seal. Combine egg yolk and water; brush top of bread with egg yolk mixture.

3. Bake in a 350° oven about 40 minutes or until golden brown. Transfer to a wire rack; cool.

Nutrition Facts per serving: 164 cal., 8 g total fat (4 g sat. fat), 65 mg chol., 280 mg sodium, 16 g carbo., 1 g fiber, 7 g pro.
Daily Values: 4% vit. A, 3% vit. C, 11% calcium, 6% iron

Pecan Streusel Coffee Cake

Make this cake ahead of time and freeze for up to a month unfrosted. Then whip it out and drizzle with glaze for a delicious breakfast treat.

Prep: 20 minutes **Bake:** 35 minutes **Oven:** 350°F
Makes: 15 servings

1	cup chopped pecans
⅔	cup packed brown sugar
2	tablespoons butter, melted
1½	teaspoons ground cinnamon
1	26½-ounce package cinnamon streusel coffee cake mix
½	cup dairy sour cream

Savory Holiday Bread

Pick a Spread If time is running short for baking bread this holiday, there's no need to panic. In only minutes, you can create a tasty butter spread to enhance purchased loaves or rolls.

• **Herb Butter:** Stir together 6 tablespoons butter or margarine, softened; ½ teaspoon dried marjoram or basil, crushed; ½ teaspoon dried thyme, crushed; and ¼ teaspoon garlic powder.

• **Garlic Butter:** Stir together 6 tablespoons butter or margarine, softened; and ½ teaspoon garlic powder.

• **Parmesan Butter:** Stir together 6 tablespoons butter or margarine, softened; ¼ cup grated Parmesan cheese; and 1 tablespoon snipped chives.

1. Grease and flour a 13×9×2-inch baking pan; set aside. For topping, in a small bowl stir together pecans, brown sugar, butter, and cinnamon.

2. Prepare the coffee cake mix according to the package directions, then stir sour cream into prepared batter. Spread half (about 3 cups) of the batter into the prepared baking pan. Sprinkle batter with the streusel mix from the package of coffee cake mix. Carefully spread with the remaining batter. Sprinkle with the topping.

3. Bake in a 350° oven for 35 to 40 minutes or until a toothpick inserted near the center comes out clean. Cool slightly in pan.

4. Meanwhile, prepare glaze from the coffee cake mix according to package directions. Drizzle glaze over warm coffee cake.

Nutrition Facts per serving: 395 cal., 20 g total fat (5 g sat. fat), 50 mg chol., 243 mg sodium, 50 g carbo., 1 g fiber, 4 g pro.
Daily Values: 2% vit. A, 7% calcium, 9% iron

Blueberry Breakfast Rolls

Blueberry Breakfast Rolls

Turn refrigerated cinnamon roll dough into a breakfast masterpiece by topping with blueberries and pecans.

Prep: 15 minutes **Bake:** 12 minutes **Cool:** 5 minutes
Oven: 375°F **Makes:** 16 rolls

1	12.4-ounce package refrigerated cinnamon rolls with icing (8)
1	cup frozen blueberries, thawed and well-drained
⅓	cup blueberry preserves
1	teaspoon finely shredded lemon peel
¼	cup chopped pecans, toasted

1. Lightly grease sixteen 2½-inch muffin cups. Remove cinnamon rolls from package; set icing aside. Cut each cinnamon roll in half crosswise. Press a roll half in bottom and about ½ inch up the side of each muffin cup.

2. In a small bowl stir together blueberries, preserves, and lemon peel. Spoon filling into muffin cups. Sprinkle with pecans.

3. Bake in a 375° oven about 12 minutes or until golden. Cool in muffin cups on a wire rack for 5 minutes. Remove from muffin cups and place on a wire rack. Cool for 5 minutes.

4. Place icing from the package in a small bowl. If necessary, stir in a little milk to make icing of drizzling consistency. Drizzle icing over rolls. Serve rolls warm.

Nutrition Facts per serving: 110 cal., 4 g total fat (1 g sat. fat), 0 mg chol., 172 mg sodium, 18 g carbo., 0 g fiber, 1 g pro.
Daily Values: 3% vit. C, 3% iron

Caramel Bubble Ring

Caramel Bubble Ring

This impressive coffee cake starts with a base of refrigerated breadsticks in cinnamon-sugar. It is then topped with pecans, caramel sauce, and maple syrup.

Prep: 25 minutes **Bake:** 35 minutes **Stand:** 1 minute
Oven: 350°F **Makes:** 10 to 12 servings

⅓	**cup chopped pecans**
¾	**cup sugar**
4	**teaspoons ground cinnamon**

2	**11-ounce packages refrigerated breadsticks (12 each)**
⅓	**cup butter or margarine, melted**
½	**cup caramel ice-cream topping**
2	**tablespoons maple-flavored syrup**

1. Generously grease a 10-inch fluted tube pan. Sprinkle half of the pecans in the bottom of the prepared pan; set aside. In a small bowl stir together sugar and cinnamon; set aside.

2. Separate each package of breadstick dough on the perforated lines into 6 spiral pieces, making 12 pieces total. Do not unroll. Cut the pieces in half crosswise. Dip each piece of dough into melted butter; roll in the sugar mixture to coat. Arrange dough pieces in the prepared pan. Sprinkle with remaining pecans over dough pieces.

3. In a measuring cup stir together caramel topping and maple-flavored syrup; drizzle over dough.

4. Bake in a 350° oven about 35 minutes or until dough is light brown, covering with foil for the last 10 minutes of baking to prevent overbrowning.

5. Let stand for 1 minute only. (If it stands for more than 1 minute, the ring will be difficult to remove from pan.) Invert the pan onto a serving platter. Remove the pan. Spoon any topping and nuts remaining in the pan onto rolls. Serve warm.

Nutrition Facts per serving: 367 cal., 13 g total fat (4 g sat. fat), 17 mg chol., 567 mg sodium, 58 g carbo., 2 g fiber, 5 g pro.
Daily Values: 4% vit. A, 1% vit. C, 3% calcium, 13% iron

Orange Biscuit Rolls

As easy as they are delicious, these gooey biscuits—baked in the shape of a cake—make winter mornings warm and cozy. If desired, garnish with twists of orange peel and fresh herbs.

Prep: 15 minutes **Bake:** 30 minutes
Cool: 30 minutes **Oven:** 375°F
Makes: 10 servings (20 biscuits)

1¼	**cups sugar**
1	**tablespoon finely shredded orange peel**
⅓	**cup orange juice**
¼	**cup butter, melted**
2	**10-ounce packages refrigerated biscuits (10 biscuits each)**

1. Grease a 10-inch fluted tube pan. Set aside.

2. In a small bowl stir together sugar and orange peel. In another small bowl combine orange juice and melted butter.

3. Separate biscuits. Dip each into the orange juice mixture, then roll in the sugar mixture.

4. Arrange the biscuits upright with flat sides together in the prepared pan. Pour any remaining orange juice mixture over biscuits.

5. Bake in a 375° oven for 30 minutes. Cool in pan on a wire rack for 1 minute only. (If it stands for more than 1 minute, the ring will be difficult to remove from pan.) Invert pan onto a serving platter. Remove the pan. Cool for 30 to 45 minutes. If desired, garnish center of ring with orange peel and fresh herbs. Serve warm.

Nutrition Facts per serving: 240 cal., 6 g total fat (2 g sat. fat), 13 mg chol., 395 mg sodium, 44 g carbo., 0 g fiber, 3 g pro.
Daily Values: 3% vit. A, 8% vit. C, 7% iron

Orange Biscuit Rolls

Pumpkin Crescent Rolls

Keep the flavors of fall going into the winter by serving a batch of these pumpkin-flavored rolls at your Christmas feast.

Prep: 20 minutes **Bake:** 9 minutes **Oven:** 400°F
Makes: 16 rolls

1¾	cups all-purpose flour
1	teaspoon baking powder
¼	teaspoon baking soda
¼	teaspoon ground nutmeg
⅛	teaspoon salt
¾	cup canned pumpkin
3	tablespoons cooking oil
2	tablespoons brown sugar
2	teaspoons granulated sugar
¼	teaspoon ground cinnamon

1. Line a large baking sheet with foil; set aside. In a medium bowl stir together flour, baking powder, baking soda, nutmeg, and salt. Set aside.

2. In a small bowl mix pumpkin, oil, and brown sugar. Add pumpkin mixture to flour mixture, stirring with a fork until combined. Form into a ball.

3. Turn dough out onto a lightly floured surface. Knead dough by folding and gently pressing for 10 to 12 strokes. Divide dough in half. Roll each half to a 10-inch circle. Cut each circle into 8 wedges. To shape, begin at the wide end of each wedge and loosely roll toward the point. Place point sides down, about 2 inches apart, on the prepared baking sheet. Slightly curve ends of rolls inward. Combine the granulated sugar and cinnamon; sprinkle over crescent rolls.

4. Bake in a 400° oven for 9 to 11 minutes or until golden. Serve warm.

Nutrition Facts per serving: 79 cal., 3 g total fat (0 g sat. fat), 0 mg chol., 54 mg sodium, 12 g carbo., 1 g fiber, 1 g pro.
Daily Values: 36% vit. A, 1% vit. C, 1% calcium, 4% iron

Morning Fruit Bread

Despite the use of healthful whole wheat, this tasty morning treat is more like a cake than bread.

Prep: 15 minutes **Bake:** 25 minutes
Cool: 20 minutes **Oven:** 400°F **Makes:** 16 servings

1	cup whole wheat flour
1	cup all-purpose flour
2	tablespoons toasted wheat germ
2½	teaspoons baking powder
¼	teaspoon ground cinnamon
¾	teaspoon salt
½	cup raisins
⅓	cup chopped almonds
¼	cup dried blueberries or snipped dried tart cherries
1	egg, beaten
1	cup milk
½	cup granulated sugar
⅓	cup cooking oil
1	cup powdered sugar
	Milk

1. Grease the bottom and ½ inch up the sides of a 9×9×2-inch baking pan; set aside. In a large bowl stir together whole wheat flour, all-purpose flour, wheat germ, baking powder, cinnamon, and salt. Stir in raisins, almonds, and dried blueberries until coated with flour. Make a well in the center of flour mixture; set aside.

2. In a medium bowl stir together the egg, 1 cup milk, granulated sugar, and oil. Add egg mixture all at once to flour mixture. Stir just until moistened (batter should be lumpy). Spoon batter into the prepared pan spreading evenly.

3. Bake in a 400° about 25 minutes or until golden brown. Cool in pan on a wire rack for 20 minutes. Cut into sixteen squares. In a small bowl combine powdered sugar and enough milk to reach drizzling consistency; drizzle over squares. Serve warm.

Nutrition Facts per serving: 195 cal., 4 g total fat (1 g sat. fat), 15 mg chol., 160 mg sodium, 31 g carbo., 2 g fiber, 4 g pro.
Daily Values: 1% vit. A, 0% vit. C, 5% calcium, 6% iron

Morning Fruit Bread

Desserts on the Double

CHOOSE FROM CAKES, PIES, TORTES, FRUITS, AND A SLEW OF CHOCOLATE CONFECTIONS to add the finishing touches to your fabulous Christmas dinner. Dazzle your guests by revealing your inner pastry chef—even if that pastry chef started with a frozen or refrigerated convenience product. When selecting purchased piecrusts, pound cakes, cheesecakes, puff pastry, and more, these dessert recipes are among the quickest (and most delicious) available today. Your guests will be impressed with the personal touches you add to modern-day products.

Peppermint-Stick Pie, page 75

Chocolate-Macaroon Cheesecake

Macaroons, small confections made of frothy egg whites, sugar, and coconut, are found in many supermarkets. As delicious as they are on their own, they're even better on this fudge-topped cheesecake.

Start to Finish: 10 minutes **Makes:** 12 servings

- 1 **30-ounce frozen New York-style cheesecake**
- 1 **12-ounce jar fudge ice-cream topping**
- 4 **soft coconut macaroon cookies, crumbled**
- ¼ **cup sliced almonds, toasted**

1. Thaw cheesecake in microwave oven according to package directions. Place on serving plate.

2. Spread fudge topping over cheesecake, allowing some to drip down the sides. Sprinkle with crumbled macaroons and almonds. Serve immediately.

Nutrition Facts per serving: 398 cal., 21 g total fat (11 g sat. fat), 47 mg chol., 417 mg sodium, 47 g carbo., 1 g fiber, 6 g pro.
Daily Values: 10% vit. A, 6% calcium, 1% iron

Cheesecakes for Every Taste There's more than one way to turn an ordinary purchased cheesecake into a "homemade" masterpiece. Consider these simple ideas.

- **Berry Delight** Place fresh raspberries or strawberries in a blender with some sugar, and process until smooth. Serve sauce drizzled over cheesecake.

- **Turtle Cheesecake** Drizzle a cheesecake with caramel and chocolate sauces. Sprinkle with chopped peanuts.

- **Holiday Cranberry Cheesecake** Stir finely shredded orange peel into whole berry cranberry sauce and serve over cheesecake.

- **Mint-Chocolate Cheesecake** Fold chopped chocolate-covered mints into whipped cream. Serve with slices of chocolate cheesecake

- **Amaretto Cheesecake** Stir amaretto liqueur into vanilla yogurt. Spoon over cheesecake and sprinkle with toasted almonds.

Chocolate-Mocha Cheesecake

There's something to be said for the ease of a store-bought cheesecake mix, especially when you can quickly turn it into a homemade dessert by adding your own personal touches. This recipe relies on the flavors of chocolate and coffee to create a tempting Christmas treat.

Prep: 15 minutes **Chill:** 1 hour **Makes:** 9 servings

- 1 **11.1-ounce package cheesecake mix**
- ⅓ **cup butter or margarine, melted**
- 1¼ **cups milk**
- 2 **teaspoons instant coffee crystals**
- ½ **cup dairy sour cream**
- ½ **cup miniature semisweet chocolate pieces**

1. In a small bowl stir together crust crumbs from the cheesecake mix and the melted butter. Press crumb mixture onto the bottom of an 8×8×2-inch baking pan.

2. In a large mixing bowl combine milk and instant coffee crystals; stir to dissolve coffee crystals. Add filling mix from the cheesecake mix. Beat with an electric mixer on medium speed just until combined. Add sour cream and beat on high speed for about 3 minutes.

3. Stir in ¼ cup of the chocolate pieces. Spread cheesecake mixture over crumb layer in baking pan. Sprinkle remaining ¼ cup chocolate pieces on top. Cover and chill for at least 1 hour or up to 24 hours. To serve, cut into squares.

Nutrition Facts per serving: 323 cal., 17 g total fat (10 g sat. fat), 27 mg chol., 351 mg sodium, 37 g carbo., 1 g fiber, 5 g pro.
Daily Values: 7% vit. A, 15% calcium, 4% iron

Nutmeg Cake with Lemon Sauce

When Columbus "discovered" America after getting lost on his way to the East Indies, he was in search of a variety of spices, including nutmeg. After getting a taste of this lightly spiced cake with lemon sauce, you'll understand why he was willing to sail halfway around the world to nab some of this fine flavoring.

Prep: 35 minutes **Bake:** 30 minutes
Cool: 30 minutes **Oven:** 350°F **Makes:** 12 servings

2	cups all-purpose flour
1	teaspoon baking powder
1	teaspoon ground nutmeg
½	teaspoon baking soda
¼	teaspoon salt
¼	cup butter, softened
¼	cup shortening
1½	cups sugar
½	teaspoon vanilla
3	eggs
1	cup buttermilk or sour milk*
1	recipe Lemon Sauce

1. Grease a 13×9×2-inch baking pan; set aside. Combine flour, baking powder, nutmeg, baking soda, and salt; set aside.

2. In a large bowl beat butter and shortening with an electric mixer on medium to high speed for 30 seconds. Add sugar and vanilla; beat until combined. Add eggs, one at a time, beating well after each addition. Alternately add flour mixture and buttermilk, beating on low speed after each addition just until combined. Spread cake batter into prepared pan.

3. Bake in a 350° oven for 30 to 35 minutes or until a wooden toothpick inserted near the center comes out clean. Cool slightly in pan on a wire rack. Serve warm cake with Lemon Sauce.

Lemon Sauce: In a small saucepan stir together ¾ cup sugar, 5 teaspoons cornstarch, and a dash of salt. Stir in 1 cup water. Cook and stir over medium heat until thickened and bubbly. Cook and stir for 2 minutes more. Remove from heat. Stir in 1 teaspoon finely shredded lemon peel, 3 tablespoons lemon juice, 2 tablespoons butter, and, if desired, 1 drop yellow food coloring.

*Note: To make sour milk, place 1 tablespoon lemon juice or vinegar in a glass measuring cup. Add enough milk to make 1 cup total liquid; stir. Let stand for 5 minutes before using.

Nutrition Facts per serving: 334 cal., 12 g total fat (5 g sat. fat), 70 mg chol., 216 mg sodium, 53 g carbo., 1 g fiber, 4 g pro.
Daily Values: 5% vit. A, 4% vit. C, 4% calcium, 6% iron

Calling for Citrus

- 1 medium lemon contains about 3 tablespoons of juice and 2 teaspoons of shredded peel.
- 1 medium lime contains approximately 2 tablespoons of juice and about 1½ teaspoons of shredded peel.
- 1 medium orange contains about ¼ to ⅓ cup of juice and 4 teaspoons of shredded peel.

Nutmeg Cake with Lemon Sauce

Festive Red Velvet Cake

With a striking red color and a luscious chocolatey flavor, this velvety cake will become a Christmas tradition for years to come. The best part is, this festive holiday cake only takes 10 minutes to prepare (see photo, front cover).

Prep: 10 minutes **Bake:** 30 minutes **Cool:** 2 hours
Oven: 350°F **Makes:** 12 servings

1	2-layer-size package German chocolate cake mix
1	1-ounce bottle red food coloring
1	16-ounce can white frosting or one 7.2-ounce package fluffy white frosting mix prepared according to package directions
	Coconut, red coarse sugar, small decorative candies
1	recipe Candy Snowflakes (optional)

1. Prepare cake mix according to the package directions. When measuring water, place red food coloring in the measuring cup first, then add enough water to make the amount called for on package. Use the 8- or 9-inch cake pan option (for 2-layer cake) and bake as directed.

2. Frost cooled cake with white frosting. Garnish with coconut, red coarse sugar, and small decorative candies. If desired, make Candy Snowflakes and decorate cake.

Candy Snowflakes: Draw snowflake designs onto waxed paper. Turn over paper so the design is face down. Place melted and slightly cooled vanilla candy coating in a pastry bag fitted with a small round tip. Pipe melted candy coating over design to make snowflakes. Let stand for 30 minutes or until set. Carefully peel the snowflakes off the waxed paper. Decorate cake as desired with snowflakes.

Nutrition Facts per serving: 410 cal., 15 g total fat (4 g sat. fat), 0 mg chol., 365 mg sodium, 59 g carbo., 1 g fiber, 3 g pro.
Daily Values: 4% iron

Triple-Nut Chocolate Torte

Nutty for nuts? Combined with devil's food cake mix and a rich chocolate mousse, this trio of hazelnuts, pecans, and almonds will satisfy even the most ardent nut lover.

Prep: 30 minutes **Bake:** 30 minutes
Chill: 4 to 24 hours **Oven:** 350°F
Makes: 12 servings

1	package 2-layer-size devil's food cake mix
¾	cup ground pecans, toasted
2	2.8-ounce packages milk chocolate or dark chocolate mousse dessert mix
½	cup chopped hazelnuts, toasted
½	cup slivered almonds, toasted and chopped

1. Grease and lightly flour two 8×1½-inch round baking pans. Set aside.

2. Prepare cake mix according to package directions; fold in pecans. Divide half of the batter evenly between the prepared pans. Cover and refrigerate remaining batter while the cake layers bake.

3. Bake in a 350° oven about 15 minutes or until a toothpick inserted in center comes out clean. Cool in pans on a wire rack for 10 minutes. Remove from pans; cool completely on wire racks.

4. Wash pans; grease and lightly flour as in Step 1. Divide remaining batter evenly between prepared pans. Bake and cool as directed in step 3.

5. Prepare mousse mixes according to package directions. Fold hazelnuts into half of the mousse and chopped almonds into the other half of mousse.

6. Place 1 of the cake layers on a cake platter. Top with half of the hazelnut mousse mixture. Top with another cake layer and half of the almond mousse mixture. Repeat layers. Cover loosely and chill in the refrigerator for 4 to 24 hours. If desired, sprinkle with additional sliced, toasted almonds.

Nutrition Facts per serving: 372 cal., 22 g total fat (5 g sat. fat), 3 mg chol., 374 mg sodium, 43 g carbo., 3 g fiber, 6 g pro.
Daily Values: 1% vit. A, 1% vit. C, 12% calcium, 15% iron

Crunchy Pound Cake Slices

Crunchy Pound Cake Slices

Chocolate hazelnut spread—made of cocoa, skim milk, and hazelnuts—was once a novelty food found only in Italian markets. Now it can be found in the peanut butter aisle of almost any grocery store.

Prep: 15 minutes **Broil:** 2 minutes
Makes: 4 servings

4	½-inch slices purchased pound cake
¼	cup chocolate hazelnut spread
½	cup roasted mixed nuts, coarsely chopped
1	pint caramel-swirl or cinnamon ice cream

1. Place the pound cake slices on a baking sheet. Broil 3 to 4 inches from heat for 1 minute on each side or until light brown. Cool slightly.

2. Spread one side of each slice with 1 tablespoon of the chocolate hazelnut spread. Sprinkle with nuts; pat gently to form an even layer. Transfer each slice to a dessert plate and top with a scoop of the ice cream. Serve immediately.

Nutrition Facts per serving: 763 cal., 45 g total fat (22 g sat. fat), 206 mg chol., 421 mg sodium, 82 g carbo., 2 g fiber, 12 g pro.
Daily Values: 19% vit. A, 19% calcium, 11% iron

Berry Trifle Cake

If fresh berries are difficult to find in the supermarket during the winter season, thaw and drain a frozen berry mixture, and serve it on the side rather than on the top of the cake.

Prep: 20 minutes **Chill:** up to 2 hours
Makes: 8 servings

1	9½-inch tart-shape sponge cake
½	cup berry or orange juice
¼	of an 8-ounce container frozen whipped dessert topping, thawed

It's All in the Mix Don't fret if you forget the dessert! With only a few added ingredients, a regular cake mix can be turned into a taste extravaganza worthy of applause.

Add one of these to the dry cake mix:
- ¾ teaspoon of ground cinnamon
- ½ teaspoon ground allspice
- ¼ teaspoon ground nutmeg

Add one of these with the eggs:
- 1 tablespoon instant coffee crystals (dissolved in specified amount of water in the cake mix directions)
- 1 tablespoon finely shredded orange peel
- 1 teaspoon maple flavoring
- ½ teaspoon almond extract

Stir one of these into the cake batter:
- 1 cup coconut
- ½ cup finely chopped toasted nuts
- ½ cup miniature semisweet chocolate pieces
- ½ cup well-drained maraschino cherries

Easy Chocolate Marble Cake To ⅓ of a white or yellow cake batter, add ½ cup chocolate-flavored syrup. Pour plain batter into the baking pans; pour chocolate batter on top of plain batter. Swirl gently with a spatula.

Chocolate Peanut Cake Stir ½ cup chopped peanuts into prepared yellow or white cake mix batter, bake as directed and serve warm with chocolate sauce.

1	6-ounce carton (⅔ cup) raspberry, strawberry, or blueberry yogurt
2	cups fresh raspberries, strawberries, blackberries, and/or blueberries

1. Place the cake on a serving plate; sprinkle with juice. Set aside.

2. For filling, in a small bowl stir together whipped topping and yogurt. Spread over cake. Cover and chill in the refrigerator up to 2 hours.

3. Arrange berries over filling. Cut into wedges.

Nutrition Facts per serving: 174 cal., 3 g total fat (2 g sat. fat), 40 mg chol., 107 mg sodium, 34 g carbo., 2 g fiber, 3 g pro.
Daily Values: 2% vit. A, 21% vit. C, 7% calcium, 7% iron

Frozen Tiramisu Squares

The word tiramisu literally means "carry me up," and this frozen coffee-brushed dessert will assuredly do just that. Layered with ice cream and covered in whipped topping, this cake is well worth the effort to make.

Prep: 30 minutes **Stand:** 15 minutes
Freeze: 4 hours **Makes:** 16 servings

2	10¾-ounce frozen loaf pound cakes
⅓	cup coffee liqueur or ⅓ cup strong coffee plus 2 tablespoons sugar
3	tablespoons instant coffee crystals
2	quarts French vanilla or custard-style ice cream, softened
2	ounces semisweet chocolate, grated*
1	8-ounce container frozen whipped dessert topping, thawed

1. Slice each frozen pound cake into 14 slices. Place half of the slices in a single layer in the bottom of a 3-quart rectangular baking dish.

2. Place coffee liqueur (or strong coffee and sugar) in a small saucepan. Stir in coffee crystals. Heat just until coffee crystals dissolve. Remove 2 tablespoons and set aside. Brush about half of the remaining coffee mixture over cake slices in dish.

3. In a large bowl stir softened ice cream; spread over cake slices in dish. Top with half of the chocolate. Arrange remaining cake slices in a single layer over the chocolate. Gently press down cake slices. Brush remaining coffee mixture over slices.

4. Stir the reserved 2 tablespoons coffee mixture into whipped topping. Spread evenly over top layer in dish. Sprinkle with remaining chocolate. Cover and freeze 4 hours or up to 1 week.

5. Let stand at room temperature for 15 minutes before serving. Cut into squares.

*Note: If desired, use a food processor to grate the semisweet chocolate.

Nutrition Facts per serving: 393 cal., 22 g total fat (14 g sat. fat), 118 mg chol., 176 mg sodium, 41 g carbo., 1 g fiber, 5 g pro.
Daily Values: 10% vit. A, 1% vit. C, 11% calcium, 4% iron

Peppermint-Stick Pie

Sometimes the easiest desserts get the best reviews, which is definitely the case with this pie. With a pre-made crumb shell and an ice cream filling, this pie takes only 10 minutes to make.

Prep: 10 minutes **Stand:** 5 minutes **Freeze:** 4 hours
Makes: 8 servings

- **3** pints (1½ quarts) peppermint ice cream
- **1** chocolate-flavored crumb pie shell
- **1** 12-ounce jar fudge ice cream topping
Coarsely crushed candy cane or striped round peppermint candies (optional)

1. In a chilled bowl stir ice cream until softened.

2. Spoon ice cream onto pie shell, spreading evenly. Return to freezer for at least 4 hours.

3. To serve, warm the fudge topping in the microwave oven according to directions on jar. Let pie stand at room temperature for 5 minutes before slicing. Serve with warmed topping. If desired, sprinkle with crushed candies.

Nutrition Facts per serving: 555 cal., 24 g total fat (13 g sat. fat), 60 mg chol., 335 mg sodium, 75 g carbo., 0 g fiber, 7 g pro.
Daily Values: 6% vit. C, 13% calcium, 53% iron

Peppermint-Stick Pie

No-Peel Apple Pie

The expression "easy as pie" surely applies to this quick version of the classical Christmas dessert. Although the apples still have to be cored and sliced, eliminating the time spent peeling the fruit cuts down on preparation.

Prep: 30 minutes **Bake:** 55 minutes **Oven:** 375°F
Makes: 8 servings

1	15-ounce package rolled refrigerated unbaked piecrust (2 crusts)
4	large cooking apples, such as Golden Delicious, Jonagold, Jonathan, McIntosh, and/or Granny Smith (2 pounds)
2	tablespoons lemon juice
½	cup granulated sugar
2	tablespoons all-purpose flour
1½	teaspoons apple pie spice
	Milk
	Coarse or granulated sugar

1. Roll out piecrust according to the package directions. Transfer 1 piecrust to a 9-inch pie plate; set crusts aside.

2. For filling, core and thinly slice unpeeled apples (there should be about 8 cups). Place apple slices in a very large bowl. Sprinkle with lemon juice; gently toss to coat. In a small bowl stir together the ½ cup granulated sugar, the flour, and apple pie spice. Sprinkle over apple slices, toss gently to coat.

3. Spoon the apple mixture into the pastry-lined pie plate. Trim pastry to edge of pie plate. Moisten edge with water. Cut out desired shapes from center of remaining crust; set shapes aside. Center remaining

No-Peel Apple Pie

crust over filling and press to seal. Crimp edge as desired. Brush the top crust with milk. If desired, top with reserved pastry cutouts; brush cutouts with milk. Sprinkle the pie with coarse sugar.

4. To prevent over browning, cover the edge of pie with foil. Bake in a 375° oven for 55 to 60 minutes or until apples are tender. If necessary, cover the top of the pie with foil for the last 5 to 10 minutes of baking to prevent the crust from over browning. Cool on a wire rack.

Nutrition Facts per serving: 354 cal., 14 g total fat (6 g sat. fat), 10 mg chol., 199 mg sodium, 56 g carbo., 3 g fiber, 2 g pro.
Daily Values: 1% vit. A, 12% vit. C, 2% calcium, 2% iron

Chocolate-Pecan Chess Pie

This cross between a chess pie and a pecan pie—with some chocolate sprinkled in for good measure—is a Southern dessert dream. For an ultra-decadent treat, garnish the pie with whipped cream and a sprinkle of toasted, chopped pecans.

Prep: 30 minutes **Bake:** 52 minutes
Oven: 450°F/350°F **Makes:** 8 servings

½	of a 15-ounce package rolled refrigerated unbaked piecrust (1 crust)
1¼	cups sugar
1	tablespoon cornmeal
4	eggs, beaten
⅓	cup half-and-half or light cream
3	tablespoons butter, melted
1	teaspoon vanilla
½	cup pecans, toasted and chopped
½	cup miniature semisweet chocolate pieces
	Sweetened whipped cream (optional)

1. Roll out piecrust according to package directions. Transfer pastry to a 9-inch pie plate (do not prick). Trim pastry ½ inch beyond edge of pie plate. Fold under extra pastry. Flute edges high. If desired, press the tines of a fork against fluted edges at evenly spaced intervals. Line pastry with a double thickness of foil. Bake in a 450° oven for 8 minutes. Remove foil; bake for 4 to 5 minutes more or until pastry is set. Reduce oven temperature to 350°.

Short Order Pie Shop Looking for more simplified pie recipes? Take your convenience piecrusts and tart shells to new levels by tossing together these simple creations.

Teeny S'Mores Pies Fill individual graham cracker tart shells with marshmallow crème and vanilla ice cream. Top each pie with hot fudge sauce.

Papayas and Cream Tarts Combine prepared vanilla pudding, dairy sour cream, and finely shredded orange peel; spoon into individual baked pastry tart shells. Top with canned papaya slices and slivered almonds.

Double-Chocolate Ice Cream Pie Substitute softened chocolate ice cream for the milk when preparing chocolate instant pudding, beating for 2 minutes. Spoon into a ready-made pie shell. Freeze for about 5 to 10 minutes before serving.

Quickened Mocha Mousse Tarts Prepare instant chocolate pudding mix according to package directions, except dissolve instant coffee crystals in the milk. Fold in thawed whipped dessert topping and spoon into individual baked phyllo or pastry shells.

Chocolate-Pecan Chess Pie

2. Meanwhile, for filling, in a large mixing bowl stir together sugar and cornmeal. Stir in eggs until combined. Gradually stir in half-and-half, melted butter, and vanilla until combined. Stir in pecans.

3. Sprinkle chocolate pieces over bottom of pastry shell. Place on the oven rack. Carefully pour filling into pastry shell over the chocolate pieces.

4. To prevent over browning, cover edge of pie with foil (being careful not to let the foil touch the filling). Bake for 40 to 45 minutes or until the center appears nearly set when shaken (edges will be puffed). Cool on a wire rack. If desired, serve with sweetened whipped cream. Refrigerate pie within 2 hours; cover for longer storage.

Nutrition Facts per serving: 456 cal., 24 g total fat (10 g sat. fat), 126 mg chol., 170 mg sodium, 55 g carbo., 1 g fiber, 6 g pro.
Daily Values: 6% vit. A, 3% calcium, 6% iron

Dutch Almond Cherry-Filled Braids

As impressive as puff pastry is to behold, it's even more beautiful when braided into this lovely dessert. Don't be intimidated by the idea of "braiding" pastry. It's just a matter of cutting and arranging the dough.

Prep: 30 minutes **Bake:** 30 minutes per braid
Stand: 20 minutes **Cool:** 15 minutes **Oven:** 375°F
Makes: 2 braids (6 servings each)

1	17.3-ounce package frozen puff pastry, thawed (2 sheets)
1	8-ounce can almond paste
¼	cup sugar
1	egg, separated
½	cup cherry preserves
¼	cup sliced almonds
	Coarse sugar

1. Line 2 large baking sheets with parchment paper. Unfold pastry sheets; place 1 pastry sheet on each prepared baking sheet.

2. For almond filling, in a medium bowl beat almond paste, sugar, and egg white with an electric mixer on medium speed until combined. Divide almond mixture evenly between pastry sheets. Spread mixture over the center of each sheet in a 3-inch strip, leaving bare a ½-inch on each end. Spread preserves over almond filling.

3. Using kitchen shears or a sharp knife, make cuts at 1-inch intervals toward the filling about 3 inches long. Starting at one end, alternately fold opposite strips of dough at an angle across the filling, overlapping ends of strips in middle. Press down gently to seal.

4. Beat egg yolk with 1 tablespoon water. Brush over braids. Sprinkle with almonds and coarse sugar. Cover lightly with plastic film and let stand for 20 minutes. Remove and discard plastic film.

5. Bake, one braid at a time, in a 375° oven for 30 to 35 minutes or until top and bottom are golden brown. Cool braids on a wire rack about 15 minutes. Cut each braid into 6 slices; serve warm.

Nutrition Facts per serving: 344 cal., 20 g total fat (1 g sat. fat), 18 mg chol., 165 mg sodium, 38 g carbo., 1 g fiber, 5 g pro.
Daily Values: 2% vit. C, 4% calcium, 3% iron

Blueberry Crisp

Searching for a light dessert? Look no further than this oat-topped spiced pie filling baked in individual custard cups. There's always room for a couple of bites of this small blueberry beauty—a perfect ending to a heavy Christmas feast.

Prep: 15 minutes **Bake:** 20 minutes
Cool: 10 minutes **Oven:** 350° F **Makes:** 6 servings

1	21-ounce can blueberry, apple, or cherry pie filling
1	tablespoon lemon juice
¼	teaspoon ground nutmeg
1	cup quick-cooking rolled oats
¼	cup shredded coconut or chopped nuts
2	tablespoons brown sugar
¼	cup butter
	Half-and-half or light cream (optional)

1. For filling, in a medium bowl stir together pie filling, lemon juice, and nutmeg. Spoon into six 6-ounce custard cups set in a shallow baking pan.

Dutch Almond Cherry-Filled Braids

2. For topping, in a clean medium bowl stir together oats, coconut, and brown sugar. Using a pastry blender, cut in butter until crumbly. Sprinkle topping over filling.

3. Bake in a 350° oven for 20 to 25 minutes or until edges are bubbly and topping is golden brown. Serve warm and, if desired, pour half-and-half over each dish of crisp.

Nutrition Facts per serving: 294 cal., 11 g total fat (6 g sat. fat), 22 mg chol., 139 mg sodium, 47 g carbo., 4 g fiber, 3 g pro.
Daily Values: 5% vit. A, 2% vit. C, 2% calcium, 8% iron

Plump Apple Dumplings with Caramel Sauce

Store-bought puff pastry and caramel ice cream topping turn the arduous task of making apple dumplings into a simple 30-minute project.

Prep: 30 minutes Bake: 35 minutes Oven: 400°F
Makes: 4 servings

**Plump Apple Dumplings
with Caramel Sauce**

½	of a 17.3-ounce package frozen puff pastry (1 sheet), thawed
4	medium cooking apples (such as Golden Delicious or Jonathan)
1	tablespoon sugar
½	teaspoon ground cinnamon
1	egg
1	teaspoon water
½	cup caramel ice cream topping
⅓	cup chopped pecans, toasted

1. Unfold puff pastry on a lightly floured surface. Roll pastry into a 14-inch square. Using a fluted pastry cutter or table knife, cut pastry into four 7-inch squares. Set aside.

2. Core apples, and if desired, peel apples. If necessary, trim bottoms of apples so they stand upright. Place an apple in the center of each pastry square. In a small bowl combine sugar and cinnamon; spoon into centers of apples.

3. In another small bowl beat egg and water with a fork. Moisten the edges of the pastry squares with egg mixture; fold corners to center over fruit. Pinch to seal, pleating and folding pastry along seams as necessary. Place dumplings in a 13×9×2-inch baking pan.

4. If desired, cut leaf shapes from pastry trimmings with a small cookie cutter or knife; score veins in leaves. For curved leaves, drape over crumpled foil on another baking sheet.

5. Brush wrapped apples and leaf cutouts with egg mixture. Sprinkle leaves with sugar. Bake in a 400° oven about 35 minutes or until fruit is tender and pastry is brown.

6. Meanwhile, for sauce, in a 2-cup glass measuring cup combine caramel topping and pecans. Microwave, uncovered, on 100% (high) power for 30 to 60 seconds or until heated through.

7. To serve, moisten the bottoms of pastry leaves with caramel sauce; place on top of the baked dumplings, gently pressing in place. Serve dumplings warm with caramel-pecan sauce.

Nutrition Facts per serving: 562 cal., 27 g total fat (1 g sat. fat), 53 mg chol., 358 mg sodium, 76 g carbo., 5 g fiber, 5 g pro.
Daily Values: 3% vit. A, 11% vit. C, 5% calcium, 4% iron

Chocolate-Peppermint Malts

Mocha Fondue

Chocolate fondue is a timeless classic, but even favorites can be updated and improved. This recipe adds a hint of coffee and recommends using store-bought meringue cookies as crispy dippers.

Start to Finish: 25 minutes **Makes:** 6 to 8 servings

1	4-ounce package sweet baking chocolate, broken up
4	ounces semisweet chocolate, chopped
⅔	cup light cream or milk
½	cup sifted powdered sugar
1	teaspoon instant coffee crystals
2	tablespoons coffee liqueur
	Assorted fruits (such as pineapple chunks, kiwifruit wedges, strawberries, pear slices, banana slices)
	Meringue cookies

1. In a medium, heavy saucepan combine sweet baking chocolate, semisweet chocolate, light cream, sugar, and coffee crystals. Heat and stir over low heat until chocolate is melted and mixture is smooth. Remove from heat; stir in liqueur.

2. Pour into a fondue pot; keep warm over low heat. Serve with fruit and cookies.

Nutrition Facts per serving: 262 cal., 14 g total fat (5 g sat. fat), 10 mg chol., 15 mg sodium, 34 g carbo., 1 g fiber, 3 g pro.
Daily Values: 2% vit. A, 3% calcium, 5% iron

Chocolate-Peppermint Malts

Chocolate malts are always in season, but with a delicious peppermint flavor, these are perfect for the holidays. Serve them as an after-dinner Christmas dessert or a special treat at the end of a long workday.

Start to Finish: 20 minutes **Makes:** 6 servings

3	cups chocolate milk
1	quart vanilla or chocolate ice cream
¼	cup malted milk powder
½	teaspoon peppermint extract
⅛	teaspoon ground cinnamon
	Coarsely crushed hard peppermint candies
6	peppermint sticks (optional)

1. In a blender combine chocolate milk, half of the ice cream, the malted milk powder, peppermint extract, and cinnamon. Cover and blend until mixture is smooth. Pour into 6 chilled, large glasses. Top each malt with a scoop of the remaining ice cream. Sprinkle with crushed candy pieces. If desired, place a peppermint stick in each glass.

Nutrition Facts per serving: 403 cal., 20 g total fat (12 g sat. fat), 104 mg chol., 205 mg sodium, 48 g carbo., 1 g fiber, 9 g pro.
Daily Values: 18% vit. A, 3% vit. C, 30% calcium, 4% iron

Pretty Pear Gingerbread Tart

Topped with cream cheese, marmalade, and fresh pear slices, this light tart is the perfect conclusion to the Christmas feast. If you can't find gingerbread cookie dough, sugar cookie dough will work just as well.

Prep: 20 minutes **Bake:** 15 minutes **Chill:** 1 hour
Oven: 375°F **Makes:** 12 servings

1	18-ounce roll refrigerated gingerbread or sugar cookie dough
1	8-ounce tub cream cheese
3	ripe medium pears, peeled, cored, and very thinly sliced

1   to 2 tablespoons lemon juice
⅓   cup orange marmalade, melted
¼   cup chopped salted pistachio
    nuts, roasted

1. For crust, line a 12-inch pizza pan with parchment paper or foil. Pat cookie dough evenly onto parchment- or foil-lined pan. Build up edges slightly. Bake in a 375° oven for 15 to 20 minutes or until edge is light brown and center appears set. Cool in pan on a wire rack.

2. Invert cooled crust onto baking sheet; remove parchment paper or foil. Place serving platter over inverted crust; invert platter and crust together.

3. Stir cream cheese to soften. Spread cream cheese over crust, leaving ½-inch border. Brush pear slices with lemon juice. Arrange pear slices in concentric circles over cream cheese. Brush melted marmalade over pears. Sprinkle with pistachio nuts. Cover and chill 1 to 4 hours. Use a pizza cutter or sharp knife to cut into wedges.

Nutrition Facts per serving: 249 cal., 10 g total fat (3 g sat. fat), 13 mg chol., 198 mg sodium, 38 g carbo., 2 g fiber, 3 g pro.
Daily Values: 1% vit. A, 5% vit. C, 4% calcium, 5% iron

Chocolate-Sauced Pears

Go ahead and splurge with these delicious Christmas pears. Each luscious fruit is fat-free and contains less than 130 calories per serving. For an extra special presentation, garnish with an orange wedge.

Prep: 15 minutes **Bake:** 30 minutes **Oven:** 375°F
Cool: 5 minutes **Makes:** 4 servings

4   small pears
2   tablespoons orange juice
2   teaspoons vanilla
½   teaspoon ground cinnamon
2   tablespoons chocolate-flavored syrup
    Orange wedges (optional)

1. Core pears from bottom ends, leaving stems intact. Peel pears. If necessary, trim bottoms of pears so they stand upright. Place pears in a 2-quart square baking dish.

2. In a small bowl stir together orange juice, vanilla, and cinnamon. Brush onto pears. Pour remaining orange juice mixture over pears.

3. Cover with foil and bake in a 375° oven for 30 to 35 minutes or until pears are tender. Remove from oven; cool slightly, about 5 minutes.

4. To serve, place warm pears, stem end up, on dessert plates. Drizzle chocolate-flavored syrup over pears. Serve warm. If desired, garnish with orange wedges.

Nutrition Facts per serving: 127 cal., 0 g total fat (0 g sat. fat), 0 mg chol., 11 mg sodium, 32 g carbo., 5 g fiber, 1 g pro.
Daily Values: 1% vit. A, 18% vit. C, 2% calcium, 3% iron

Chocolate-Sauced Pears

Simplified Sweets

SAVE TIME; MAKE MORE! When holiday goodies are this easy to make, your trays of Christmas sweets will be overflowing with impressive variety. Long-time favorites are reinvented with simpler ingredients, making them a snap to make, bake, and eat. Melted caramel candies re-create tasty toffee, caramel ice cream topping saves the day in a speedy version of peanut brittle, and the lengthy process of chilling and rolling sugar cookies is eliminated in a revamped recipe. Make several batches of these Christmas confections, then fill platters and gift bags for friends, neighbors, and co-workers. Don't forget to save plenty for yourself and your own holiday parties!

Peppermint Thins, page 91

Browned Butter Cookies

Browned Butter Cookies acquire their nutty essence from frosting flavored with lightly browned butter. The French term for browned butter is "beurre noisette," referring to butter cooked to a light hazelnut color.

Prep: 25 minutes **Bake:** 10 minutes per batch
Oven: 350°F **Makes:** 56 cookies

½	cup butter, softened
1½	cups packed brown sugar
1	teaspoon baking soda
½	teaspoon baking powder
¼	teaspoon salt
2	eggs
1	teaspoon vanilla
2½	cups all-purpose flour
1	8-ounce carton dairy sour cream
1	cup coarsely chopped walnuts, toasted
1	recipe Browned Butter Icing

1. Lightly grease a baking sheet; set aside. In a large mixing bowl beat butter with an electric mixer on medium to high speed for 30 seconds. Add brown sugar, baking soda, baking powder, and salt. Beat until combined, scraping sides of bowl occasionally. Beat in eggs and vanilla until combined. Alternately add flour and sour cream to mixture, beating on low speed after each addition. Stir in walnuts.

2. Drop dough by rounded teaspoons 2 inches apart on prepared baking sheet. Bake in a 350° oven about 10 minutes or until edges are light brown. Transfer cookies to a wire rack and let cool. Frost with Browned Butter Icing.

Browned Butter Icing: In a small saucepan heat ½ cup butter over medium heat until butter turns the color of light brown sugar. Remove saucepan from heat. Stir in 4 cups sifted powdered sugar and enough boiling water (2 to 4 tablespoons) to make icing smooth and easy to spread. Frost the cooled cookies immediately after preparing frosting. If the frosting becomes grainy, soften with a few more drops of hot water.

Nutrition Facts per cookie: 132 cal., 6 g total fat (2 g sat. fat), 19 mg chol., 67 mg sodium, 19 g carbo., 0 g fiber, 1 g pro.
Daily Values: 3% vit. A, 2% calcium, 3% iron

Crackled Sugar Cookies

This sugar cookie recipe allows you to skip the refrigeration step, but requires a longer baking time at a lower temperature. To keep them tender to the bite, don't allow the cookies to over brown in the oven.

Prep: 25 minutes **Bake:** 18 minutes per batch
Oven: 300°F **Makes:** 48 cookies

½	cup butter, softened
½	cup shortening
2	cups sugar
1	teaspoon cream of tartar
½	teaspoon baking soda
⅛	teaspoon salt
3	egg yolks
1	tablespoon milk
½	teaspoon vanilla
2	cups all-purpose flour

1. In a large mixing bowl beat butter and shortening with an electric mixer on medium to high speed for 30 seconds. Add sugar, cream of tartar, baking soda, and salt. Beat until combined, scraping sides of bowl occasionally. Beat in egg yolks, milk, and vanilla until combined. Beat in as much of the flour as possible with the mixer. Using a wooden spoon, stir in any remaining flour. If necessary, knead dough until smooth.

2. Shape dough into 1-inch balls. Place 2 inches apart on an ungreased baking sheet. Bake in a 300° oven about 18 minutes or until the tops are slightly crackled and cookies are light brown. Cool on baking sheet for 1 minute. Transfer cookies to a wire rack and let cool.

Make-Ahead Tip: Prepare as directed through step 1. Shape dough into 1-inch balls. Arrange balls in a single layer on a baking sheet. Cover and freeze for 1 to 2 hours or until firm. Transfer balls to a self-sealing freezer bag or a freezer container. Seal, label, and freeze up to 3 months. To bake cookies, place frozen dough balls 2 inches apart on an ungreased baking sheet. Bake in a 300° oven about 20 minutes or until the tops are slightly crackled and cookies are light brown. Cool as directed above.

Nutrition Facts per serving: 90 cal., 5 g total fat (2 g sat. fat), 19 mg chol., 41 mg sodium, 12 g carbo., 0 g fiber, 1 g pro.
Daily Values: 2% vit. A, 2% iron

Fairy Dust Cookies

Fairy Dust Cookies

When sprinkled with colored sugar and crushed hard candies, these cookies sparkle like Christmas tree ornaments. Delight young children by letting them help decorate these colorful little sweets.

Prep: 30 minutes **Bake:** 10 minutes per batch
Oven: 350°F **Makes:** about 84 cookies

1	cup butter, softened
1	cup powdered sugar
1	cup granulated sugar
1	teaspoon baking soda
1	teaspoon cream of tartar
1	teaspoon salt
1	cup cooking oil
2	eggs
2	teaspoons almond extract
4½	cups all-purpose flour
	Plain or colored sugar or
1	recipe Almond Frosting
	Crushed hard candies (optional)

1. In a large mixing bowl beat butter with an electric mixer on medium to high speed for 30 seconds. Add powdered sugar, the 1 cup granulated sugar, the baking soda, cream of tartar, and salt. Beat until combined, scraping sides of bowl occasionally. Beat in oil, eggs, and almond extract just until combined. Beat in as much of the flour as possible with the mixer. Using a wooden spoon, stir in any remaining flour.

2. Drop dough from a rounded teaspoon 2 inches apart onto an ungreased baking sheet. With the bottom of a glass dipped in granulated sugar, gently flatten balls to about ¼-inch thickness. Sprinkle with plain or colored granulated sugar or leave plain for frosting. Bake in a 350° oven for 10 to 12 minutes or until edges just begin to brown. Transfer cookies to a wire rack and let cool. If desired, frost cooled cookies with Almond Frosting and sprinkle with crushed candies.

Almond Frosting: In a small mixing bowl beat ½ cup butter with an electric mixer on medium to high speed until fluffy. Beat in ½ teaspoon vanilla and ¼ teaspoon almond extract. Alternately add 2½ cups powdered sugar and 3 tablespoons half-and-half, light cream, or milk, beating until smooth. If necessary beat in up to 1 cup additional powdered sugar to achieve spreading consistency. If desired, stir in a few drops of food coloring to tint frosting. Makes about 2 cups.

Nutrition Facts per cookie: 83 cal., 5 g total fat (2 g sat. fat), 11 mg chol., 61 mg sodium, 9 g carbo., 0 g fiber, 1 g pro.
Daily Values: 2% vit. A, 2% iron

Cashew, Chocolate, and Butterscotch Cookies

Candy Cane Shortbread

Perfect for the holidays, these shortbread cookies will satisfy everyone with a soothing peppermint flavor and melt-in-your-mouth buttery texture.

Prep: 30 minutes **Bake:** 11 minutes per batch
Oven: 325° F **Makes:** about 36 cookies

1	cup butter, softened
¾	cup sugar
½	teaspoon baking powder
¼	teaspoon salt
¼	teaspoon peppermint extract
2	cups all-purpose flour
3	tablespoons finely crushed candy canes or striped round peppermint candies
2	ounces semisweet chocolate or white chocolate, chopped (optional)
1	teaspoon shortening (optional)

1. In a large mixing bowl beat butter with an electric mixer on medium to high speed for 30 seconds. Add sugar, baking powder, salt, and peppermint extract. Beat until combined, scraping sides of bowl occasionally. Stir in flour until combined. Form mixture into a ball.

2. On a lightly floured surface, knead dough until smooth. Divide dough in half. On the floured surface, roll half of the dough to ¼-inch thickness. Using a 2½-inch cookie cutter, cut dough into desired shapes. Place cookies 1 inch apart on ungreased baking sheets. Repeat with remaining dough, re-rolling as needed.

3. Bake in a 325° oven for 10 minutes. Remove cookies from oven and sprinkle with crushed candy canes. Return to oven and bake 1 to 3 minutes more or until edges just start to brown. Transfer cookies to a wire rack; let cool.

4. If desired, combine chocolate and shortening in a heavy small saucepan. Cook and stir over low heat until melted. Drizzle over the cooled cookies.

Nutrition Facts per cookie: 88 cal., 5 g total fat (3 g sat. fat), 14 mg chol., 58 mg sodium, 9 g carbo., 0 g fiber, 1 g pro.
Daily Values: 3% vit. A, 2% iron

Cashew, Chocolate, and Butterscotch Cookies

Cashew, chocolate, and butterscotch pieces turn regular oatmeal cookies into eye-popping delights. These sturdy cookies are perfect for shipping to friends and relatives who live across the country.

Prep: 20 minutes **Bake:** 6 minutes per batch
Oven: 375°F **Makes:** 48 cookies

1	cup butter, softened
1	cup packed brown sugar
½	cup granulated sugar
1½	teaspoons baking soda
½	teaspoon salt
2	eggs
1	teaspoon vanilla
2¼	cups all-purpose flour
2	cups rolled oats
1	cup coarsely chopped cashews
1	cup semisweet chocolate pieces
½	cup butterscotch-flavored pieces

1. In a large mixing bowl beat the butter with an electric mixer on medium to high speed for 30 seconds. Add brown sugar, granulated sugar, baking soda, and salt; beat until combined, scraping sides of bowl occasionally. Beat in eggs and vanilla until combined. Beat in as much flour as possible with the mixer. Using a wooden spoon, stir in any remaining flour, rolled oats, cashews, chocolate pieces, and butterscotch pieces.

2. Drop dough by rounded teaspoons 2 inches apart onto an ungreased baking sheet. Bake in a 375° oven for 6 to 7 minutes or until edges are golden. Transfer cookies to a wire rack; let cool.

Nutrition Facts per cookie: 145 cal., 7 g total fat (4 g sat. fat), 20 mg chol., 99 mg sodium, 18 g carbo., 1 g fiber, 2 g pro.
Daily Values: 3% vit. A, 1% calcium, 4% iron

Chewy Coconut Macaroons

During the Great Depression, coconut was a luxury. Macaroon recipes of that era often preserved the precious ingredient by replacing or combining it with cereal, like cornflakes. Luckily coconut is more affordable today and this substitution isn't necessary.

Prep: 15 minutes **Bake:** 20 minutes per batch
Oven: 325°F **Makes:** 30 cookies

2	3½-ounce cans flaked coconut (2⅔ cups)
⅔	cup sugar
⅓	cup all-purpose flour
¼	teaspoon salt
4	egg whites
½	teaspoon almond extract
2	ounces semisweet chocolate (optional)
½	teaspoon shortening (optional)

1. Lightly grease and flour a large baking sheet. In a medium bowl combine coconut, sugar, flour, and salt. Stir in egg whites and almond extract.

2. Drop egg white mixture by rounded teaspoons 2 inches apart onto prepared baking sheet. Bake in a 325° oven for 20 to 25 minutes or until edges are golden. Transfer to a wire rack; let cool.

3. If desired, in a heavy small saucepan, combine chocolate and shortening; heat and stir over low heat until melted. Drizzle over the cooled cookies.

Nutrition Facts per cookie: 55 cal., 3 g total fat (2 g sat. fat), 0 mg chol., 27 mg sodium, 8 g carbo., 0 g fiber, 1 g pro.

Chewy Coconut Macaroons

87

Maple-Cinnamon Wedges

Who says refrigerated cookie dough doesn't compare to homemade? These tasty wedges start with store-bought dough, but with the added flavors and unique shape, no one will know the dough wasn't made from scratch.

Prep: 15 minutes **Bake:** 20 minutes
Oven: 350°F **Makes:** 30 wedges

1	18-ounce roll refrigerated sugar cookie dough
¼	cup all-purpose flour
3	tablespoons butter, melted
2	tablespoons pure maple syrup or maple-flavored syrup
¼	cup packed brown sugar
¼	cup finely chopped pecans
½	teaspoon ground cinnamon

1. Line a 13×9×2-inch baking pan with foil. Lightly grease the foil; set aside. In a large bowl combine cookie dough and flour; stir or knead until well mixed. Press dough evenly onto the prepared pan.

2. In a small bowl combine melted butter and maple syrup. Drizzle syrup mixture over dough, spreading evenly. In another small bowl combine brown sugar, pecans, and cinnamon. Sprinkle evenly over syrup layer in pan.

3. Bake in a 350° oven about 20 minutes or until edges are firm (center will be soft). Cool completely on a wire rack. Use foil to lift from pan. Cut into

Super-Simple Sugar Cookies (See photo, front cover)
Knead ½ cup all-purpose flour, ¼ cup at a time, into refrigerated sugar cookie dough. On a lightly floured surface, roll out dough to ⅛-inch thickness. Cut into desired shapes (re-roll dough as necessary to make desired number of cookies). Place cookies 1 inch apart on an ungreased baking sheet. Bake according to package directions; cool cookies on wire racks. If desired, tint white canned frosting with food coloring and decorate sugar cookies. Top with colored sugars, non-pareils, and other small candies. Makes about 26 (3-inch) cookies.

15 bars; cut each bar in half diagonally to make wedges. Store wedges in a tightly covered container for up to 3 days.

Nutrition Facts per cookie: 105 cal., 5 g total fat (2 g sat. fat), 8 mg chol., 81 mg sodium, 14 g carbo., 0 g fiber, 1 g pro.
Daily Values: 1% vit. A, 2% calcium, 2% iron

Orange-Iced Fruitcake Cookies

The prep time for these cookies is a little longer than it is for many of the other recipes in this book, but that's because so much dough is produced. With a yield of 8 dozen cookies, this recipe is perfect to prepare for large cookie exchanges.

Prep: 45 minutes **Bake:** 12 minutes per batch
Oven: 350°F **Makes:** 96 cookies

½	cup butter, softened
½	cup shortening
¾	cup granulated sugar
¾	cup packed brown sugar
1½	teaspoons baking soda
1½	teaspoons ground cinnamon
½	teaspoon baking powder
½	teaspoon salt
2	eggs
2	teaspoons vanilla
4	cups all-purpose flour
1	20-ounce can crushed pineapple, well-drained
1	8-ounce package chopped dates
1	cup chopped walnuts
½	cup dried cherries or cranberries
½	cup golden raisins
1	teaspoon finely shredded orange peel
1	recipe Orange Icing

1. Lightly grease a baking sheet; set aside. In a large mixing bowl beat butter and shortening with an electric mixer on medium to high speed for 30 seconds. Add granulated sugar, brown sugar, baking soda, cinnamon, baking powder, and salt. Beat until combined, scraping sides of bowl occasionally. Beat in eggs and vanilla until combined. Beat in as much flour as possible. Stir in any remaining flour. Stir in pineapple, dates, walnuts, dried cherries, raisins, and orange peel.

2. Drop dough by rounded teaspoons 2 inches apart on prepared baking sheet. Bake in a 350° oven for 12 to 15 minutes or until edges are light brown. Transfer to a wire rack; let cool. Frost the cooled cookies with Orange Icing.

Orange Icing: In a medium bowl combine 2 cups powdered sugar, 2 tablespoons softened butter, and 2 tablespoons orange juice. Gradually add additional orange juice until icing reaches desired consistency. Stir in 1 teaspoon finely shredded orange peel. Spread on cookies.

Nutrition Facts per cookie: 80 cal., 3 g total fat (1 g sat. fat), 8 mg chol., 45 mg sodium, 13 g carbo., 1 g fiber, 1 g pro.
Daily Values: 1% vit. A, 1% vit. C, 1% calcium, 2% iron

Thumbprint Sugar Plum Pies

While any flavor of fruit preserves or jam can be used to make this tasty version of thumbprint cookies, plum jam brings to mind sugar plums—the traditional holiday favorite.

Prep: 30 minutes Bake: 10 minutes per batch
Oven: 375°F Makes: 24 cookies

²⁄₃	cup butter, softened
²⁄₃	cup packed brown sugar
2	egg yolks
1	tablespoon milk
1	teaspoon vanilla
¼	teaspoon ground cinnamon
1¾	cups all-purpose flour
²⁄₃	cup coarse raw sugar, granulated sugar, coarse sugar, or pearl sugar
½	teaspoon ground cinnamon
1	slightly beaten egg white
1	tablespoon water
¼	cup plum, cherry, or apricot preserves or jam

1. Lightly grease a baking sheet or line a baking sheet with parchment paper; set aside.

2. In a large bowl beat butter with an electric mixer on medium to high speed for 30 seconds. Add brown sugar and beat until combined, scraping sides of bowl occasionally. Beat in egg yolks, milk,

Thumbprint Sugar Plum Pies

vanilla, and the ¼ teaspoon ground cinnamon until combined. Beat in as much flour as possible with the mixer. Using a wooden spoon, stir in any remaining flour.

3. In a small bowl combine raw sugar and the ½ teaspoon cinnamon. In another small bowl whisk together egg white and water. Shape dough into 1-inch balls. Roll the balls in egg white mixture, then in sugar-cinnamon mixture. Place the balls 1 inch apart on the prepared baking sheet. Press your thumb into the center of each ball.

4. Bake in a 375° oven for 10 to 12 minutes or until edges are slightly firm. Cool on baking sheet for 1 minute. Transfer to a wire rack; let cool. Just before serving, fill the centers with preserves.

Nutrition Facts per cookie: 140 cal., 6 g total fat (3 g sat. fat), 40 mg chol., 44 mg sodium, 20 g carbo., 0 g fiber, 1 g pro.
Daily Values: 4% vit. A, 1% vit. C, 1% calcium, 3% iron

Carrot Cake Cookies

These quick-to-make cookies use a cake mix and a few extra ingredients to cut down on time spent baking during the holiday season.

Prep: 30 minutes **Bake:** 10 minutes per batch
Oven: 350°F **Makes:** about 36 cookies

2	eggs, slightly beaten
½	cup cooking oil
½	teaspoon vanilla
1	2-layer spice or carrot cake mix
½	cup finely shredded carrot (1 medium)
½	cup golden raisins
½	cup finely chopped walnuts or pecans, toasted if desired (optional)
½	teaspoon vanilla
1	16-ounce can cream cheese frosting
¼	cup finely chopped walnuts or pecans, toasted if desired (optional)

1. In a large mixing bowl combine eggs, oil, and vanilla. Add cake mix, carrot, raisins, the ½ cup nuts (if desired), and vanilla. Stir until combined and no lumps remain.

2. Drop dough by rounded teaspoonfuls 2 inches apart onto an ungreased baking sheet. Bake in a 350° oven for 10 to 12 minutes or until edges are light brown. Transfer to a wire rack; let cool. Frost with cream cheese frosting. If desired, sprinkle with the ¼ cup nuts.

Nutrition Facts per cookie: 152 cal., 6 g total fat (2 g sat. fat), 12 mg chol., 129 mg sodium, 22 g carbo., 0 g fiber, 1 g pro.
Daily Values: 4% vit. A, 3% calcium, 2% iron

Little Lemon Snowbites

If you've never had lemon curd, now is the time to give this citrusy spread a try. Made from sugar, butter, egg yolks, and fresh lemon juice, lemon curd is a cooked mixture that becomes quite thick. It is perfect for spreading on breads and pastries. When combined with whipped topping, lemon curd is sensational on these easy-to-make cookies.

Prep: 25 minutes **Bake:** 7 minutes per batch
Oven: 375°F **Makes:** about 24 sandwich cookies

1	17½-ounce package sugar cookie mix
¼	cup crushed hard lemon candies
⅔	cup purchased lemon curd
⅔	cup frozen whipped dessert topping, thawed
2	tablespoons powdered sugar

1. Line a baking sheet with parchment or foil; set aside. Prepare cookie mix according to package directions. Stir in crushed candies. If necessary, cover and chill dough about 1 hour.

2. Roll dough into 1-inch balls. Place balls 2 inches apart on prepared baking sheet. Bake in a 375° oven for 7 to 9 minutes or until edges are firm and cookies are light brown on bottom. Cool on baking sheet for 1 minute. Transfer to a wire rack; let cool.

3. For filling, in small bowl stir together lemon curd and whipped topping; set aside. To assemble cookies, place a rounded teaspoon of filling on the bottom side of a cookie; top with another cookie,

Little Lemon Snowbites

top-side-up. Repeat with remaining cookies and filling. Sprinkle tops of cookies with powdered sugar. Refrigerate filled cookies for up to 3 days or freeze for up to 1 month.

Nutrition Facts per sandwich: 169 cal., 7 g total fat (3 g sat. fat), 26 mg chol., 87 mg sodium, 25 g carbo., 1 g fiber, 1 g pro.
Daily Values: 3% vit. A, 2% iron

Chocolate Cappuccino Cookies

Chocolate, chocolate, chocolate—and espresso! The flavor of this scrumptious cookie is undeniably perfect. Brimming with both white and dark chocolate pieces, these treats will be the first cookies to disappear from the dessert tray.

Prep: 30 minutes **Bake:** 8 minutes per batch
Cool: 2 minutes **Oven:** 350°F
Makes: about 48 cookies

3	tablespoons water
1	tablespoon instant espresso coffee powder
1	19.5- or 19.8-ounce package fudge brownie mix
1	egg
3	tablespoons cooking oil
¼	teaspoon ground cinnamon
1½	cups dark chocolate pieces, semisweet chocolate pieces, and/or white baking pieces
	Milk chocolate kisses (optional)

1. Lightly grease a baking sheet or line a baking sheet with parchment paper; set aside. In a small bowl combine water and espresso coffee powder; stir until dissolved; set aside.

2. In a large mixing bowl combine brownie mix, egg, oil, cinnamon, and the espresso mixture. Beat with an electric mixer on low speed until combined, scraping sides of bowl occasionally. Using a wooden spoon, stir in chocolate pieces.

3. Drop dough by rounded teaspoons 1 inch apart onto prepared baking sheets or shape into 1-inch balls and place 1 inch apart on prepared baking sheets. Bake in a 350° oven about 8 minutes or until

edges are just set (centers will appear doughy). Do not overbake. Cool on baking sheet for 2 minutes. If desired, place a chocolate kiss on each cookie. Transfer to a wire rack; let cool. Store cookies in an airtight container at room temperature for up to 24 hours. Freeze for longer storage.

Nutrition Facts per cookie: 85 cal., 4 g total fat (1 g sat. fat), 5 mg chol., 34 mg sodium, 13 g carbo., 1 g fiber, 1 g pro.
Daily Values: 3% iron

Peppermint Thins

For easy cleanup after dipping these holiday-inspired cookies, place waxed paper under the wire rack to catch the vanilla candy drippings.

Start to Finish: 35 minutes **Makes:** 40 cookies

24	ounces vanilla candy coating, chopped
3	tablespoons shortening
⅛	teaspoon peppermint oil or peppermint candy flavoring
1	9-ounce package chocolate wafer cookies or 40 chocolate graham cracker squares
¼	cup coarsely crushed peppermint candy canes*

1. In a medium, heavy saucepan combine candy coating and shortening. Cook and stir over low heat until melted. Stir in peppermint oil. Keep warm over low heat, stirring occasionally.

2. Dip one wafer cookie at a time into the melted candy coating mixture. Remove with a fork and place on wire rack. While coating is still wet, sprinkle with crushed candy canes. If necessary, chill dipped cookies in refrigerator to set.

*Note: To crush candy canes, place them in a heavy plastic bag. Crush bag lightly with a meat mallet. Empty bag of crushed candy into a fine wire mesh strainer. Shake strainer over sink to remove excessive candy dust.

Nutrition Facts per cookie: 140 cal., 7 g total fat (5 g sat. fat), 1 mg chol., 50 mg sodium, 17 g carbo., 0 g fiber, 1 g pro.
Daily Values: 1% calcium, 1% iron

Golden-Flecked Chocolate Bars

1. Line a 9×9×2-inch baking pan with foil and lightly grease the foil; set aside. Using a sharp knife cut cookie dough in 4 equal portions. For crust, press 3 portions of the cookie dough evenly onto bottom of prepared pan; set aside.

2. For filling, in a medium mixing bowl beat cream cheese with an electric mixer on medium speed until smooth. Add sugar, egg, and vanilla, beating on low speed until combined. Spread filling evenly over crust. Dot filling with the remaining portion of cookie dough.

3. Bake in 350° oven for 28 to 30 minutes or until top is light brown and filling is set. Cool on a wire rack. Cut into bars. Cover and refrigerate.

Double Chocolate Cream Bars: Prepare as above, except beat ¼ cup unsweetened cocoa powder into the filling before spreading over the crust. Continue as directed above.

Nutrition Facts per bar: 120 cal., 6 g total fat (3 g sat. fat), 18 mg chol., 76 mg sodium, 14 g carbo., 0 g fiber, 1 g pro.
Daily Values: 2% vit. A, 1% calcium, 3% iron

Golden-Flecked Chocolate Bars

The top of this fudgelike filling is dotted with bits of leftover crust and baked until golden brown. Let the bars cool completely before cutting because the filling needs time to set up.

Prep: 20 minutes **Bake:** 35 minutes **Oven:** 350°F
Makes: about 25 bars

1	cup butter, softened
½	cup sugar
⅛	teaspoon salt
2	cups all-purpose flour
1	14-ounce can (1¼ cups) sweetened condensed milk
1	cup semisweet chocolate pieces
½	cup chopped walnuts or pecans
½	teaspoon vanilla

1. For crust, in a large mixing bowl beat butter with an electric mixer on medium to high speed for 30 seconds. Add sugar and salt; beat until

Chocolate Chip Cream Bars

These delicious bars are given the status of the ultimate chocolate chip cookie! Not only are they simplified by using purchased cookie dough for the base, but their yum-yum quotient goes up several notches with a filling similar to cheesecake that is spread across the top.

Prep: 20 minutes **Bake:** 28 minutes **Oven:** 350°F
Makes: 30 bars

1	18-ounce package or roll refrigerated chocolate chip cookie dough
1	8-ounce package cream cheese, softened
½	cup sugar
1	egg
½	teaspoon vanilla

combined, scraping sides of bowl occasionally. Beat in flour on low speed until combined. Press two-thirds of the crust mixture onto the bottom of an ungreased 13×9×2-inch baking pan.

2. For filling, in a medium saucepan combine sweetened condensed milk and chocolate pieces. Stir over low heat until chocolate melts and mixture is smooth. Remove from heat. Stir in nuts and vanilla. Spread hot mixture over the crust. Dot with the remaining crust mixture.

3. Bake in a 350° oven about 35 minutes or until golden. Cool on a wire rack. Cut into squares.

Nutrition Facts per bar: 213 cal., 13 g total fat (6 g sat. fat), 26 mg chol., 87 mg sodium, 24 g carbo., 1 g fiber, 3 g pro.
Daily Values: 6% vit. A, 1% vit. C, 5% calcium, 4% iron

Peanut Brittle Bars

Peanut brittle is a holiday classic, but if you have ever spent the afternoon pulling and stretching the candy across a pan, you know it's not easy to make. This recipe gives you homemade goodness and ease by substituting a purchased caramel ice cream topping for the cooked syrup.

Prep: 15 minutes **Bake:** 24 minutes **Oven:** 350°F
Makes: 36 bars

2	cups all-purpose flour
½	cup packed brown sugar
⅔	cup butter
2	cups cocktail peanuts
1	cup milk chocolate pieces
1	12½-ounce jar caramel ice cream topping
3	tablespoons all-purpose flour

1. Line a 15×10×1-inch baking pan with foil. Grease foil; set pan aside. For crust, in a medium bowl combine the 2 cups flour and the brown sugar. Using a pastry blender, cut in butter until mixture is crumbly. Press mixture onto the bottom of the prepared pan. Bake in a 350° oven about 12 minutes or until golden.

2. Sprinkle peanuts and milk chocolate pieces over warm crust. In a small bowl stir together caramel topping and the 3 tablespoons flour. Drizzle over top.

Peanut Brittle Bars

Building Better Bars

• Always use the pan size that is recommended in the recipe: pans that are too small will cause the bars to be too thick to cook in the appropriate time; pans that are too large will result in thin, unappealing bars.

• Try lining the pan with heavy foil—allowing extra to hang over the edges—to better remove the bars from the pan. Once the pan has cooled after baking, lift the bars from the pan by holding the foil, and then place the bars on a cutting board. Gently peel away the foil and cut into squares with a large chef's knife.

• For bars with layered ingredients, use a spatula to press firmly down on the top after the last layer is added to the pan. This will help the layers stick together better when the bars are cut. Always cool the pan completely before attempting to cut the bars.

3. Bake in the 350° oven for 12 to 15 minutes more or until caramel is bubbly. Cool on a wire rack. Carefully lift foil; gently peel it away from edges. Cut into bars.

Nutrition Facts per bar: 172 cal., 9 g total fat (3 g sat. fat), 10 mg chol., 81 mg sodium, 20 g carbo., 1 g fiber, 3 g pro.
Daily Values: 2% vit. A, 2% calcium, 3% iron

Easy Gingerbread Bars

Gingerbread originated in the Middle Ages, referring to a spiced confection that was bestowed upon knights before battle. Today the term gingerbread defines both the cookie and cake that are made with honey or molasses, ginger, and other spices.

Prep: 10 minutes **Bake:** 20 minutes **Oven:** 350°F
Makes: 24 bars

1	14½-ounce package gingerbread mix
¾	cup water
1	egg
1	7-ounce package tropical blend mixed dried fruit bits
1	cup chopped pecans
1	cup sifted powdered sugar
⅛	teaspoon ground ginger
3 to 4 teaspoons milk	

1. Grease a 13×9×2-inch baking pan; set aside. In a medium mixing bowl combine gingerbread mix, water, egg, fruit bits, and pecans; stir just until combined. Spread batter onto the prepared pan.

2. Bake in a 350° oven for 20 to 25 minutes or until a wooden toothpick inserted near the center comes out clean. Cool on a wire rack.

3. For glaze, in a small bowl stir together powdered sugar, ginger, and enough milk to make a glaze of drizzling consistency. Drizzle glaze over baked dough. Cut into bars.

Nutrition Facts per bar: 148 cal., 6 g total fat (1 g sat. fat), 9 mg chol., 123 mg sodium, 24 g carbo., 0 g fiber, 2 g pro.
Daily Values: 1% calcium, 3% iron

Candied Cherry Squares

For an extraordinary punch of cherry flavor, this recipe suggests using kirsch, a cherry brandy made from distilling the fruit's pits and juice. If you prefer to avoid alcohol in your cooking and baking—or don't want to purchase kirsch just to use one tablespoon— vanilla extract is an option.

Prep: 25 minutes **Bake:** 30 minutes **Oven:** 350°F
Makes: 16 bars

½	cup butter, softened
½	cup granulated sugar
¼	cup packed brown sugar
1	egg
1	tablespoon cherry brandy (Kirsch), cherry liqueur, or 1 teaspoon vanilla
1¼	cups all-purpose flour
½	cup miniature semisweet chocolate pieces
½	cup candied cherries, chopped
1	recipe Powdered Sugar Icing (optional)

1. Lightly grease an 8×8×2-inch baking pan; set aside. In a large mixing bowl beat butter with an electric mixer on medium to high speed for 30 seconds. Add granulated sugar and brown sugar. Beat until combined, scraping sides of bowl occasionally. Beat in egg and cherry brandy. Beat in as much flour as possible with the mixer. Stir in any remaining flour. Stir in chocolate pieces; gently fold in candied cherries.

2. Spread evenly onto prepared baking pan. Bake in a 350° oven for 30 to 35 minutes or until golden and the top springs back when lightly touched. Cool on a wire rack. If desired, drizzle with Powdered Sugar Icing. Cut into squares.

Powdered Sugar Icing: In a small bowl stir together ½ cup powdered sugar and enough milk (2 to 3 teaspoons) to make an icing of drizzling consistency.

Nutrition Facts per bar: 175 cal., 8 g total fat (4 g sat. fat), 29 mg chol., 49 mg sodium, 24 g carbo., 0 g fiber, 2 g pro.
Daily Values: 4% vit. A, 1% calcium, 4% iron

Scandinavian Almond Bars

Almonds are available in many forms, including blanched, sliced, whole, smoked, slivered, chopped, and candied. For this recipe, sliced almonds are the most attractive version to use.

Prep: 15 minutes **Bake:** 12 minutes per batch
Oven: 325°F **Makes:** 48 bars

1¾	cups all-purpose flour
2	teaspoons baking powder
¼	teaspoon salt
½	cup butter, softened
1	cup sugar
1	egg
½	teaspoon almond extract
	Milk
½	cup sliced almonds, coarsely chopped
1	recipe Almond Icing

1. In a medium bowl stir together flour, baking powder, and salt; set aside. In a large mixing bowl beat butter with an electric mixer on medium to high speed for 30 seconds. Add sugar; beat until combined, scraping sides of bowl occasionally. Beat in egg and almond extract until combined. Add flour mixture; beat until combined.

2. Divide dough into 4 equal portions. Form each portion into 12-inch long roll. Place two rolls 4 to 5 inches apart on an ungreased baking sheet. Using your hands, flatten each roll until it is 3 inches wide. Repeat with remaining rolls on another cookie sheet. Brush flattened rolls with milk and sprinkle with almonds.

3. Bake, one sheet at a time, in a 325° oven for 12 to 15 minutes or until edges are light brown. While still warm, slice diagonally into 1-inch-wide pieces. Transfer pieces to wire racks; let cool. Drizzle with Almond Icing.

Almond Icing: In a small bowl stir together 1 cup sifted powdered sugar, ¼ teaspoon almond extract, and enough milk (3 to 4 teaspoons) to make an icing of drizzling consistency.

Nutrition Facts per bar: 69 cal., 3 g total fat (1 g sat. fat), 10 mg chol., 38 mg sodium, 10 g carbo., 0 g fiber, 1 g pro.
Daily Values: 1% vit. A, 1% calcium, 2% iron

Scandinavian Almond Bars

The Irresistible Almond Who knew? The nut that we think of as an almond is actually the edible kernel, or seed, of a tree fruit. Similar to stone fruits, such as peaches, the flesh of the almond's fruit is allowed to reach maturity and dry, at which point the shell-covered seed is extracted.

Along with its lip-smacking flavor and enormous versatility in both sweet and savory dishes, the almond is also a nutritional powerhouse. Packed with vitamin E, potassium, magnesium, and fiber (all shown to aid in heart health), these little nuts also contain monounsaturated fat, which lowers bad cholesterol. So next time you're looking for an easy way to dress up salads, dinners, and desserts, consider the healthful, nutty goodness of almonds.

Foolproof Fudge

If candy thermometers and elaborate cooking methods typically discourage you from indulging in homemade fudge, you'll be delighted with this simplified recipe.

Prep: 15 minutes **Cook:** 8 minutes **Chill:** 4 hours
Makes: about 4½ pounds (120 pieces)

1	cup butter
3	cups semisweet chocolate pieces
2	tablespoons vanilla
4½	cups sugar
1	12-ounce can evaporated milk
1	to 2 cups chopped walnuts or pecans (optional)

1. Line a 13×9×2-inch baking pan with foil, extending it over the edges of the pan. Butter the foil; set pan aside.

2. In a large mixing bowl combine butter, chocolate pieces, and vanilla; set aside.

3. In a 5- to 6-quart Dutch oven combine sugar and evaporated milk. Cook and stir over medium-high heat until mixture boils. Reduce heat to medium and continue cooking, stirring constantly, for 8 minutes. (Adjust heat as necessary to maintain a steady boil without allowing mixture to boil over sides of pan.)

4. Pour milk mixture over chocolate mixture in the bowl; stir to combine. Beat with an electric mixer on medium speed about 2 minutes or until smooth and creamy. If desired, stir in nuts.

5. Quickly spread fudge evenly into the prepared pan. Cover and chill 4 hours or until firm. When fudge is firm, use foil to lift it out of pan. Cut fudge into 1-inch squares. Store tightly covered in the refrigerator for up to 2 weeks.

Nutrition Facts per piece: 66 cal., 3 g total fat (2 g sat. fat), 5 mg chol., 15 mg sodium, 10 g carbo., 0 g fiber, 1 g pro.
Daily Values: 1% vit. A, 1% calcium, 1% iron

P.B. and Chocolate Fudge

Peanut butter and chocolate create an age-old combination that delights taste buds year after year. Coming together once again, this well-loved pair works its magic in a decadently smooth Christmas fudge.

Prep: 20 minutes **Chill:** 2 hours
Makes: about 3 pounds (64 pieces)

2	cups sugar
½	cup evaporated milk
1⅓	cups creamy or chunky peanut butter
1	7-ounce jar marshmallow crème
1½	cups semisweet chocolate pieces
½	cup finely chopped peanuts

1. Line an 8×8×2-inch baking pan with foil, extending it over the edges of the pan. Butter the foil; set pan aside.

2. In a medium saucepan combine sugar and evaporated milk. Cook and stir over medium-high heat until mixture boils. Reduce heat to medium; continue cooking for 3 minutes, stirring occasionally. Remove from heat.

3. Immediately stir in peanut butter, marshmallow crème, and chocolate pieces. Stir until chocolate is melted and mixture is well combined. Quickly spread fudge evenly onto the prepared pan. Sprinkle with peanuts, pressing them lightly into the fudge.

4. Cover and chill for 2 to 3 hours or until firm. When fudge is firm, use foil to lift it out of pan. Cut fudge into 1-inch squares. Store tightly covered in the refrigerator for up to 1 week.

Nutrition Facts per piece: 91 cal., 5 g total fat (1 g sat. fat), 1 mg chol., 35 mg sodium, 12 g carbo., 1 g fiber, 2 g pro.
Daily Values: 1% vit. C, 1% calcium, 1% iron

Foolproof Fudge and P.B. and Chocolate Fudge

Quick Toffee Delight

Quick Toffee Delight

Prepared with crunchy pecans, a graham cracker crust, and a decadent layer of chocolate, this quick version of toffee will easily become an all-time favorite.

Prep: 10 minutes **Bake:** 2 minutes **Chill:** 15 minutes
Oven: 300°F **Makes:** 20 pieces

	Nonstick cooking spray
12	graham cracker squares
24	vanilla caramels, unwrapped
2	tablespoons milk or water
1	cup chopped pecans
2	cups dark chocolate pieces or semisweet chocolate pieces

1. Line a 13×9×2-inch baking pan with foil. Lightly coat foil with cooking spray. Cover bottom of pan with a single layer of graham crackers, breaking them as needed to fit. Set aside.

2. In a medium microwave-safe bowl combine caramels and milk. Microwave, uncovered, on high (100% power) for 2 to 3 minutes or until caramels are melted, stirring once. Quickly pour caramel mixture over graham crackers.

3. Sprinkle pecans over warm caramel layer. With a rubber spatula, lightly press pecans into caramel. Sprinkle chocolate pieces over the top.

4. Bake in a 300° oven about 2 minutes or until chocolate pieces soften (they will still hold their shape). Spread the softened pieces with a knife or metal spatula to cover caramel evenly. Chill about 15 minutes or until firm. Use foil to lift toffee out of pan. Remove foil. On a cutting board, cut or break the toffee into pieces.

Nutrition Facts per piece: 174 cal., 10 g total fat (3 g sat. fat), 0 mg chol., 56 mg sodium, 24 g carbo., 2 g fiber, 2 g pro.
Daily Values: 2% calcium, 5% iron

Marbled Mint Candy

These tasty goodies are simple to prepare and make for a lovely presentation when arranged on a platter.

Prep: 20 minutes **Chill:** 30 minutes
Makes: about 1½ pounds (about 32 pieces)

⅓	cup semisweet mint-flavored chocolate pieces or semisweet chocolate pieces
1	pound vanilla-flavored candy coating, cut up
¾	cup finely crushed candy canes or finely crushed striped round peppermint candies

1. Line a baking sheet with foil; set aside. In a small saucepan heat chocolate pieces over low heat until melted and smooth, stirring constantly. Remove saucepan from heat.

2. In a 2-quart saucepan melt candy coating over low heat. Remove saucepan from heat. Stir in crushed candy. Pour mixture onto the prepared baking sheet. Spread to about a ¼-inch thickness; drizzle with the melted chocolate. Gently zigzag a narrow metal spatula through the chocolate and peppermint layers to create a marbled look.

3. Chill candy about 30 minutes or until firm. (Or let candy stand at room temperature for several hours until firm.) Use foil to lift candy from the baking sheet; carefully break candy into pieces. Store tightly covered for up to 2 weeks.

Nutrition Facts per serving: 103 cal., 5 g total fat (4 g sat. fat), 0 mg chol., 2 mg sodium, 15 g carbo., 0 g fiber, 0 g pro.
Daily Values: 1% calcium

Fruitcake Candy Tarts

Prepared in individual cupcake liners, these sweet little treats are a combination of white chocolate and fruit bits heaped on a vanilla wafer. For extra holiday appeal, look for festively decorated mini-cupcake liners at supermarkets and craft stores.

Prep: 25 minutes **Chill:** 30 minutes **Makes:** 25 tarts

45	vanilla wafer cookies
25	midget foil cupcake liners (1¾ inches in diameter)
4	ounces vanilla candy coating, cut up
4	ounces white chocolate baking squares, cut up
2	teaspoons shortening
1	cup mixed dried fruit bits
½	cup dried cranberries

1. Place a vanilla wafer cookie in the bottom of each cupcake liner. Set cupcake liners and the remaining cookies aside.

2. In a medium microwave-safe bowl combine candy coating, white chocolate, and shortening. Microwave on high (100% power) about 2 minutes or until melted, stirring twice.

3. Coarsely crush the remaining 20 cookies. Gently stir crushed cookies, fruit bits, and cranberries into melted white chocolate mixture. Drop mixture from a rounded teaspoon into prepared foil cups. Chill about 30 minutes or until firm.

Nutrition Facts per serving: 127 cal., 5 g total fat (3 g sat. fat), 1 mg chol., 42 mg sodium, 19 g carbo., 0 g fiber, 1 g pro.
Daily Values: 1% calcium, 2% iron

Rocky Road Clusters

This four-ingredient recipe is as easy as they come. You don't even have to measure out the chocolate pieces or the marshmallows.

Prep: 20 minutes **Chill:** 1 hour **Makes:** about 50

1	12-ounce package semisweet chocolate pieces (2 cups)
1	cup creamy peanut butter
1	10½-ounce package tiny marshmallows (5½ cups)
1½	cups honey roasted or dry roasted peanuts

1. Line two baking sheets with waxed paper; set aside. In a heavy, medium saucepan combine chocolate pieces and peanut butter; cook and stir over medium-low heat until mixture is melted and smooth. Remove from heat.

2. In a large bowl combine marshmallows and peanuts. Pour chocolate mixture over the top; stir well to coat marshmallows and peanuts. Drop by heaping tablespoons onto prepared baking sheets. Chill for 1 hour or until set. Store in airtight container in the refrigerator for up to 2 weeks.

Nutrition Facts per servings: 98 cal., 6 g total fat (2 g sat. fat), 0 mg chol., 45 mg sodium, 11 g carbo., 1 g fiber, 3 g pro.
Daily Values: 2% iron

Snack Truffles

Make a batch of these scrumptious little morsels to wrap and bestow on any unexpected gift-givers.

Start to Finish: 30 minutes **Makes:** 30 truffles

½	cup flaked coconut
3	tablespoons powdered sugar
¾	cup coarsely chopped walnuts
8	ounces pitted dates
½	cup raisins
½	cup dried cranberries
⅓	cup flaked coconut
1	tablespoon unsweetened cocoa powder
¼	teaspoon ground cinnamon
¼	cup creamy peanut butter

1. In a food processor combine the ½ cup coconut and the powdered sugar. Cover and process until coconut is finely chopped. Transfer mixture to a shallow dish; set aside.

2. For truffles, in the food processor place walnuts, dates, raisins, cranberries, the ⅓ cup coconut, the cocoa powder, and cinnamon. Cover and process or blend until finely chopped, stopping to scrape sides as necessary. Add peanut butter. Cover and process until mixture is moist enough to form a ball.

3. Using your hands, shape the mixture into 1-inch balls. Roll the balls in the coconut mixture, gently patting the mixture onto sides of the balls. Transfer truffles to a storage container. Cover and store at room temperature for up to 7 days.

Nutrition Facts per piece: 86 cal., 4 g total fat (2 g sat. fat), 0 mg chol., 21 mg sodium, 12 g carbo., 1 g fiber, 2 g pro.
Daily Values: 1% calcium, 2% iron

Tropical Snowballs

Although "tropical snowball" is a contradiction in terms, make a batch and you will understand how these little candies were named.

Prep: 30 minutes **Chill:** 1 hour **Makes:** about 24

- 1 **8-ounce tub cream cheese spread with pineapple**
- ¼ **cup powdered sugar**
- 1 **cup crisp rice cereal, crushed**
- ½ **cup tropical blend mixed dried fruit bits**
- ⅓ **cup finely chopped macadamia nuts**
- ¾ **cup shredded or flaked coconut**

1. In a medium bowl stir together cream cheese and powdered sugar. Stir in cereal, fruit bits, and macadamia nuts.

2. Place coconut in a shallow dish or a small bowl. Using a small scoop or a rounded teaspoon, drop scoops of cream cheese mixture into coconut. Roll to coat with coconut and shape into balls. Place the balls on a waxed paper-lined tray or baking pan.

3. Cover and chill about 1 hour or until firm. Refrigerate in airtight container for up to 1 week.

Nutrition Facts per piece: 80 cal., 5 g total fat (3 g sat. fat), 7 mg chol., 61 mg sodium, 8 g carbo., 1 g fiber, 1 g pro.
Daily Values: 3% vit. A, 2% calcium, 1% iron

Tropical Snowballs and Snack Truffles

Angel Kisses

The heavenly name of these sweet little meringues makes them a perfect cookie for the holidays.

Prep: 15 minutes **Bake:** 20 minutes per batch
Stand: 30 minutes **Oven:** 300°F
Makes: about 36 cookies

2	egg whites
¼	teaspoon vanilla
⅛	teaspoon cream of tartar
⅛	teaspoon almond extract
⅔	cup sugar
½	cup almond brickle pieces

1. Let egg whites stand in a medium mixing bowl at room temperature for 30 minutes. Lightly grease a baking sheet or line a baking sheet with parchment paper; set aside.

2. Add vanilla, cream of tartar, and almond extract to the egg whites. Beat with an electric mixer on high speed until soft peaks form (tips curl). Gradually add sugar, 1 tablespoon at a time, beating until stiff peaks form (tips stand straight). Fold in almond brickle pieces.

3. Drop mixture by rounded teaspoons 1½ inches apart onto prepared baking sheet. Bake in a 300° oven about 20 minutes or until firm and bottoms are light brown. Cool cookies on parchment or foil on a wire rack. Store in an airtight container for up to a week.

Nutrition Facts per cookie: 23 cal., 1 g total fat (0 g sat. fat), 0 mg chol., 10 mg sodium, 5 g carbo., 0 g fiber, 0 g pro.

Sweet-and-Salty Peanut Rolls

After these peanut-covered cream cheese rolls are sliced, place two pieces in candy papers, which are available at hobby stores. Because the recipe yields so many slices, these sweet and salty bites are perfect for cookie exchanges with friends.

Prep: 30 minutes **Chill:** 3 hours
Makes: about 84 pieces

1	3-ounce package cream cheese, softened
¼	cup butter, softened
4¼	cups powdered sugar
1	teaspoon vanilla
½	cup finely chopped honey roasted peanuts
2	to 3 teaspoons milk

1. In a large mixing bowl beat cream cheese and butter with an electric mixer on medium to high speed for 30 seconds. Gradually beat in powdered sugar and vanilla until combined. Shape mixture into a ball. Divide mixture into thirds.

2. Shape each third into a 9-inch long log, about 1 inch in diameter. Spread peanuts in a single layer on a piece of waxed paper. Brush logs lightly with milk. Roll the logs in peanuts to coat, reshaping logs as necessary.

3. Wrap logs in waxed paper or plastic wrap. Chill about 3 hours or until firm enough to slice. To serve, cut rolls into ¼-inch slices. Cover and store in the refrigerator for up to 2 weeks.

Nutrition Facts per piece: 33 cal., 1 g total fat (1 g sat. fat), 3 mg chol., 11 mg sodium, 5 g carbo., 0 g fiber, 0 g pro.
Daily Values: 1% vit. A

Managing Meringues Crispy meringue cookies are made from a whipped mixture of egg whites and sugar, which is baked at very low temperatures to obtain a dry, crispy texture.

- **Keep it clean.** Wash utensils and bowls with hot, soapy water prior to use, and discard eggs if the yolk breaks in the white.

- **Warming up.** Let the egg whites sit out at room temperature for about 30 minutes prior to beating them. This will give the whites more volume once beaten.

- **First the soft peaks.** When beating the egg whites, wait for soft peaks (slight curl to tips) to form before adding the sugar.

- **Then the stiff peaks.** After slowly adding the sugar, continue to beat the mixture until the sugar is dissolved and stiff peaks form (the tips will now stand straight).

- **Easy does it.** Baking these airy cookies at low temperatures, then turning off the oven and allowing them to dry in the oven, makes them crisp and airy.

Strawberry Meringue Stars

Strawberry Meringue Stars

Try to keep these little morsels the same size or they may not dry out in the specified time.

Prep: 20 minutes **Bake:** 18 minutes per batch
Stand: 45 minutes **Oven:** 300°F
Makes: about 90 cookies

- 3   **egg whites**
- 1   **teaspoon white vinegar**
- ⅛   **teaspoon salt**
- ¾   **cup sugar**
- ½   **of a 3-ounce package (about 3 tablespoons) strawberry-flavored gelatin**
- 6   **ounces bittersweet chocolate and/or white chocolate, melted (optional)**
       Sifted powdered sugar (optional)

1. Let egg whites stand in a medium mixing bowl at room temperature for 30 minutes. Line a large cookie sheet with parchment paper or foil; set aside.

2. Add vinegar and salt to egg whites. Beat with an electric mixer on high speed until soft peaks form (tips curl). Gradually add sugar and the dry gelatin, beating until stiff peaks form (tips stand straight).

3. Spoon mixture into a pastry bag with a large star tip (at least ½-inch opening). Pipe stars, about 1 inch wide and 1 inch tall, onto prepared cookie sheet. Bake in 300° oven for 18 to 20 minutes or until dry but not brown. Turn off oven and let meringues dry in oven for another 15 minutes.

4. Peel meringues from paper or foil and let cool on wire racks. If desired, decorate meringue stars by dipping tops or bottoms in melted chocolate, drizzling chocolate over tops of meringue stars, or sprinkling with powdered sugar. Place on waxed paper until chocolate is set Store in an airtight container for up to a week.

Nutrition Facts per cookie: 9 cal., 0 g total fat (0 g sat. fat), 0 mg chol., 8 mg sodium, 2 g carbo., 0 g fiber, 0 g pro.

Save-the-Day
Slow Cooker

THANKS TO THE RENAISSANCE of the slow cooker, a plethora of exciting new recipes, many of which are perfect for holiday feasts, has emerged just for this special cooking appliance. Rather than trying to juggle the timing of several different dishes emerging from the oven at one time, put your mind at ease by allowing the slow cooker to help with at least one recipe on the day of the big feast. You're bound to find an irresistible recipe choice, from meat to potatoes or vegetables to soups, that will put the finishing touches on your Christmas celebration and eliminate the pressures of dinner preparation.

Festive Cheesy Potatoes, page 107

Fruit and Pecan Stuffing

Although definitely a savory herbed dish, this stuffing also has a touch of sweetness from the apple juice and dried fruit. Perfect when paired with any roasted meat, the stuffing is exceptional when served alongside turkey and chicken.

Prep: 25 minutes **Cook:** 4½ to 5 hours (low-heat setting) or 2¼ to 2½ hours (high-heat setting)
Makes: 10 to 12 side-dish servings

½	cup apple juice
1	6-ounce package mixed dried fruit bits (1½ cups)
1	cup finely chopped celery (2 stalks)
½	cup sliced green onion (4)
½	cup butter or margarine
2	tablespoons snipped fresh parsley
1	teaspoon dried sage, crushed
½	teaspoon dried thyme, crushed
½	teaspoon dried marjoram, crushed
½	teaspoon salt
¼	teaspoon black pepper
10	cups dry bread cubes*
½	cup broken pecans, toasted
1	to 1½ cups chicken broth

1. In a small saucepan heat apple juice until boiling. Stir in dried fruit. Remove from heat; cover and let stand until needed.

Fruit and Pecan Stuffing

2. Meanwhile, in a medium saucepan cook celery and green onion in butter over medium heat until tender but not brown; remove from heat. Stir in parsley, sage, thyme, marjoram, salt, and pepper.

3. Place dry bread cubes in a large bowl. Add the undrained fruit, the vegetable mixture, and pecans. Drizzle with enough of the broth to moisten, tossing lightly. Transfer stuffing mixture to a 3½- or 4-quart slow cooker.

4. Cover and cook on low-heat setting for 4½ to 5 hours or on high-heat setting for 2¼ to 2½ hours.

*Note: To prepare the 10 cups dry bread cubes, cut 14 to 16 bread slices into ½-inch cubes and spread in a large roasting pan. Bake in a 300°F oven for 10 to 15 minutes or until dry, stirring twice.

Nutrition Facts per serving: 279 cal., 15 g total fat (7 g sat. fat), 27 mg chol., 528 mg sodium, 33 g carbo., 2 g fiber, 4 g pro.
Daily Values: 9% vit. A, 5% vit. C, 6% calcium, 10% iron

Sage Dressing

Whether you call it dressing or stuffing, the combination of bread cubes, herbs, and vegetables is a classic few holiday meals go without. This savory version spends the day in a slow cooker, rather than in the oven or in the bird.

Prep: 20 minutes **Cook:** 4 to 5 hours (low-heat setting) **Makes:** 8 to 10 side-dish servings

12	cups dry bread cubes*
2	cups sliced celery (4 stalks)
½	cup finely chopped onion (1 medium)
¼	cup snipped fresh parsley
1½	teaspoons dried sage, crushed
½	teaspoon dried marjoram, crushed
¼	teaspoon black pepper
1½	cups chicken broth
¼	cup butter or margarine, melted

1. In a large bowl combine dry bread cubes, celery, onion, parsley, sage, marjoram, and pepper.

2. Pour broth and butter over bread mixture; toss. Transfer mixture to a 3½- to 5-quart slow cooker.

3. Cover and cook dressing on low-heat setting for 4 to 5 hours.

*Note: To prepare the 12 cups dry bread cubes, cut 16 to 18 bread slices into ½-inch cubes and spread in a large roasting pan. Bake in a 300°F oven for 10 to 15 minutes or until dry, stirring twice.

Nutrition Facts per serving: 200 cal., 8 g total fat (3 g sat. fat), 17 mg chol., 593 mg sodium, 28 g carbo., 2 g fiber, 5 g pro.
Daily Values: 10% vit. A, 6% vit. C, 10% calcium, 12% iron

Caramelized Onions and Potatoes

Low heat and plenty of cooking time transform sliced onions and succulent new potatoes into a savory side dish. Match it with full-flavored meat dishes, such as roasted turkey or beef tenderloin, to complete the meal.

Prep: 15 minutes **Cook:** 6 to 7 hours (low-heat setting) or 3 to 3½ hours (high-heat setting)
Makes: 6 side-dish servings

1½	pounds tiny new potatoes, halved
2	large sweet onions (such as Vidalia), cut into thin wedges (2 cups)
¼	cup butter, melted
½	cup beef or chicken broth
3	tablespoons brown sugar
½	teaspoon salt
¼	teaspoon freshly ground pepper

1. In a 3½- or 4-quart slow cooker place potatoes and onions. In a small bowl combine melted butter, broth, brown sugar, salt, and pepper. Pour mixture over onions and potatoes in the cooker.

2. Cover and cook on low-heat setting for 6 to 7 hours or on high-heat setting for 3 to 3½ hours. Stir gently before serving. Serve with a slotted spoon.

Nutrition Facts per serving: 194 cal., 8 g total fat (5 g sat. fat), 22 mg chol., 356 mg sodium, 28 g carbo., 3 g fiber, 3 g pro.
Daily Values: 6% vit. A, 29% vit. C, 3% calcium, 10% iron

1. Lightly coat the liner of a 3½- or 4-quart slow cooker with cooking spray. Add sweet potatoes, apple pie filling, raisins, the 3 tablespoons butter, and the apple pie spice; mix well.

2. Cover and cook on low-heat setting for 6 to 8 hours or on high-heat setting for 3 to 4 hours.

3. Meanwhile, for candied pecans, in a heavy large skillet combine pecans, sugar, and the 2 tablespoons butter. Cook and stir over medium heat for 8 to 10 minutes or until sugar mixture clinging to the nuts turns golden and starts to melt. Pour the nut mixture onto a large piece of foil; cool completely. When the nut mixture is cool, coarsely crush.

4. To serve, top each serving of potatoes with some of the candied pecans.

Nutrition Facts per serving: 332 cal., 14 g total fat (4 g sat. fat), 16 mg chol., 84 mg sodium, 52 g carbo., 6 g fiber, 3 g pro.
Daily Values: 287% vit. A, 34% vit. C, 6% calcium, 8% iron

Sweet Baby Carrots

With an apple jelly and dill glaze, these baby carrots and tiny onions make a tasty side dish for the holiday table. Start simmering them in the morning and by the time dinner is done, the carrots will be ready to glaze.

Prep: 10 minutes **Cook:** 6 to 7 hours (low-heat setting) or 3 to 3½ hours (high-heat setting)
Stand: 2 minutes **Makes:** 8 to 10 side-dish servings

2	16-ounce packages peeled baby carrots
1	pound boiling onions (about 16), peeled, or one 16-ounce package frozen small whole onions
½	teaspoon dried dill
¾	cup water
1	cup apple jelly

1. In a 4½- to 5½-quart slow cooker combine carrots and onions. Sprinkle with dill. Add water.

2. Cover and cook on low-heat setting for 6 to 7 hours or on high-heat setting for 3 to 3½ hours.

Apple-Spiced Sweet Potatoes

Apple-Spiced Sweet Potatoes

Americans have enjoyed candied sweet potatoes since Colonial times when cooks first sweetened them with maple syrup. This version includes sweet apples and is ideal for the holidays because the potatoes can cook in a slow cooker while other foods bake in the oven.

Prep: 20 minutes **Cook:** 6 to 8 hours (low-heat setting) or 3 to 4 hours (high-heat setting)
Makes: 10 side-dish servings

	Nonstick cooking spray
3½	to 4 pounds sweet potatoes, peeled and cut into 2-inch chunks
1	20-ounce can apple pie filling
⅔	cup golden raisins
3	tablespoons butter or margarine, cut into cubes
1½	teaspoons apple pie spice
1	cup coarsely chopped pecans
⅓	cup sugar
2	tablespoons butter or margarine

3. Using a slotted spoon, remove carrots and onions from cooker. For sauce, gently stir apple jelly into liquid in cooker; let stand for 2 to 3 minutes or until jelly is melted. Stir sauce. Return carrots and onions to sauce in cooker. Stir gently to coat vegetables. Serve with slotted spoon.

Nutrition Facts per serving: 178 cal., 0 g total fat (0 g sat. fat), 0 mg chol., 53 mg sodium, 43 g carbo., 5 g fiber, 2 g pro.
Daily Values: 574% vit. A, 19% vit. C, 5% calcium, 4% iron

Festive Cheesy Potatoes

For anyone who loves potatoes, this classy side dish will hit the spot. With the added flavors of bacon, green onions, smoked Gouda and provolone cheeses, this tasty treat is made with packaged frozen potatoes.

Prep: 20 minutes **Cook:** 5 to 6 hours (low-heat setting) **Makes:** 12 side-dish servings

- 1 **28-ounce package frozen loose-pack diced hash brown potatoes with onion and peppers, thawed**
- 1 **10¾-ounce can condensed cream of chicken with herbs soup**
- 1 **8-ounce package cream cheese, cubed**
- 1 **cup finely shredded smoked Gouda cheese (4 ounces)**
- 1 **cup finely shredded provolone cheese (4 ounces)**
- ¾ **cup milk**
- ¼ **cup finely chopped leek or thinly sliced green onion**
- ½ **teaspoon black pepper**
- 4 **slices bacon, crisp-cooked, drained, and crumbled (optional)**

1. In a 3½- or 4-quart slow cooker combine thawed potatoes, soup, cream cheese, Gouda cheese, provolone cheese, milk, leek, and pepper.

2. Cover and cook on low-heat setting for 5 to 6 hours. If desired, stir in bacon before serving.

Nutrition Facts per serving: 216 cal., 14 g total fat (8 g sat. fat), 39 mg chol., 534 mg sodium, 16 g carbo., 2 g fiber, 8 g pro.
Daily Values: 12% vit. A, 14% vit. C, 18% calcium, 6% iron

Wild Rice Pilaf with Squash

Inspire some appreciative table conversation with this unusual winter side dish. A combination of squash, wild rice, and citrus, this recipe will cook by itself all afternoon, and then delight your guests with a flavor-packed punch when dinner is ready.

Prep: 20 minutes **Cook:** 4 to 5 hours (low-heat setting) or 2 to 3 hours (high-heat setting)
Makes: 8 to 10 side-dish servings

- 2 **large oranges**
- 3 **cups peeled, seeded winter squash cut into bite-size pieces (such as butternut)**
- 2 **4.1- to 4.5-ounce packages long grain and wild rice mix with herbs (not quick-cooking)**
- ¼ **cup packed brown sugar**
- 2 **14-ounce cans chicken broth**

1. Finely shred the peel from one of the oranges. Measure 1 teaspoon of finely shredded orange peel; set aside. Squeeze juice from both oranges. Measure ⅔ cup orange juice; set aside.

2. In a 3½- or 4-quart slow cooker combine squash, rice mix and the contents of rice seasoning packets, and brown sugar. Add the reserved orange peel and the orange juice. Pour broth over all ingredients. Stir to combine.

3. Cover and cook on low-heat setting for 4 to 5 hours or on high-heat setting for 2 to 3 hours. Stir gently before serving.

Nutrition Facts per serving: 170 cal., 1 g total fat (0 g sat. fat), 0 mg chol., 931 mg sodium, 37 g carbo., 1 g fiber, 4 g pro.
Daily Values: 81% vit. A, 33% vit. C, 5% calcium, 8% iron

Turkey Roast Chablis

This recipe is the perfect dish for a small holiday gathering when a whole bird is too much. Serve the delectable white wine gravy with mounds of creamy mashed potatoes and a crisp green salad on the side.

Prep: 20 minutes **Cook:** 10 to 12 hours (low-heat setting) or 4½ to 5½ hours (high-heat setting); plus 10 minutes **Makes:** 6 to 8 main-dish servings

¾   **cup Chablis or other dry white wine**
½   **cup chopped onion (1 medium)**
1   **clove garlic, minced**
1   **bay leaf**
1   **3- to 3½-pound frozen boneless turkey roast, thawed**
1   **teaspoon dried rosemary, crushed**
¼   **teaspoon black pepper**
⅓   **cup half-and-half, light cream, or milk**
2   **tablespoons cornstarch**
⅛   **teaspoon salt**

1. In a 3½- to 6-quart slow cooker combine white wine, onion, garlic, and bay leaf. If turkey roast is wrapped in netting, remove it and discard. If gravy packet is included, remove it from roast; if desired, refrigerate packet for another use. Combine rosemary and pepper. Rub turkey roast with the rosemary mixture. Place roast in cooker.

2. Cover and cook on low-heat setting for 10 to 12 hours or on high-heat setting for 4½ to 5½ hours. Transfer turkey to a serving platter; cover with foil to keep warm.

3. For gravy, strain cooking juices; discard solids. Skim fat from juices. Measure 1⅓ cups of the juices into a small saucepan. Combine half-and-half, cornstarch, and salt; stir into juices. Cook and stir until thickened. Cook and stir for 2 minutes more. Slice turkey. Spoon some gravy over turkey. Pass remaining gravy with the turkey.

Nutrition Facts per serving: 324 cal., 6 g total fat (3 g sat. fat), 125 mg chol., 1594 mg sodium, 19 g carbo., 0 g fiber, 41 g pro.
Daily Values: 1% vit. A, 2% vit. C, 3% calcium, 28% iron

Cherried Pork Roast

This family-friendly pork roast can be simmered with a variety of other dried fruits, such as coarsely chopped dried cranberries, apricots, or golden raisins. Although the recipe recommends serving the meat with noodles or rice, any side dish will do.

Prep: 20 minutes **Cook:** 7 to 9 hours (low-heat setting) or 3½ to 4½ hours (high-heat setting)
Makes: 6 to 8 main-dish servings

1   **2- to 2½-pound boneless pork shoulder roast**
2   **tablespoons cooking oil**
1   **tablespoon quick-cooking tapioca**
1   **teaspoon dried thyme, crushed**
½   **teaspoon black pepper**
1   **medium onion, cut into wedges**
1   **cup dried sweet cherries**
½   **cup apple juice or apple cider**
3   **to 4 cups hot cooked noodles or rice**
2   **tablespoons snipped fresh parsley**

1. Trim fat from meat. If necessary, cut meat to fit into a 3½- to 4½-quart slow cooker. In a large skillet brown meat on all sides in hot oil. Drain off fat from skillet.

2. Transfer meat to cooker. Sprinkle tapioca, thyme, and pepper over meat. Add onion and dried cherries to cooker. Pour apple juice over all.

3. Cover and cook on low-heat setting for 7 to 9 hours or on high-heat setting for 3½ to 4½ hours. Transfer meat to a cutting board. Using 2 forks, break meat into bite-size chunks. Toss hot cooked noodles with parsley. Serve pork roast and cherry sauce with noodles.

Nutrition Facts per serving: 475 cal., 16 g total fat (5 g sat. fat), 127 mg chol., 122 mg sodium, 47 g carbo., 3 g fiber, 35 g pro.
Daily Values: 6% vit. A, 8% vit. C, 6% calcium, 35% iron

Cherried Pork Roast

Old-Fashioned Rice Pudding

Sweet, comforting and deliciously old-fashioned, this Christmas classic gains new life from the addition of dried fruit. If you like, hide a whole, shelled almond in the dessert before you begin cooking it. Whoever finds the traditional treat supposedly has good luck throughout the year.

Prep: 10 minutes **Cook:** 2 to 3 hours (low-heat setting) **Makes:** 12 to 14 servings

	Nonstick cooking spray
4	cups cooked rice
1	12-ounce can evaporated milk
1	cup milk
1/3	cup sugar
1/4	cup water
3	tablespoons butter or margarine, softened
1	tablespoon vanilla
1	teaspoon ground cinnamon
1	cup raisins, dried cranberries, dried cherries, or dried currants

1. Coat the liner of a 3½- or 4-quart slow cooker with cooking spray; set aside. In a large bowl combine cooked rice, evaporated milk, milk, sugar, and water. Stir in butter, vanilla, cinnamon, and raisins. Stir well to combine. Transfer rice mixture to the slow cooker.

2. Cover and cook on low-heat setting for 2 to 3 hours. Stir well before serving.

Nutrition Facts per serving: 204 cal., 6 g total fat (3 g sat. fat), 18 mg chol., 73 mg sodium, 34 g carbo., 1 g fiber, 4 g pro.
Daily Values: 5% vit. A, 2% vit. C, 11% calcium, 6% iron

Slow-Cooked Apple Betty

This full-flavored comfort food consists of fresh apples, brown sugar, and apple butter— all of which are slow-cooked with a topping of soft cinnamon-raisin bread. The dessert is delicious served alone, but if desired, top with vanilla ice cream and drizzle liberally with caramel topping.

Prep: 25 minutes **Cook:** 4 hours (low-heat setting)
Stand: 30 minutes **Makes:** 6 to 8 servings

	Nonstick cooking spray
5	tart cooking apples, peeled, cored and sliced (5 cups)
3/4	cup packed brown sugar
2/3	cup apple butter
1/2	cup water
5	cups soft cinnamon-raisin bread cut into 1/2-inch cubes (about 5 slices)
1/3	cup butter, melted
	Vanilla ice cream and/or caramel ice cream topping (optional)

1. Lightly coat the liner of a 3 ½- or 4-quart slow cooker with cooking spray; set aside.

2. In a bowl combine apples, brown sugar, apple butter, and water; toss until coated. Place bread cubes in a medium bowl; drizzle with the melted butter, tossing until mixed.

3. Place half of the buttered bread cubes in the prepared cooker. Pour all of the apple mixture over bread cubes. Sprinkle the remaining bread cubes over the apple mixture.

4. Cover and cook on low-heat setting about 4 hours. Remove liner from cooker, if possible, or turn off cooker. Let stand, uncovered, about 30 minutes to cool slightly before serving.

5. To serve, spoon warm dessert into dessert dishes. If desired, top with ice cream and/or caramel ice cream topping.

Nutrition Facts per serving: 492 cal., 12 g total fat (7 g sat. fat), 29 mg chol., 209 mg sodium, 97 g carbo., 5 g fiber, 2 g pro.
Daily Values: 11% vit. A, 9% vit. C, 6% calcium, 8% iron

Mixed Berry Cobbler

Mixed Berry Cobbler

How easy it is to serve a warm and comforting dessert for Christmas—especially when it bakes by itself in the slow cooker all afternoon. Muffin mix, frozen berries, and blueberry pie filling make the prep for this dessert a snap.

Prep: 15 minutes **Cook:** 3 hours (low-heat setting) plus 1 hour (high-heat setting) **Stand:** 30 minutes
Makes: 8 to 10 servings

       Nonstick cooking spray
1   12- to 14-ounce package frozen mixed berries
1   21-ounce can blueberry pie filling
¼   cup sugar
1   6½-ounce package blueberry or triple-berry muffin mix
⅓   cup water
2   tablespoons cooking oil
       Frozen whipped dessert topping, thawed (optional)

1. Lightly coat the liner of a 3½- or 4-quart slow cooker with cooking spray; set aside.

2. In the bottom of prepared cooker combine frozen mixed berries, blueberry pie filling, and sugar. Mix well.

3. Cover and cook on low-heat setting for 3 hours. Turn cooker to high-heat setting. In a medium bowl combine muffin mix, water, and oil; stir just until combined. Spoon muffin mixture over berry mixture. Cover and cook for 1 hour more or until a wooden toothpick inserted into the center of muffin mixture comes out clean. Remove liner from cooker, if possible, or turn off cooker. Let stand, uncovered, for 30 to 45 minutes to cool slightly.

4. To serve, spoon warm cobbler into dessert dishes. If desired, top with whipped dessert topping.

Nutrition Facts per serving: 257 cal., 7 g total fat (1 g sat. fat), 1 mg chol., 155 mg sodium, 50 g carbo., 4 g fiber, 1 g pro.
Daily Values: 11% calcium, 1% iron

"Gingerbread" Houses Without the Gingerbread

SINCE THE DAYS OF OLD, GINGERBREAD HOUSES have been a time-honored Christmas tradition worthy of re-creating anew each holiday season. From the spicy cookie walls to the sweet candy pathways, miniature homes built from edible goodies delight children and adults alike.

Despite the best of intentions, creating tiny candy-decorated houses from scratch each year can quickly become time consuming. The best way to save time is to eliminate the step of making, baking, and cutting out gingerbread pieces for the frame of the house. Instead use purchased items, such as graham crackers and pretzel sticks to create a house that looks authentic and requires only a fraction of the time to construct. For Christmas ease and simplicity, give these two "gingerbread" structures a try.

Graham Cracker Birdhouse, page 116

Rustic Pretzel Log Cabin

Rustic Pretzel Log Cabin

The gingerbread is eliminated from this "gingerbread" house to simplify the Christmas tradition of making little houses from tasty sweets. With the convenience of pretzels, crackers, and a chocolate wafer, this candy house takes a fraction of the time to prepare!

Prep: 45 minutes **Stand:** 4 hours
Makes: 1 log cabin

24	ounces (1½ pounds) vanilla-flavored candy coating, melted*
42	large pretzel rods (about 1¼ packages)
4	square waffle-style pretzels (snaps)
13	pretzel sticks (optional)
1½	cups canned vanilla frosting
	Assorted candies for decorating
4	graham cracker rectangles
5	square whole-wheat crackers
	Christmas Trees, page 115 (optional)

1. Spoon some of the melted candy coating into a small self-sealing plastic bag. Seal bag and snip off a small corner. Set aside.

2. Using a serrated knife, cut 7 pretzel rods in half crosswise for the side walls and inside supports of the log cabin.

3. Lay 1 of the half pretzel rods on a sheet of waxed paper. Pipe a line of candy coating along a long side of the pretzel rod. Press another half pretzel rod into the candy coating to attach. Repeat with 3 more half pretzel rods. Pipe additional candy coating between the pretzel rods to fill in the cracks. This makes one side wall. Repeat with 5 more halved pretzel rods to form the other side wall. Use candy coating to attach 1 waffle-style pretzel to each side wall for windows. If desired, break 4 small pretzel sticks in half and use candy coating to attach 2 halves along each side of the waffle-style pretzel to make shutters.

4. For the roof, use candy coating to attach 19 whole pretzel rods in the same way as for the side walls. For the front wall, use candy coating to attach 7 whole pretzel rods in the same way as for the side walls. For the back wall, use candy coating to attach 5 whole pretzel rods in the same way as for the side walls. For the front (the set of 7 pretzel rods) use candy coating to attach 5 pretzel sticks for the door and a waffle-style pretzel to each side of the door for windows. If desired, break 4 pretzel sticks in half and place 2 halves along each side of the waffle-style pretzel to make shutters. Place canned frosting in a small self-sealing plastic bag. Seal bag and snip off a small corner. Fill in the windows of the waffle-style pretzels with frosting. Decorate front and side walls with small candies as desired. Let pieces stand at least 1 hour to dry before assembling.

5. To assemble cabin, pipe a line of candy coating along a short end of the back wall (the set of 5 whole pretzel rods) and a side wall. Let stand for 1 to 2 minutes to allow the candy coating to set slightly. Press edges together to form a right angle. Pipe some candy coating along a long side of a half pretzel rod (using a serrated knife, cut pretzel rod to the same height as the walls if necessary). Press half pretzel rod into the corner of the two walls as a support. Brace the walls upright with small drinking glasses. Repeat with the front wall and remaining side wall. Use icing to attach remaining corners, using a half pretzel rod in each corner. Let pieces stand at least 30 minutes to dry. See Step 5 illustration at right.

6. Pipe candy coating along the tops of front and back walls. Place graham cracker rectangles over the roof, cutting with a serrated knife to fit. Let stand for 15 minutes to set. Pipe candy coating all over the surface of the graham cracker rectangles. Place roof piece (the set of 19 pretzel rods) across the top so that there is an overhang over the front. Using a serrated knife, cut 2 pretzel logs to fit in the space between the side walls and the roof. Fill in any gaps on the cabin with canned frosting. For the snow-lined roof, pipe a thick layer of canned frosting around the roof line of the house. With the back of a small spoon, spread the frosting to form the snow mounds. See Step 6 illustration at right.

Step 5: Form right angles with the cabin wall; hold the walls in place with drinking glasses until the coating dries.

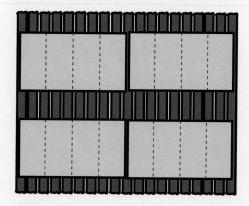

Step 6: Pretzel rod roof attached to four graham crackers for support.

7. Attach crackers along front of house for porch. Using a serrated knife, cut to fit the 2 remaining pretzel logs for the posts on the front porch. Secure with melted candy coating. If desired, arrange trees around log cabin.

Christmas Trees: Invert ice cream sugar cones and coat them with white or green-tinted frosting. If desired, decorate with candies.

Snowman: Roll 2 marshmallows into balls. Use a little icing to attach the balls together. Flatten gumdrops and shape into a hat and scarf; attach to marshmallows. Add pretzel sticks for arms.

*Note: Melt the candy coating 8 ounces at a time. You will need about that much for each step in the assembling process.

Graham Cracker Birdhouse, rear view

Graham Cracker Birdhouse

The back of this birdhouse is left open to give you a peep inside at the shredded wheat nest and the jelly bean eggs. Although it takes some time to construct, this little birdhouse is well worth the effort.

Start to Finish: 2 hours **Stand:** 3 hours
Makes: 1 house

- **1** recipe Royal Icing
- **11** graham cracker rectangles
- **1** shredded wheat biscuit
- **3** to 4 jelly beans or other small egg-shaped candies
- **1** round shortbread cookie with a hole in the center
  Colored sprinkles
- **1** braided pretzel stick or pretzel rod
  Fresh rosemary sprigs (optional)
  Small cinnamon candies (optional)
  Sunflower seeds, pumpkin seeds, sesame seeds (optional)
  Small square wheat crackers (optional)

1. Spoon about 1 cup of the Royal Icing into a pastry bag fitted with a small star or round tip. Cover the surface of the remaining icing with waxed paper and chill up to 2 days.

2. For the base, on a waxed paper-lined tray or baking sheet, place 3 graham crackers together with the short sides nearest you and long sides touching each other. Pipe icing along the edges to seal crackers together. Using a serrated knife and a sawing motion, cut the top ¼ from each of 7 of the remaining crackers (use perforations as a guide, if present). Attach 3 of these smaller pieces to the base with icing, placing the long side of each smaller piece to the short side of each cracker rectangle. This will be the front of the base. (You will have 4 extra small cracker pieces left over.) See Step 1 illustration at right.

3. For the front of the house, stand one of the cut crackers, long side down, on the base, centering it along the seam where the larger and smaller crackers meet. For the sides of the house, use icing to attach two of the remaining cut crackers to the front piece, arranging them perpendicular to the front piece (see Step 2 illustration at right). Cut the remaining whole cracker in half. (You will have one extra half cracker piece.) Use icing to attach the cracker half on the inside of the house front with a point side up (cracker point should extend about 1½ inches above the house front). (See Step 3 illustration at right.) Let stand about 30 minutes or until set.

4. Gently break the wheat biscuit apart for the nest. Use icing to attach biscuit pieces to the base between the sides of the house. For eggs, attach jelly beans to nest with icing. Spread some of the icing over the shortbread cookie to coat (thin with water, if necessary to make it spreadable). Decorate with sprinkles. Place on waxed paper until dry.

5. For the bird hole, use icing to attach the cookie to the house front. For the perch, cut pretzel stick or rod to the desired length and use icing to attach to the house front underneath the cookie.

6. For roof, use icing to attach two of the remaining cut crackers on each side of the cracker point, allowing the crackers to overhang about ½ inch over the front of the house (see Step 4 illustration at right). Use icing to attach the remaining cut crackers to finish the roof. Pipe icing around the roof edge to resemble snow. If desired, scatter icing with sprinkles. Allow house to stand at least 3 hours to set.

7. If desired, attach small rosemary sprigs and small cinnamon candies with icing around the edge of the bird house. If desired, sprinkle sunflower seeds, pumpkin seeds, and sesame seeds around the edge of the birdhouse and make a trail to the birdhouse with small square wheat crackers.

Royal Icing: In a large mixing bowl combine 3 tablespoons meringue powder, ½ cup warm water, one 16-ounce package powdered sugar (4¼ cups), 1 teaspoon vanilla, and ½ teaspoon cream of tartar. Beat with an electric mixer on low speed until combined; beat on high speed for 7 to 10 minutes or until mixture is stiff. Makes about 4 cups.

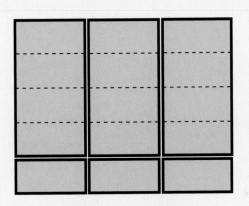

Step 1: Use three whole graham crackers and three of the cut ¼ sections of the crackers for the base of the birdhouse.

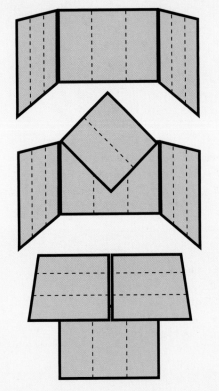

Step 2: Construct the walls from three cut graham crackers, standing them up on their long sides. Arrange the side pieces perpendicular to the front piece.

Step 3: Attach cracker half on the inside of the house front with a point side up.

Step 4: For roof, attach two of remaining cut crackers to each side of cracker point. Attach remaining cut crackers to finish roof.

Edible Gifts in a Jiff

HOME-BAKED CHRISTMAS GOODIES add to the joy and closeness of the holiday season. They also take precious time to make. When you're in a hurry, but still want to give personal gifts from the heart, look no further than the kitchen. Create gifts in a jar by adding a few simple ingredients (many of which are already in the pantry) to an attractive glass container. Or in a few quick minutes, prepare tasty little nibbles for friends to munch on at work or at home. Thoughtful gifts don't have to be expensive or time-consuming—they just have to show you care.

Little Peppermint Cakes, page 123

Easy Banana-Nut Loaf

Everybody loves home-baked goods during the holidays, but few have the extra time it takes to prepare those sweets. With this easy recipe, you'll have delicious bread, perfect for gifts, in no time.

Prep: 25 minutes **Bake:** 45 minutes **Oven:** 350°F
Makes: 2 loaves (32 servings)

2	cups self-rising flour*
1	cup packed light brown sugar
1	cup mashed ripe banana (3 bananas)
½	cup butter, softened
3	tablespoons milk
2	eggs
1	cup chopped walnuts, toasted

1. In a large mixing bowl combine 1 cup of the self-rising flour and the brown sugar. Add banana, butter, and milk. Beat with an electric mixer on low speed until combined. Beat on high speed for 2 minutes. Add eggs and the remaining flour. Beat until combined. Stir in walnuts. Pour into 2 greased 8×4×2-inch loaf pans.

2. Bake in a 350° oven for 45 to 50 minutes or until a wooden toothpick inserted near the centers comes out clean. Cool in pans for 10 minutes. Remove loaves from pans; cool completely on wire racks. Wrap and store overnight for easier slicing.

*Note: To substitute all-purpose flour for the self-rising flour, use 2 cups all-purpose flour, 2 teaspoons baking powder, ½ teaspoon baking soda, and ¼ teaspoon salt.

Nutrition Facts per serving: 116 cal., 6 g total fat (2 g sat. fat), 8 mg chol., 124 mg sodium, 16 g carbo., 1 g fiber, 2 g pro.
Daily Values: 2% vit. A, 2% vit. C, 4% calcium, 4% iron

Surprise Cereal Bars

The surprises, tiny marshmallows and colorful milk-chocolate candies, peek from the edges of these cereal bars. They can be individually wrapped, tied with ribbons, and placed in small Christmas stockings.

Prep: 30 minutes **Stand:** 20 minutes
Makes: 24 bars

1	cup sugar
1	cup light corn syrup
1½	cups peanut butter
6	cups crisp rice cereal
1	cup tiny marshmallows
½	cup red and green candy-coated milk chocolate pieces

1. Line a 13×9×2-inch baking pan with foil, extending foil beyond the ends of the pan; butter foil and set foil-lined pan aside. In a large saucepan

Surprise Cereal Bars

stir together sugar and corn syrup. Bring just to boiling, stirring to dissolve sugar. Remove from heat. Stir in peanut butter until melted. Stir in cereal until evenly coated.

2. Spread about half of the mixture in the prepared pan. Sprinkle with marshmallows and candy pieces. Spoon remaining cereal mixture over candy and spread evenly to cover. Let stand until firm. Cut cereal mixture into squares.

To Store: Place bars in layers separated by waxed paper in an airtight container; cover. Store at room temperature for up to 1 week. Do not freeze.

Nutrition Facts per serving: 215 cal., 9 g total fat (2 g sat. fat), 0 mg chol., 164 mg sodium, 32 g carbo., 1 g fiber, 5 g pro.
Daily Values: 2% vit. A, 2% vit. C, 1% calcium, 4% iron

Chocolate-Dipped Eggnog Spritz Sticks

Chocolate-Dipped Eggnog Spritz Sticks

The use of nutmeg, rum extract, and egg is where the eggnog comes from in this recipe's name. Tie a bundle of these chocolate-dipped sticks together with a pretty bow, or place several in a decorative holiday mug to give to neighbors as a Christmas treat.

Prep: 30 minutes **Bake:** 7 minutes **Oven:** 375°F
Makes: 30 cookies

¾	cup butter, softened
½	cup sugar
1	teaspoon baking powder
¼	teaspoon ground nutmeg
¼	teaspoon salt
1	egg
1	teaspoon rum extract
1 ¾	cups all-purpose flour
1	cup semisweet chocolate pieces
1	tablespoon shortening
	Red and green candy sprinkles (optional)

1. In a large bowl beat butter with an electric mixer on medium to high speed for 30 seconds. Add sugar, baking powder, nutmeg, and salt. Beat until combined, scraping sides of bowl occasionally.

Beat in egg and rum extract until combined. Beat in as much of the flour as possible with the mixer. Stir in any remaining flour.

2. Pack unchilled dough into a cookie press fitted with a small star plate. Force dough through press to form 4-inch sticks, about 1 inch apart, onto an ungreased baking sheet.

3. Bake in a 375° oven for 7 to 9 minutes or until the edges are firm but not brown. Transfer to a wire rack and cool.

4. Place spritz sticks on a sheet of waxed paper. In a small, heavy saucepan melt chocolate and shortening over low heat, stirring frequently. Dip one end of each stick into the melted chocolate letting excess drip off. If desired, decorate with candy sprinkles. Place on waxed paper. Let stand until chocolate is set.

Nutrition Facts per cookie: 112 cal., 7 g total fat (3 g sat. fat), 20 mg chol., 64 mg sodium, 12 g carbo., 1 g fiber, 1 g pro.
Daily Values: 3% vit. A, 1% calcium, 3% iron

Easy Cranberry-Orange Ring

Starting with frozen sweet roll dough, this delectable gift features a multitude of holiday flavors. The joy this bread brings is well worth the time spent preparing it.

Prep: 40 minutes **Rise:** 1¼ hours **Bake:** 20 minutes
Cool: 1 hour **Oven:** 350°F
Makes: 1 ring (16 servings)

- ¾ **cup snipped dried cranberries**
- 2 **tablespoons orange juice**
- 1 **16-ounce loaf frozen sweet roll dough, thawed**
- 2 **teaspoons butter, melted**
- ¼ **cup packed brown sugar**
- 2 **tablespoons finely chopped pecans**
- 1 **tablespoon all-purpose flour**
- 1 **teaspoon finely shredded orange peel**
- ¼ **teaspoon ground cinnamon**
- ¼ **teaspoon ground nutmeg**
- ⅛ **teaspoon ground cloves**
- 1 **teaspoon butter, melted**
- 1 **recipe Orange Icing**

1. Line a large baking sheet with foil; grease foil. Set baking sheet aside. In a medium bowl stir together cranberries and orange juice; set aside.

2. On a lightly floured surface roll dough into a 15×9-inch rectangle (if dough is difficult to roll, let rest a few minutes and try again). Brush with the 2 teaspoons melted butter. Drain cranberries; return cranberries to bowl.

3. Add brown sugar, pecans, flour, orange peel, cinnamon, nutmeg, and cloves to cranberries. Sprinkle cranberry mixture evenly over dough. Starting from a long side, roll up into a spiral; seal edge. Place, seam side down, on prepared baking sheet. Bring ends together to form a ring. Moisten ends with waterc; pinch together to seal the ring. Using kitchen scissors or a sharp knife, cut from the outside edge toward center, leaving about 1 inch attached. Repeat around the edge at 1-inch intervals. Gently turn each slice slightly so the same side faces upward.

4. Cover; let rise in a warm place until nearly double (1¼ to 1½ hours). Brush ring with the 1 teaspoon melted butter.

5. Bake in a 350° oven about 20 minutes or until golden. Remove ring from foil and cool completely on a wire rack. Drizzle Orange Icing over ring. Let stand until icing sets.

Orange Icing: In a small bowl stir together ½ cup powdered sugar, ¼ teaspoon finely shredded orange peel, and enough orange juice (1 to 3 teaspoons) to make an icing of drizzling consistency.

Nutrition Facts per serving: 140 cal., 3 g total fat (1 g sat. fat), 18 mg chol., 59 mg sodium, 26 g carbo., 1 g fiber, 2 g pro.
Daily Values: 1% vit. A, 2% vit. C, 2% calcium, 5% iron

Easy Cranberry-Orange Ring

Little Peppermint Cakes

These tiny triangular petits fours are flavored with peppermint and coated in a surprisingly delicious fondant frosting made from white chocolate and canned frosting. Wrap several of these in a small decorated box for a gift or place on a platter to present to holiday visitors.

Start to Finish: 30 minutes **Makes:** 15 cakes

1	10¾-ounce frozen loaf pound cake, thawed
1	16-ounce can vanilla frosting
2	to 3 drops peppermint extract
1	drop red food coloring
4	ounces white chocolate baking squares with cocoa butter, chopped
¼	teaspoon peppermint extract
54	small peppermint candies (optional)

1. Using a serrated knife, cut cake into ten ½-inch slices. Set aside.

2. For peppermint filling, in a small bowl stir together ¼ cup of the frosting, the 2 to 3 drops peppermint extract, and the red food coloring. Spread five of the cake slices with the filling. Top each with a plain cake slice, making a sandwich. Cut each sandwich into 3 pieces, starting from center of one long side and cutting to each opposite corner, making 15 triangular-shaped pieces; set aside.

3. For icing, in a heavy, small saucepan cook and stir chopped white chocolate over low heat until melted. Add remaining frosting; heat over low heat, stirring until smooth. Stir in ¼ teaspoon peppermint extract. Keep saucepan over low heat.

4. Insert a fork into the side of a cake piece. Holding the cake over the saucepan, spoon on enough icing to cover sides and top. Using another fork, gently push the cake piece onto a wire rack set over a piece of waxed paper. If necessary, spoon icing onto side of cake where fork was inserted. If desired, arrange three peppermint candies on each cake. Repeat with remaining cake pieces, icing, and peppermint candies. Let stand until icing sets.

Nutrition Facts per cake: 256 cal., 12 g total fat (5 g sat. fat), 24 mg chol., 139 mg sodium, 35 g carbo., 0 g fiber, 2 g pro.
Daily Values: 2% vit. A, 2% calcium, 2% iron

Maple-Pecan Pie in a Jar

Turn this recipe-in-a-jar into a full-size gift basket by including a purchased piecrust and a new holiday-themed pie plate. The recipient will then have all the necessary elements needed to assemble this decadent maple-flavored pie. And maybe you will be able to sample a piece when it's made!

Prep: 10 minutes **Bake:** 45 minutes
Stand: 15 minutes **Oven:** 350°F **Chill:** up to 2 weeks
Makes: 1 jar (enough for one 9-inch pie, 8 servings)

⅔	cup dark corn syrup
⅔	cup sugar
⅓	cup pure maple syrup or maple-flavored syrup
⅓	cup butter, melted
1	teaspoon vanilla
1¾	cups pecan halves, toasted

1. In a medium bowl stir together corn syrup, sugar, maple syrup, butter, and vanilla until well combined. Add pecan halves, stirring to combine. Transfer mixture to a 2½ cup jar or food-safe container. Seal; attach directions for making Maple-Pecan Pie. If giving as a gift, recipient can store jar in refrigerator for up to 2 weeks.

2. To make Maple-Pecan Pie: Remove pecan mixture from refrigerator; let stand at room temperature for 15 minutes. In a large bowl slightly beat 3 *eggs* until combined. Add contents of jar to eggs, stirring to combine. Pour the filling into an unbaked *9-inch pastry shell*. To prevent over browning, cover edges of the pie with foil. Bake in a 350°F oven for 25 minutes. Remove foil. Bake for 20 to 25 minutes more or until a knife inserted near the center comes out clean. Cool completely on a wire rack. Cover and refrigerate within 2 hours.

Nutrition Facts per serving: 577 cal., 36 g total fat (8 g sat. fat), 101 mg chol., 199 mg sodium, 63 g carbo., 3 g fiber, 6 g pro.
Daily Values: 7% vit. A, 5% calcium, 11% iron

Dried Cherry Scone Mix

2. To make Dried Cherry Scones: In a small bowl combine dried cherries and 2 tablespoons brandy or apricot nectar. Let stand for 15 minutes. Empty the contents of the jar into a medium bowl; make a well in the center of the flour mixture. In another small bowl stir together 1 beaten egg and ⅓ cup half-and-half. Add egg mixture and dried cherry mixture all at once to flour mixture. Using a fork, stir ingredients just until moistened.

3. Turn out dough onto a lightly floured surface; quickly knead by folding and gently pressing for 12 to 15 strokes or until nearly smooth. Pat or lightly roll dough into a 7-inch circle. Cut into 8 wedges, dipping a knife into flour between cuts. Place wedges 1 inch apart on an ungreased baking sheet. Brush tops with 1 tablespoon half-and-half or light cream. Sprinkle with 2 teaspoons sugar. Bake in a 400°F oven for 12 to 15 minutes or until browned. Transfer to a wire rack; cool slightly. Serve warm. If desired, serve with Maple-Nut Butter.

Nutrition Facts per scone: 293 cal., 14 g total fat (4 g sat. fat), 31 mg chol., 177 mg sodium, 34 g carbo., 1 g fiber, 5 g pro.
Daily Values: 1% vit. A, 5% calcium, 9% iron

Maple-Nut Butter: In a small bowl stir together ½ cup chopped toasted pecans, ½ cup softened butter, and 1 teaspoon pure maple syrup or maple-flavored syrup. Chill until serving time (up to 3 days). Soften to room temperature before serving. Makes about 1 cup.

Dried Cherry Scone Mix

Treat someone to an easy-does-it Christmas breakfast by giving that person a decorative basket filled with the fixings for these delightful scones: the scone mix, a 2-ounce bottle of brandy or an individual-size can of apricot nectar, and a container of Maple-Nut Butter.

Prep: 10 minutes **Bake:** 12 minutes **Oven:** 400°F
Store: up to 1 month **Makes:** 8 scones

2	cups all-purpose flour
3	tablespoons sugar
1	tablespoon baking powder
¼	teaspoon salt
6	tablespoons shortening
¼	cup chopped pecans, toasted
½	cup dried tart red cherries

1. In a medium bowl stir together flour, sugar, baking powder, and salt. Using a pastry blender, cut in shortening until mixture resembles coarse crumbs. Add pecans; toss. Spoon into a 1-quart glass jar. Wrap dried cherries in plastic film; place the packet on top of mix in jar. Seal; attach directions for making Dried Cherry Scones. Store in a cool, dry place for up to 1 month. Makes 1 jar (enough mix to make 8 scones).

Gingerbread Scone Mix

Gift wrap a jar of this spicy scone mix with a jar of your favorite honey or purchased lemon curd. Warm-from-the-oven scones are exceptional when accompanied by a bit of either delicious spread.

Prep: 15 minutes **Bake:** 10 minutes **Oven:** 400°F
Store: up to 1 month **Makes:** 6 scones

3¾	cups all-purpose flour
½	cup packed brown sugar
2	tablespoons baking powder
2	teaspoons ground ginger
1	teaspoon ground cinnamon
½	teaspoon salt
¼	teaspoon baking soda

¼   **teaspoon ground cloves**
¼   **teaspoon ground nutmeg**
¾   **cup shortening**

1. In a large bowl combine flour, brown sugar, baking powder, ginger, cinnamon, salt, baking soda, cloves, and nutmeg. Using a pastry blender, cut in shortening until mixture resembles coarse crumbs. Divide flour mixture evenly among three 1-pint glass jars. Seal; attach the directions for making Gingerbread Scones to each jar. Store in a cool, dry place for up to 1 month. Makes 3 jars (enough mix in each jar for 6 scones).

2. To make Gingerbread Scones: Empty the contents of 1 jar into a medium bowl; make a well in center of flour mixture. In a small bowl stir together 1 beaten egg, 2 tablespoons milk, and 1 tablespoon molasses. Add egg mixture to flour mixture; stir just until moistened.

3. Turn out dough onto a lightly floured surface; quickly knead by folding and gently pressing for 10 to 12 strokes or until nearly smooth. Pat or lightly roll dough into a 6-inch circle. Cut into 6 wedges, dipping a knife into flour between cuts. Place wedges 1 inch apart on an ungreased baking sheet. Brush with milk and sprinkle with coarse or granulated sugar. Bake in a 400°F oven for 10 to 12 minutes or until bottoms are browned. Transfer to a wire rack; cool slightly. Serve warm.

Nutrition Facts per scone: 592 cal., 27 g total fat (7 g sat. fat),
36 mg chol., 512 mg sodium, 78 g carbo., 2 g fiber, 9 g pro.
Daily Values: 1% vit. A, 13% calcium, 23% iron

Gift-Bag Fudgy Brownies

Give the young cooks in your life the chance to assist with the holiday gift-giving. Christmas presents containing dry, pre-measured ingredients are great afternoon projects that will keep little hands busy.

Prep: 20 minutes **Bake:** 30 minutes **Cool:** 2 hours
Oven: 350°F **Store:** up to 1 month
Makes: 32 brownies

1   **cup granulated sugar**
⅔   **cup unsweetened cocoa powder**
½   **teaspoon baking soda**
1⅓ **cups all-purpose flour**

1   **cup packed brown sugar**
1   **6-ounce package semisweet chocolate pieces**
1   **cup chopped pecans or walnuts, toasted**

1. In a clean 2-quart plastic bag layer ingredients in the following order: granulated sugar, cocoa powder, baking soda, flour, brown sugar, chocolate pieces, and nuts. Tie the top of the bag with decorative ribbon. Place bag in a decorative container. Store in a cool, dry place for up to 1 month.

2. Attach these directions on a gift tag: Lightly grease a 13×9×2-inch baking pan; set aside. In a large bowl stir together the contents of the bag with 1 cup butter, melted, and 2 slightly beaten eggs. Spread mixture in prepared pan. Bake for 30 minutes in a 350°F oven. Cool in pan on a wire rack.

Nutrition Facts per brownie: 178 cal., 10 g total fat (4 g sat. fat),
29 mg chol., 70 mg sodium, 21 g carbo., 1 g fiber, 2 g pro.
Daily Values: 4% vit. A, 3% calcium, 5% iron

Gift-Bag Fudgy Brownies

Lemon Tea Bread Mix

Whether you decide to bake the bread yourself or give jars of the mix for the holidays, this is the ideal gift for anyone who enjoys entertaining. Lemon tea bread makes a first-rate addition to any breakfast, brunch, or afternoon tea party menu. If desired, wrap the mix with a fresh lemon and new loaf pan.

Prep: 10 minutes **Bake:** 30 minutes **Oven:** 350°F
Store: up to 1 month **Makes:** two 5³⁄₄×3×2-inch
loaves (8 servings each) or one 8×4×2-inch loaf
(16 servings)

3¹⁄₃	cups all-purpose flour
1½	cups sugar
4	teaspoons poppy seeds
1	tablespoon baking powder
1	teaspoon salt
1	teaspoon baking soda
½	teaspoon ground nutmeg

1. In a large bowl combine flour, sugar, poppy seeds, baking powder, salt, baking soda, and nutmeg. Divide flour mixture between two 1-quart glass jars. Seal; attach directions for making Lemon Tea Bread to each jar. Store in a cool, dry place for up to 1 month. Makes 2 jars (enough mix in each jar for two 5³⁄₄×3×2-inch loaves or one 8×4×2-inch loaf of bread).

2. To make Lemon Tea Bread: Grease bottom and ½ inch up the sides of two 5³⁄₄×3×2-inch loaf pans or one 8×4×2-inch loaf pan. Empty the contents of 1 jar into a medium bowl; make a well in center of the flour mixture. Set aside.

3. Finely shred enough peel from 1 lemon to yield 1½ teaspoons shredded peel. Squeeze lemon to yield 2 to 3 tablespoons lemon juice.

4. In a small bowl stir together 1 egg, ³⁄₄ cup milk, ¼ cup cooking oil, 1 teaspoon of the finely shredded lemon peel and 1 tablespoon of the lemon juice. Add egg mixture all at once to flour mixture. Stir just until moistened (batter should be lumpy). Spoon batter into prepared pan(s). Bake in a 350°F oven for 30 to 35 minutes for the 5³⁄₄×3×2-inch pans, 45 to 50 minutes for the 8×4×2-inch pan, or until a toothpick inserted near center(s) comes out clean. Cool in pan(s) on wire rack(s) for 10 minutes. Remove from pan(s). Cool completely on wire rack(s). Wrap and store overnight before slicing.

5. Just before serving, combine ½ cup sifted powdered sugar, remaining ½ teaspoon finely shredded lemon peel, and enough of the remaining lemon juice to make an icing of drizzling consistency. Drizzle over the loaf or loaves. If desired, garnish with lemon peel strips.

Nutrition Facts per serving: 214 cal., 5 g total fat (1 g sat. fat), 14 mg chol., 279 mg sodium, 40 g carbo., 1 g fiber, 3 g pro.
Daily Values: 1% vit. A, 2% vit. C, 44% calcium, 1% iron

Christmas Macaroon Mix

Why do the baking when a jar full of ingredients works just as well for a gift? If you line up several containers to fill at once, you can produce many of your Christmas presents in one fell swoop.

Prep: 15 minutes **Bake:** 15 minutes **Oven:** 325°F
Store: up to 1 month **Makes:** 30 cookies

2²⁄₃	cups flaked coconut (7 ounces)
²⁄₃	cup sugar
½	cup chopped toasted almonds
¼	cup all-purpose flour
¼	teaspoon salt

Lemon Tea Bread Mix

¼ cup chopped candied red and/or
  green cherries
2 tablespoons finely chopped candied
  orange peel

1. In a clean 1-quart jar or covered container layer coconut, sugar, almonds, flour, salt, candied cherries, and candied orange peel. Seal; attach the directions for making Christmas Macaroons to jar. Store in a cool, dry place for up to 1 month.

2. To make Christmas Macaroons: Line baking sheets with parchment paper or foil. Grease foil, if using. In a large mixing bowl stir together the contents of the jar. Add 3 slightly beaten egg whites, stirring well to combine. Drop mixture by teaspoons, 2 inches apart, onto prepared baking sheets. Bake in a 325°F oven for 15 to 18 minutes or until cookies are light brown. Transfer to a wire rack and cool.

Nutrition Facts per serving: 83 cal., 5 g total fat (4 g sat. fat), 0 mg chol., 57 mg sodium, 9 g carbo., 1 g fiber, 2 g pro.
Daily Values: 1% calcium, 1% iron

Triple Fruit Fruitcake Mix

Bring back the time-honored Christmas tradition of sharing the gift of fruitcake without actually making it. Supply the ingredients in a jar so the recipient can bake this holiday cake whenever time allows or whenever a fruitcake craving strikes.

Prep: 20 minutes **Bake:** 45 minutes **Oven:** 325°F
Store: up to 1 month
Makes: 1 cake or loaf (12 servings)

1½ cups all-purpose flour
1¼ teaspoons apple pie spice
½ teaspoon baking powder
¼ teaspoon baking soda
¼ teaspoon salt
⅔ cup packed brown sugar
½ cup snipped dried apricots
½ cup dried cranberries
½ cup snipped golden figs (Calimyrna)
⅓ cup chopped almonds
2 tablespoons diced candied orange
  peel

1. In a small bowl stir together flour, apple pie spice, baking powder, baking soda, and salt. In a 1-quart glass jar, container, or bag, layer flour mixture, brown sugar, apricots, cranberries, figs, almonds, and orange peel. Seal; attach the directions for making Triple Fruit Fruitcake. Store in a cool, dry place for up to 1 month.

2. To Make Triple Fruit Fruitcake: Grease and lightly flour a 6-cup fluted tube pan or an 8×4×2-inch loaf pan; set aside. Empty the contents of the jar into a large bowl. Add 2 slightly beaten eggs, ½ cup orange juice, ¼ cup melted butter, 2 tablespoons light corn syrup, and 1 teaspoon vanilla. Stir until well combined. Spread batter into the prepared pan. Bake in a 325°F oven about 45 minutes for the tube pan or about 55 minutes for loaf pan, or until a wooden toothpick inserted near the center comes out clean. Cool cake in pan on a wire rack for 10 minutes. Remove from pan; cool thoroughly on a wire rack.

Poke holes into cake using a toothpick or bamboo skewer. Soak an approximately 20×16-inch piece of 100-percent cotton cheesecloth in 3 tablespoons brandy or orange juice. Wrap cake in soaked cheesecloth. Wrap tightly in foil. Refrigerate cake for 24 hours. Remove foil and drizzle with 2 tablespoons brandy or orange juice. Rewrap with foil and refrigerate for 1 to 5 days. Let stand at room temperature 1 hour before serving. If desired, sprinkle with sifted powdered sugar.

Nutrition Facts per serving: 171 cal., 2 g total fat (0 g sat. fat), 0 mg chol., 92 mg sodium, 37 g carbo., 3 g fiber, 3 g pro.
Daily Values: 4% vit. A, 3% vit. C, 5% calcium, 9% iron

Fruitcake Facts Composed of dried fruit, nuts, fruit rinds, and a dense cake batter, fruitcakes are a traditional gift most often shared during the holiday season. After baking and cooling, the fruitcake is covered in cheesecloth that is soaked in brandy, rum, wine, or fruit juice, and stored for several weeks. This storage method improves the flavor and texture of the holiday cake, and assuming the cheesecloth is remoistened occasionally, the fruitcake can be kept for years.

Heavenly Hot Fudge Sauce

Chocoholics will rave about this velvety, fudgy sauce, which can be poured over cake or ice cream. Be sure to keep the heat low while melting the chocolate to prevent it from scorching.

Prep: 15 minutes **Stand:** 45 minutes
Chill: up to 1 week **Makes:** 4 jars
(a scant 1 cup sauce in each jar) 32 servings total)

8	ounces semisweet chocolate pieces (1⅓ cups)
½	cup butter
1⅓	cups sugar
1⅓	cups whipping cream

1. In a heavy medium saucepan combine chocolate pieces and butter; cook and stir over low heat until melted. Stir in sugar. Gradually stir in whipping cream. Bring to boiling; reduce heat to low. Boil gently for 8 minutes, stirring frequently. Remove from heat. Let stand at room temperature about 45 minutes or until cooled.

2. Divide sauce among 4 half-pint glass jars. Seal; attach directions for reheating Heavenly Hot Fudge Sauce to each jar. Refrigerate for up to 1 week.

3. To reheat Heavenly Hot Fudge Sauce: Empty the contents of 1 glass jar into a small saucepan. Heat over medium-low heat just until warm. Serve warmed sauce over ice cream, fruit, pound cake, angel food cake, or other desserts.

Nutrition Facts per 2 tablespoons sauce: 122 cal., 8 g total fat
(5 g sat. fat), 22 mg chol., 25 mg sodium, 13 g carbo., 1 g fiber, 1 g pro.
Daily Values: 5% vit. A, 1% calcium, 1% iron

Roasted Red Pepper Spread

Don't think this spread is only for lovers of spicy food. It features sweet red peppers that have been roasted for a mellow flavor.

Prep: 15 minutes **Chill:** up to 1 week
Makes: 4 jars (about ¾ cup spread in each jar)

4	7-ounce jars roasted red sweet peppers, drained
½	cup tomato paste
4	teaspoons sugar
1	teaspoon dried thyme, crushed
1	teaspoon salt
½	teaspoon garlic powder
⅛	teaspoon cayenne pepper

1. In a blender or food processor combine sweet peppers, tomato paste, sugar, thyme, salt, garlic powder, and cayenne pepper. Cover and blend or process until nearly smooth. Divide pepper mixture among 4 half-pint glass jars. Seal; attach serving suggestions for Red Pepper Spread to each jar. Store in the refrigerator for up to 1 week.

Serving suggestions for Red Pepper Spread: Serve with assorted crackers or toasted baguette slices, spread on sandwiches, or use as a condiment for grilled burgers.

Nutrition Facts per tablespoon: 8 cal., 0 g total fat (0 g sat. fat),
0 mg chol., 50 mg sodium, 2 g carbo., 0 g fiber, 0 g pro.
Daily Values: 58% vit. C, 1% iron

Split Pea and Tortellini Soup Mix

Soup mugs and a jar of this sensational soup mix will make an exceptional gift for even the most hard-to-please person on your gift list.

Prep: 10 minutes **Cook:** 50 minutes
Store: up to 6 months **Stand:** 8 to 24 hours
Makes: 4 servings

⅓	cup dry split peas
1	tablespoon instant chicken bouillon granules
1	tablespoon dried minced onion

Split Pea and Tortellini Soup Mix

1 ½ teaspoons dried basil, crushed
1 ½ teaspoons dried thyme, crushed
½ teaspoon garlic powder
¼ teaspoon black pepper
½ cup dried chopped carrots
¼ cup snipped dried tomatoes
   (not oil-packed)
3 ounces dried cheese-filled tortellini
   (⅔ cup)

1. Rinse split peas. Spread split peas in a single layer on paper towels; let stand for 8 to 24 hours or until completely dry.

2. In a 1-pint glass jar layer in the following order: chicken bouillon granules, dried minced onion, basil, thyme, garlic powder, pepper, dried carrots, the split peas, dried tomatoes, and tortellini. Seal; attach directions for making Split Pea Tortellini Soup. Store in a cool, dry place for up to 6 months. Makes 1 jar (enough mix to make 4 servings).

3. To make Split Pea Tortellini Soup: Empty the contents of the jar into a 3-quart saucepan; add 5 cups water. Bring to boiling; reduce heat. Cover and simmer about 50 minutes or until peas are tender. If desired, stir in 1 cup chopped cooked ham.

Nutrition Facts per serving: 213 cal., 3 g total fat (3 g sat. fat), 0 mg chol., 960 mg sodium, 37 g carbo., 6 g fiber, 10 g pro.
Daily Values: 625% vit. A, 21% vit. C, 13% calcium, 13% iron

Busy-Day
Dinners
for
December

BUSTLING AND EXCITING, busy and hectic—no matter how you choose to describe the month leading up to Christmas, you're sure to agree there's little time to squeeze in complicated dinners. So when you gaze into the pantry and wonder what you can possibly concoct from sauerkraut and hash brown potatoes, or pineapple chunks and frozen chicken, check this chapter for a quick, delicious answer. Even with all the shopping, baking, card writing, mailing, and visiting that comes with the season, it is possible to prepare a meal that is both satisfying and simple.

Two-Tomato Pasta, page 138

Saucy Sloppy Joes

As well as being a super-quick dinner, these sloppy joes are the perfect way to use any type of leftover beef roast. Serve a complete meal by purchasing deli potato salad or other tasty side dishes.

Prep: 20 minutes **Cook:** 30 minutes
Makes: 6 to 8 servings

¼	cup chopped onion
¼	cup chopped celery
2	tablespoons chopped green sweet pepper
1	clove garlic, minced
1	tablespoon butter or margarine
3	cups chopped cooked beef (about 1 pound)
1	cup bottled barbecue sauce
1½	teaspoons vinegar
1½	teaspoons Worcestershire sauce
½	teaspoon dry mustard
¼	teaspoon black pepper
6	to 8 hamburger buns, split and toasted

1. In a large skillet cook onion, celery, sweet pepper, and garlic in hot butter until tender.

2. Stir in beef, barbecue sauce, vinegar, Worcestershire sauce, dry mustard, and pepper. Bring to boiling; reduce heat. Cover and simmer for 20 minutes. Cook, uncovered, for 5 to 10 minutes more or until desired consistency is reached. Serve on toasted hamburger buns.

Nutrition Facts per serving: 341 cal., 13 g total fat (5 g sat. fat),
65 mg chol., 634 mg sodium, 28 g carbo., 2 g fiber, 25 g pro.
Daily Values: 2% vit. A, 10% vit. C, 8% calcium, 23% iron

Speedy Turkey Wraps

Purchase your choice of flavored, plain, or whole wheat tortillas for these turkey roll-ups. Or forget about a wrap and layer the fixings into a hoagie bun.

Start to Finish: 15 minutes **Makes:** 4 wraps

¼	cup cream cheese, softened
¼	cup basil pesto
4	8- to 10-inch flavored, plain, or whole wheat tortillas
8	ounces deli shaved or sliced smoked turkey breast
2	cups shredded lettuce or assorted fresh sprouts (such as radish, sunflower, or broccoli sprouts)
½	cup chopped tomato and/or ripe avocado

1. In a small bowl stir together cream cheese and pesto. Spread the cheese mixture over one side of each tortilla. Arrange turkey and lettuce on each tortilla. Top with tomato. Roll up.

Nutrition Facts per wrap: 313 cal., 18 g total fat (4 g sat. fat),
42 mg chol., 852 mg sodium, 20 g carbo., 1 g fiber, 18 g pro.
Daily Values: 40% vit. A, 16% vit. C, 6% calcium, 11% iron

Chicken Tacos

A taco is still a taco (and just as tasty), even if it's with chicken instead of beef. If you don't have prepared leftover chicken to use, buy frozen chopped, cooked chicken or canned chicken at the supermarket.

Start to Finish: 30 minutes **Makes:** 6 servings

	Nonstick cooking spray
1	cup chopped onion (1 large)
1	clove garlic, minced
2	cups chopped cooked, chicken (10 ounces)
1	8-ounce can tomato sauce
1	4-ounce can diced green chile peppers, drained
½	teaspoon chili powder (optional)
¼	teaspoon ground cumin (optional)

12   taco shells or twelve 6- to 8-inch corn
      or flour tortillas, warmed*
2   cups shredded lettuce
1   medium tomato, seeded and chopped
½   cup shredded Monterey Jack cheese
      (2 ounces)

1. Coat a large skillet with cooking spray. Cook onion and garlic in the skillet over medium heat about 5 minutes or until onion is tender.

2. Stir in the chicken, tomato sauce, chile peppers, and, if desired, chili powder and ground cumin. Cook and stir until heated through.

3. Divide chicken mixture among taco shells or warm tortillas. Top with lettuce, tomato, and cheese. Roll up tortillas, if using.

***Note:** To warm tortillas, wrap them tightly in foil. Heat in a 350°F oven about 10 minutes or until heated through.

Nutrition Facts per serving: 279 cal., 13 g total fat (4 g sat. fat), 50 mg chol., 417 mg sodium, 23 g carbo., 3 g fiber, 19 g pro.
Daily Values: 7% vit. A, 18% vit. C, 16% calcium, 10% iron

Tuna Salad with a Twist

Green pepper and creamy Italian dressing put a delicious spin on regular, run-of-the-mill tuna salad. Accompany this easy-to-make sandwich with pickles and chips or On-the-Side Coleslaw (see page 139), for a quick break in the busy holiday season.

Start to Finish: 15 minutes Makes: 4 servings

1   12-ounce can chunk white tuna
      (water-pack), drained and broken
      into chunks
⅓   cup bottled creamy Italian salad
      dressing
⅓   cup chopped green sweet pepper
2   bagels (such as sesame seed, poppy
      seed, garlic, or plain), split
4   slices provolone, Swiss, or mozzarella
      cheese (about 4 ounces total)
8   red and/or yellow cherry tomatoes,
      halved, or 4 tomato slices

Tuna Salad with a Twist

1. In a medium bowl combine tuna, salad dressing, and sweet pepper. Set aside. Place bagel halves, cut side up, on the rack of a broiler pan. Broil 4 to 5 inches from the heat for 1 minute or until toasted.

2. Place a cheese slice on each bagel half. Spoon tuna mixture over cheese slice. Broil for 2 to 4 minutes or until cheese is melted. Top with halved cherry tomatoes.

Nutrition Facts per serving: 385 cal., 19 g total fat (7 g sat. fat), 55 mg chol., 1,094 mg sodium, 23 g carbo., 1 g fiber, 31 g pro.
Daily Values: 11% vit. A, 23% vit. C, 254% calcium, 2% iron

Caraway Potato Chowder

A combination of potatoes, ham, sauerkraut, and caraway make this quick-and-easy soup a weeknight favorite. Adjust the amount of caraway seed to fit your family's preferences.

Start to Finish: 30 minutes
Makes: 4 main-dish servings (about 6 cups)

4	cups frozen shredded hash brown potatoes
1	14-ounce can chicken broth
½	cup chopped onion (1 medium)
2½	cups milk
¼	cup all-purpose flour
1½	to 2 teaspoons caraway seeds, crushed
¼	teaspoon black pepper or lemon-pepper seasoning
8	ounces cooked ham or smoked turkey sausage, chopped (1½ cups)
1	8-ounce can sauerkraut, rinsed and drained
1	recipe Rye Croutons

1. In a large saucepan combine frozen potatoes, broth, and onion. Bring to boiling; reduce heat. Cover and simmer about 10 minutes or until potatoes are tender. Do not drain. Slightly mash the potato mixture.

2. In a medium bowl stir together milk and flour. Stir into the potato mixture. Stir in caraway seeds and pepper. Cook and stir until thickened and bubbly. Cook and stir for 1 minute more.

3. Stir in ham and sauerkraut. Cook and stir until heated through. To serve, ladle chowder into individual bowls. Sprinkle with Rye Croutons.

Rye Croutons: Cut two ½-inch slices rye bread into cubes. Toss bread cubes with 2 tablespoons melted butter or margarine. Spread bread cubes in a shallow baking pan. Bake in a 300° oven for 10 to 15 minutes or until bread cubes are dry and crisp, stirring once. Cool completely before using.

Nutrition Facts per serving: 378 cal., 15 g total fat (6 g sat. fat), 62 mg chol., 1,761 mg sodium, 42 g carbo., 5 g fiber, 20 g pro.
Daily Values: 10% vit. A, 80% vit. C, 22% calcium, 14% iron

Quick Fix-Ups Depend on the supermarket deli to supply some quick side dishes to the dinner table. Personalize these purchased sides by tossing in a few additions.

• **Veggie Macaroni Salad:** Add ½ cup thawed frozen peas and 2 tablespoons sliced radishes to 1 pint macaroni salad.

• **Meal-Worthy Three-Bean Salad:** Add 1 cup cooked and drained shell macaroni, ½ cup cubed cheddar cheese, and 6 ounces cooked ham strips to 1 pint of three-bean salad.

• **Italian-Style Three-Bean Salad:** Add ½ cup sliced hearts of palm; 1 medium tomato, chopped; and ½ teaspoon dried Italian seasoning, crushed, to 1 pint three-bean salad.

Stroganoff-Sauced Beef Roast

With the help of purchased beef roast, button mushrooms, and sour cream dip, you can create this all-time favorite comfort food in just 30 minutes.

Prep: 15 minutes **Cook:** 15 minutes
Makes: 3 to 4 servings

1	16-ounce package cooked beef pot roast with gravy
2	cups button mushrooms
½	cup dairy sour cream French onion dip
2	cups hot cooked noodles

1. Transfer beef with gravy to a large skillet (leave meat whole). Remove stems from mushrooms; halve or quarter mushrooms. Add mushrooms to skillet. Cover and cook over medium-low heat for 15 minutes or until heated through, stirring mushrooms once and turning roast over halfway through cooking time.

Easy Shepherd's Pie

2. Use a wooden spoon to break meat into bite-size pieces. Stir onion dip into meat mixture; heat through (do not boil). Stir in hot cooked noodles.

Nutrition Facts per serving: 542 cal., 7 g total fat (11 g sat. fat), 99 mg chol., 787 mg sodium, 46 g carbo., 4 g fiber, 8 g pro.
Daily Values: 2% calcium, 20% iron

Easy Shepherd's Pie

Cold winter nights are the perfect occasion to make this warm and comforting one-dish meal. Mop up any leftover sauce with thick chunks of Italian bread, generously smeared with butter.

Prep: 20 minutes **Bake:** 20 minutes
Stand: 10 minutes **Oven:** 375°F **Makes:** 4 servings

1	17-ounce package refrigerated cooked beef tips with gravy
2	cups loose-pack frozen mixed vegetables
1	10¾-ounce can condensed tomato bisque soup
1	tablespoon Worcestershire sauce
1	teaspoon dried minced onion

½	teaspoon dried thyme, crushed
⅛	teaspoon black pepper
1	20-ounce package refrigerated mashed potatoes
½	cup shredded cheddar cheese (2 ounces)

1. In a large saucepan combine beef tips with gravy, mixed vegetables, soup, Worcestershire sauce, dried onion, thyme, and pepper. Bring to boiling over medium heat, stirring occasionally. Transfer to a greased 2-quart baking dish.

2. Place mashed potatoes in a large bowl; stir until nearly smooth. Spoon potatoes into 6 mounds on top of meat mixture.

3. Bake, uncovered, in a 375° oven for 20 to 25 minutes or until heated through and bubbly on edges. Sprinkle with cheese. Let stand for 10 minutes before serving.

Nutrition Facts per serving: 438 cal., 15 g total fat (6 g sat. fat), 64 mg chol., 1,570 mg sodium, 49 g carbo., 5 g fiber, 27 g pro.
Daily Values: 80% vit. A, 63% vit. C, 19% calcium, 20% iron

Creamy Tuna Mac

Most of the ingredients for this simple dinner are probably already in your kitchen. With the tasty additions of roasted red pepper and flavored sour cream dip, this is a mac and cheese recipe even adults will enjoy eating.

Start to Finish: 25 minutes **Makes:** 4 servings

1	7¼-ounce package macaroni and cheese dinner mix
½	cup frozen peas
¼	cup butter or margarine, softened
¼	cup milk
½	cup dairy sour cream ranch-, onion-, or chive-flavor dip
1	6-ounce can solid white tuna, drained and broken into chunks
½	cup roasted red sweet peppers, drained and chopped

1. Cook macaroni from dinner mix according to package directions, except add the peas the last 2 minutes of cooking. Drain. Continue preparing mix with butter and milk according to package.

2. Stir sour cream dip into the macaroni mixture. Gently stir in tuna and roasted red peppers just until combined. Heat through.

Nutrition Facts per serving: 474 cal., 21 g total fat (11 g sat. fat), 80 mg chol., 962 mg sodium, 49 g carbo., 2 g fiber, 23 g pro.
Daily Values: 20% vit. A, 90% vit. C, 16% calcium, 19% iron

Easy Sweet-and-Sour Chicken

Finally! Here is a homemade sweet-and-sour chicken recipe that doesn't require complicated frying procedures for the meat.

Start to Finish: 30 minutes **Makes:** 4 servings

1	8-ounce can pineapple tidbits (juice pack)
2	small red and/or green sweet peppers, cut into 1-inch pieces
¼	cup red wine vinegar or vinegar
3	tablespoons sugar
2	tablespoons cornstarch
2	tablespoons soy sauce
½	teaspoon instant chicken bouillon granules
1	9-ounce package frozen diced, cooked chicken, thawed
1	8-ounce can sliced water chestnuts, drained
1½	cups quick-cooking rice (optional)

1. Drain pineapple, reserving juice. Add enough water to reserved juice to measure 1½ cups. Pour juice mixture into a medium saucepan. Add peppers. Bring to boiling; reduce heat. Cover and cook for 2 minutes or until peppers are crisp-tender.

2. In a small bowl stir together vinegar, sugar, cornstarch, soy sauce, and chicken bouillon granules. Stir into sweet pepper mixture. Cook and stir until thickened and bubbly. Cook and stir for 2 minutes more. Gently stir in chicken, pineapple, and water chestnuts. Cook and stir until heated through. If desired, serve over hot cooked rice.

Nutrition Facts per serving: 379 cal., 4 g total fat (0 g sat. fat), 34 mg chol., 777 mg sodium, 70 g carbo., 2 g fiber, 20 g pro.
Daily Values: 29% vit. A, 158% vit. C, 20% calcium, 11% iron

In-a-Pinch Ingredients Certain ingredients can be kept for long periods of time in the refrigerator, freezer, or pantry—perfect to use for a last minute side dish or recipe addition.

- Boned and trimmed meat or fish (frozen)
- Rice pilaf or pasta mixes
- Dried potato flakes
- Refrigerated mashed potatoes
- Canned soup, stock, broth, or instant bouillon granules
- Canned legumes (cannellini, Great Northern, pinto)
- Canned vegetables (corn, green beans, peas)
- Frozen chopped onions, pepper, or loose-pack vegetables
- Bottled minced garlic, roasted red pepper, or pesto
- Bottled lemon juice
- Worcestershire sauce, hot sauce, or soy sauce
- Dried gravy mixes
- Bottled marinara and Alfredo sauces
- Ketchup, mustard, teriyaki sauce, or steak sauce

Chicken Teriyaki

Spice up busy December days by whipping up a batch of this Asian-inspired chicken dish. For a complete meal, make instant rice or rely on a package of purchased fried rice.

Start to Finish: 30 minutes Makes: 4 servings

12	ounces skinless, boneless chicken breast halves
½	cup chicken broth
3	tablespoons reduced-sodium soy sauce
2	tablespoons rice vinegar
1	tablespoon honey
2	teaspoons cornstarch
¼	teaspoon ground black pepper
1	tablespoon cooking oil
1	tablespoon finely chopped fresh ginger
1	teaspoon bottled minced garlic
1	cup bias-sliced carrots (2 medium)
1	cup sliced red sweet pepper
1	cup fresh pea pods, tips and strings removed, or frozen pea pods, thawed
¼	cup thinly sliced green onions (2)
1	8-ounce can sliced water chestnuts, drained

1. Cut chicken into 1-inch pieces; set aside.

2. For sauce, in a small bowl stir together the chicken broth, soy sauce, vinegar, honey, cornstarch and pepper. Set aside.

3. Pour oil into a wok or large skillet. (If necessary, add more oil during cooking.) Heat over medium-high heat. Add ginger and garlic to wok; cook and stir for 15 seconds. Add carrots and red sweet pepper; cook and stir for 2 minutes. Add pea pods and green onions; cook and stir for 2 to 3 minutes more or until vegetables are crisp-tender. Remove vegetables from wok.

4. Add chicken to wok; cook and stir for 3 to 4 minutes or until chicken is no longer pink. Push chicken from center of wok. Stir sauce; add to center of wok. Cook and stir until thickened and bubbly. Return vegetables to wok. Stir in water chestnuts. Cook and stir for 1 to 2 minutes more or until heated through.

Nutrition Facts per serving: 261 cal., 7 g total fat (1 g sat. fat), 50 mg chol., 635 mg sodium, 27 g carbo., 3 g fiber, 23 g pro.
Daily Values: 100% vit. A, 132% vit. C, 19% calcium, 8% iron

Chicken Teriyaki

One-Pot Pesto Pasta

Packed with basil, pine nuts, and olive oil, purchased pesto is convenient for basil-lovers everywhere. Not only does it drastically cut down on the prep time for the busy holiday cook, but it adds quick and exceptional flavor to a variety of dishes. Use any leftovers to enjoy with crackers and cheese, or spice up marinara sauce.

Prep: 15 minutes **Cook:** 25 minutes
Makes: 4 servings

1	pound sweet Italian sausage or ground beef
3	cups reduced-sodium chicken broth
8	ounces spaghetti, broken
3	tablespoons purchased basil pesto
¼	cup finely shredded Parmesan cheese (1 ounce)

1. Crumble sausage into a large saucepan; cook until brown, stirring occasionally. Drain off the fat.

2. Add broth to saucepan; bring to boiling. Gradually add spaghetti. Reduce heat. Cover and simmer about 25 minutes or until spaghetti is tender and most of the liquid is absorbed, stirring occasionally. Remove saucepan from heat. Stir in pesto. Transfer to a serving dish. Sprinkle with Parmesan cheese.

Nutrition Facts per serving: 659 cal., 35 g total fat (12 g sat. fat), 84 mg chol., 1,253 mg sodium, 46 g carbo., 1 g fiber, 29 g pro.
Daily Values: 1% vit. A, 2% vit. C, 9% calcium, 17% iron

Two-Tomato Pasta

Fresh tomato and dried tomato are tossed with oregano, pine nuts, veggies, and hot cooked pasta in this low-calorie pasta dinner. For a complete meal, add 12 ounces of sliced Italian sausage links.

Start to Finish: 30 minutes
Makes: 6 side-dish servings

8	ounces dried penne or dried spaghetti or two 9-ounce packages refrigerated pasta
1	cup green sweet pepper strips or purchased shredded carrot
¼	cup sliced green onion (2)

Two-Tomato Pasta

1   **tablespoon olive oil**
2   **cups chopped fresh tomatoes**
      (4 medium)
2   **teaspoons dried oregano, crushed**
½   **teaspoon salt**
⅛   **teaspoon black pepper**
¼   **cup snipped, oil-packed dried**
      tomatoes
2   **tablespoons pine nuts, toasted**
      Sliced black olives (optional)

1. Prepare pasta according to package directions. Drain pasta well.

2. In a large skillet cook sweet pepper and green onion in hot olive oil until crisp-tender. Stir in fresh tomatoes, oregano, salt, and pepper. Cook and stir until heated through. Place drained pasta in a large bowl. Add dried tomatoes and pine nuts; toss to combine. If desired, sprinkle with sliced olives.

Nutrition Facts per serving: 206 cal., 5 g total fat (1 g sat. fat), 0 mg chol., 212 mg sodium, 34 g carbo., 3 g fiber, 7 g pro.
Daily Values: 14% vit. A, 55% vit. C, 3% calcium, 12% iron

Two-Tomato Pasta with Sausage: In a large skillet cook sausage until brown. Drain off the fat. Set sausage aside. Prepare Two-Tomato Pasta as directed above except stir in sausage with the fresh tomatoes. Makes 6 main-dish servings.

Nutrition Facts per serving: 370 cal., 18 g total fat (6 g sat. fat), 38 mg chol., 212 mg sodium, 34 g carbo., 3 g dietary fiber, 15 g pro.
Daily Values: 14% vit. A, 56% vit. C, 4% calcium, 14% iron.

On-the-Side Coleslaw

Prepare this quick-to-fix blend of cabbage, sweet pepper, and creamy vinegar dressing as a healthful accompaniment to a variety of sandwiches. (See Tuna Salad with a Twist, page 133.)

Start to Finish: 15 minutes
Makes: 4 to 6 side-dish servings

2   **tablespoons sugar**
2   **tablespoons vinegar**
1   **tablespoon water**
2   **tablespoons salad oil**
½   **teaspoon celery seeds**
      Dash salt

Cook Once, Eat Twice

• **Double Up.** Many recipes can be doubled, then packaged and frozen. They are perfect for a quick meal whenever you're in a hurry. Next time you make a casserole, stew, or slow-braised meat, double the recipe and reap the benefits on a busy day. Keep in mind that cooked potatoes become mealy after being frozen, so eliminate them from the recipe, or cook and add them just before serving.

• **Change it Up.** If the idea of eating leftovers seems less than appealing, try tweaking the recipe the next day to transform it into a slightly different dish. Chili one day could be a pasta sauce the next day when combined with extra tomato sauce, broccoli florets, and shredded cheddar cheese.

• **Be Creative.** Another way to use leftovers without actually making the same dish is to purchase and cook extra of one or more of the main ingredients at the same time. If you cook 2 pounds of ground beef, 1 pound can be used one night for chili, while the other pound can be tightly-covered and refrigerated for use a couple of days later. When you're ready to use it, making a quick ground beef stroganoff or spaghetti sauce will be a snap.

      Dash black pepper
2   **tablespoons dairy sour cream**
4   **cups shredded cabbage with carrot**
      (coleslaw mix)
¼   **cup chopped green sweet pepper**

1. For dressing, in a small saucepan combine sugar, vinegar, and water; heat and stir until the sugar dissolves. In a blender combine the sugar mixture, salad oil, celery seeds, salt, and black pepper; cover and blend until well mixed. Add sour cream; cover and blend until combined.

2. In a large bowl combine shredded cabbage and sweet pepper; add dressing. Toss to coat. Serve immediately. (Or cover and chill in the refrigerator for up to 4 hours. Stir before serving.)

Nutrition Facts per serving: 117 cal., 8 g total fat (2 g sat. fat), 3 mg chol., 56 mg sodium, 11 g carbo., 2 g fiber, 1 g pro.
Daily Values: 21% vit. A, 53% vit. C, 4% calcium, 1% iron

Fast and Fancy
New Year's
Celebration

WHAT BETTER REASON TO USE YOUR BEST CHINA and don those stylish clothes you never get to wear? It's New Year's Eve and the perfect time for a party! Whether you want to serve an intimate candlelight dinner for two or a fancy meal with a group of friends, you can find the perfect options in this elegant chapter. Whether you're looking for an appetizer, a main-dish, or a dessert, these recipes will help you and your loved ones start the year with a delicious bang!

Broiled Lobster Tails , page 151

Stuffed Eggs

Deviled eggs typically contain a spicy component, such as hot pepper sauce or mustard. Although this recipe is not technically a deviled version because it contains neither, you can add one or the other if you choose.

Start to Finish: 40 minutes **Makes:** 12 servings

6	eggs
¼	cup mayonnaise or salad dressing
2	tablespoons finely chopped ham
⅛	teaspoon ground white or black pepper
	Paprika or snipped fresh parsley

1. Place eggs in a single layer in a medium saucepan. Add enough cold water to just cover the eggs. Bring to a boil over high heat (water will have large rapidly breaking bubbles). Remove from heat; let stand, covered, for 15 minutes. Drain.

2. Run cold water over the eggs, or place in ice water until cool enough to handle. Drain.

3. To peel, gently tap each egg on the counter. Roll the egg between the palms of your hands. Peel off egg shell, starting at the large end.

4. Halve eggs lengthwise and remove yolks. Push yolks through a fine sieve with the back of a spoon. Mix yolks with mayonnaise, ham, and pepper. Stuff egg white halves with yolk mixture. Refrigerate until serving time. Sprinkle eggs lightly with paprika before serving.

Nutrition Facts per serving: 74 cal., 6 g total fat (1 g sat. fat), 110 mg chol., 78 mg sodium, 0 g carbo., 0 g fiber, 3 g pro.
Daily Values: 3% vit. A, 1% calcium, 2% iron

Garlic and Spinach Dip with Pita Wedges

These little bites are perfect to serve with all kinds of dips, as well as with soups and salads. For more pita chip ideas, check out Chip Change-Up on the next page.

Start to Finish: 20 minutes
Makes: about 4 cups dip (16 appetizer servings)

2	10¾-ounce cans condensed cream of mushroom soup with roasted garlic
2	10-ounce packages frozen chopped spinach, thawed and well drained

Stuffed Eggs

Fast and Fancy New Year's Celebration

1   cup shredded carrot (2 medium)
¼   teaspoon cayenne pepper
½   cup milk (optional)
1   recipe Toasted Pita Wedges
      or tortilla chips

1. In a medium saucepan stir together soup, spinach, carrot, and cayenne pepper. Cook and stir over medium heat until heated through. If necessary, stir in milk to create dipping consistency.

2. Transfer to a serving dish. Serve with Toasted Pita Wedges or tortilla chips.

Toasted Pita Wedges: Split 8 pita bread rounds in half horizontally; cut each half into 6 wedges. Place wedges, cut sides up, in a single layer on 2 ungreased baking sheets. Bake in a 375°F oven for 7 to 9 minutes or until light brown. Store in an airtight container for up to 5 days.

Nutrition Facts per ¼ cup dip and 6 wedges: 116 cal., 1 g total fat (0 g sat. fat), 2 mg chol., 466 mg sodium, 22 g carbo., 2 g fiber, 4 g pro.
Daily Values: 121% vit. A, 5% vit. C, 6% calcium, 5% iron

Layered Black Bean Dip

Need a last-minute appetizer to feed your guests this New Year's Eve? With only four ingredients, this crowd-pleasing dip can be whipped together and baked even after your guests arrive.

Prep: 10 minutes **Bake:** 20 minutes **Oven:** 350°F
Makes: 8 to 10 appetizer servings

1   15-ounce can black beans, rinsed and
      drained
¾   cup bottled salsa
2   cups shredded Monterey Jack cheese
      with jalapeño peppers or Monterey
      Jack cheese (8 ounces)
1   medium avocado, halved, seeded,
      peeled, and chopped
5   cups tortilla chips (6 ounces)

1. In a large bowl mash beans and salsa. Stir 1 cup of the cheese into the bean mixture. Spread the bean mixture in a 9-inch pie plate. Top with avocado and sprinkle with the remaining 1 cup cheese.

Chip Change-Up: For a taste explosion with crispy dippers, follow these recipes when making chips from pitas or tortillas.

Moroccan Pita Chips: Stir together ¼ cup olive oil, ½ teaspoon curry powder, ¼ teaspoon ground cumin, and ¼ teaspoon ground red pepper. Split 3 pita bread rounds in half horizontally, and brush both sides of each cut round with the oil mixture. Stack the rounds; cut stack into 8 wedges. Arrange half of the wedges in a single layer on a 15×10×1-inch baking pan. Bake in a 350°F oven for 8 to 10 minutes or until crisp. Repeat with remaining wedges. Store in an airtight container for up to 1 week.

Peppery Pita Chips: Split 4 large pita bread rounds in half horizontally. Lightly spray the cut side of each pita bread round with nonstick cooking spray. Sprinkle with ½ to ¾ teaspoon pepper and ½ to ¾ teaspoon onion or garlic powder. Stack rounds; cut stack into 6 wedges. Arrange half of the wedges in a single layer on a 15×10×1-inch baking pan. Bake in a 350°F oven for 10 to 12 minutes or until crisp. Repeat with remaining wedges. Store in an airtight container up to 1 week.

Focaccia-Style Chips: Cook ⅔ cup finely chopped onion in 2 tablespoons melted butter or margarine for 3 to 5 minutes or until tender. Stir in 1 teaspoon dried Italian seasoning, crushed. Brush evenly over one side of four 8-inch tortillas. Cut each tortilla into eight wedges. Spread wedges in a single layer on an ungreased 15×10×1-inch baking pan. Bake in a 350°F oven for 8 to 10 minutes or until wedges are crisp and edges are browned.

2. Bake, uncovered, in a 350° oven about 20 minutes or until heated through and cheese is melted. Serve warm with tortilla chips.

Nutrition Facts per serving: 291 cal., 18 g total fat (7 g sat. fat), 25 mg chol., 448 mg sodium, 25 g carbo., 6 g fiber, 12 g pro.
Daily Values: 12% vit. A, 8% vit. C, 27% calcium, 8% iron

143

Alpine Cheese Soup

Rolled oats give this creamy soup extra body, while leeks, Gruyère cheese, and a sprinkling of bacon ensure a rich and savory flavor. With only 25 minutes of preparation, you'll have plenty of time to finish the rest of the meal.

Prep: 25 minutes **Cook:** 25 minutes
Makes: 6 side-dish servings

4	slices bacon, cut up
½	cup chopped onion (1 medium)
½	cup chopped celery (1 stalk)
1	medium leek (white part only), halved lengthwise and sliced (⅓ cup)
2	14-ounce cans reduced-sodium chicken broth
½	cup quick-cooking rolled oats
¼	teaspoon black pepper
¾	cup shredded process Gruyère or Swiss cheese (3 ounces)
¼	cup whipping cream, half-and-half, or light cream
2	teaspoons dried parsley (optional)

1. In a large saucepan cook bacon until crisp. Drain bacon, reserving drippings in saucepan.

2. Cook onion, celery, and leek in the reserved bacon drippings over medium heat about 5 minutes or until tender. Stir in broth, oats, and pepper. Bring to boiling; reduce heat. Simmer, covered, for 20 minutes. Remove from heat. Stir in cheese until melted. Cool slightly.

3. Place half of the soup in a blender or food processor. Cover and blend or process until smooth. Repeat with remaining soup. Return all of the soup to saucepan; stir in cream. Heat through, but do not boil. Ladle into soup bowls; sprinkle with crumbled bacon and parsley.

Nutrition Facts per serving: 160 cal., 11 g total fat (6 g sat. fat), 31 mg chol., 523 mg sodium, 8 g carbo., 1 g fiber, 7 g pro.
Daily Values: 6% vit. A, 3% vit. C, 12% calcium, 4% iron

Mushroom and Leek Soup

Leeks and gourmet mushrooms transform this broth-based soup into a taste delight, while the smooth flavor of Madeira wine adds the finishing touch. If you choose to purchase a bottle of Madeira for this recipe, remember the flavor meshes well with a variety of other soups and sauces.

Prep: 25 minutes **Cook:** 15 minutes
Makes: 6 to 8 side-dish servings (5½ cups)

3	slices bacon, coarsely chopped
3	medium leeks, trimmed, rinsed, and thinly sliced
2	cloves garlic, minced
8	ounces assorted sliced mushrooms, such as shiitake, cremini, or button, sliced (3 cups)
1	teaspoon dried Italian seasoning, crushed
2	14-ounce cans reduced-sodium chicken broth
1	cup frozen peas
2	tablespoons Madeira wine (optional)
	Salt and black pepper
	Finely shredded Parmesan cheese (optional)

1. In a large saucepan cook bacon over medium heat until crisp. Remove bacon; reserve drippings in saucepan. Drain bacon and set aside.

2. Add leeks and garlic to hot drippings in saucepan. Cook and stir for 3 minutes. Add mushrooms and Italian seasoning. Cook and stir about 5 minutes more or just until mushrooms are tender. Stir in broth, peas, and, if desired, Madeira wine. Cook and stir until heated through. Season to taste with salt and pepper.

3. To serve, ladle soup into warm bowls. Sprinkle each serving with the bacon and, if desired, Parmesan cheese.

Nutrition Facts per serving: 112 cal., 7 g total fat (2 g sat. fat), 7 mg chol., 459 mg sodium, 8 g carbo., 2 g fiber, 5 g pro.
Daily Values: 15% vit. A, 11% vit. C, 2% calcium, 6% iron

Solid Gold Squash Soup

Solid Gold Squash Soup

Winter and summer squash differ in that summer types have thin, edible skin, such as that of a zucchini. Winter types, such as pumpkins, have a tough rind that is typically not eaten. Other varieties of winter squash include butternut, acorn, and spaghetti.

Start to Finish: 15 minutes
Makes: 4 side-dish servings

¼	cup finely chopped onion
1	to 2 teaspoons curry powder
½	teaspoon ground ginger
1½	teaspoons olive oil or cooking oil
2	12-ounce packages frozen cooked winter squash, thawed
1	cup reduced-sodium chicken broth
1	cup apple juice or apple cider
⅛	teaspoon salt
½	cup plain yogurt or dairy sour cream Finely chopped pistachio nuts (optional)

1. In a medium saucepan cook and stir onion, curry powder, and ginger in hot oil over medium heat for 2 minutes. Stir in squash, broth, apple juice, and salt; heat through. Ladle soup into bowls. Top each serving with yogurt. If desired, sprinkle with pistachios.

Hint: The night before you plan to make this recipe, place the packages of frozen squash in a bowl or shallow dish to thaw in the refrigerator.

Nutrition Facts per serving: 171 cal., 2 g total fat (1 g sat. fat), 2 mg chol., 243 mg sodium, 36 g carbo., 3 g fiber, 5 g pro.
Daily Values: 163% vit. A, 20% vit. C, 11% calcium, 11% iron

Volcano Potatoes

A mountain of mashed potatoes is transformed into a delectable "volcano" by adding whipping cream and cheese to a well in the center of the potatoes. Although it takes more than an hour in the oven to bake, starting with refrigerated potatoes cuts prep time significantly.

Prep: 15 minutes **Bake:** 65 minutes
Oven: 300°F/375°F **Makes:** 6 side-dish servings

2	24-ounce packages refrigerated mashed potatoes
½	cup whipping cream
½	cup shredded Gruyère, Havarti, or American cheese (2 ounces)
	Black pepper

1. Place potatoes in a 1½-quart casserole. Bake, covered, in a 300° oven for 50 minutes.

2. Meanwhile, in a chilled medium mixing bowl beat whipping cream with an electric mixer on medium speed until soft peaks form (tips curl). Gently fold in cheese.

3. Increase oven temperature to 375°. Remove casserole from oven; uncover. With a large spoon make a hole in the center of the potatoes by pushing potatoes from the center to the sides; spoon the whipping cream mixture into the hole. Sprinkle pepper over top.

4. Return to oven and bake, uncovered, for 15 to 20 minutes more or until the top is golden.

Nutrition Facts per serving: 286 cal., 14 g total fat (6 g sat. fat), 38 mg chol., 379 mg sodium, 31 g carbo., 2 g fiber, 8 g pro.
Daily Values: 8% vit. A, 65% vit. C, 13% calcium, 6% iron

Garlicky Green Beans

After all the time spent on the rest of the holiday meal, vegetable side dishes can sometimes be overlooked. Simple yet delicious, these green beans will command attention without taking precious time away from the preparation of spotlight dishes.

Prep: 15 minutes **Cook:** 13 minutes
Makes: 8 side-dish servings

1½	pounds fresh green beans, cleaned and ends trimmed
3	tablespoons butter or margarine
3	cloves garlic, minced
¾	teaspoon black pepper

1. In a large saucepan or 4-quart Dutch oven cook green beans in boiling salted water about 12 minutes or until crisp-tender. Drain. Set aside.

Volcano Potatoes

2. In the same pan melt butter. Add garlic and pepper; cook for 1 minute. Return green beans to pan; toss to coat beans with butter mixture. Serve beans immediately while hot.

Nutrition Facts per serving: 66 cal., 5 g total fat (2 g sat. fat), 12 mg chol., 37 mg sodium, 6 g carbo., 3 g fiber, 2 g pro.
Daily Values: 12% vit. A, 16% vit. C, 3% calcium, 5% iron

Pasta with Three Cheeses

The good news is that this delicious pasta dish also contains the vegetable portion of the meal, which means one less dish to cook.

Start to Finish: 30 minutes
Makes: 4 servings

10	ounces packaged dried medium shell macaroni or rotini pasta
2	cups frozen loose-pack cauliflower, broccoli, and carrots
1	cup milk
1	3-ounce package cream cheese, cut up
¼	teaspoon coarsely ground black pepper
¾	cup shredded Swiss, cheddar, or fontina cheese (3 ounces)
¼	cup grated Parmesan cheese (1 ounce)

1. In a large saucepan cook pasta according to package directions, except add frozen vegetables the last 5 minutes of cooking. Drain and set aside.

2. In the same saucepan combine milk, cream cheese, and pepper. Cook and stir over low heat until cream cheese is melted.

3. Return pasta and vegetables to saucepan; toss to coat with cream cheese mixture. Gently stir in the shredded cheese and the Parmesan cheese. Transfer to a serving bowl. If desired, sprinkle with additional grated Parmesan cheese.

Nutrition Facts per serving: 488 cal., 17 g total fat (10 g sat. fat), 52 mg chol., 233 mg sodium, 61 g carbo., 3 g fiber, 22 g pro.
Daily Values: 42% vit. A, 23% vit. C, 32% calcium, 14% iron

Pasta with Three Cheeses

Roasted Asparagus

The most economical time to buy asparagus is when it naturally begins to grow during early spring, although most supermarkets offer hothouse asparagus year-round. What better time to splurge on this deliciously tender vegetable than during the holidays?

Prep: 10 minutes **Roast:** 20 minutes **Oven:** 400°F
Makes: 4 to 6 side-dish servings

2	pounds fresh asparagus, trimmed
2	tablespoons olive oil
	Dash salt
1	ounce shaved Parmesan cheese
¼	teaspoon black pepper

1. Arrange oven racks to middle and lower third of oven. Divide asparagus and spread on 2 shallow baking pans. Drizzle each with 1 tablespoon oil and salt; toss to coat.

2. Roast in a 400° oven for 10 minutes. Switch pans between the racks and roast about 10 minutes more or until stalks are tender. Sprinkle with Parmesan cheese and pepper.

Nutrition Facts per serving: 113 cal., 9 g total fat (2 g sat. fat), 5 mg chol., 158 mg sodium, 5 g carbo., 3 g fiber, 5 g pro.
Daily Values: 18% vit. A, 10% vit. C, 12% calcium, 15% iron

Baked Risotto

Baked Risotto

Traditional risotto requires several minutes of stirring to acquire the desired creamy texture of the dish. To speed the process along, this simplified version bakes all the ingredients in the oven and relies on canned soup to obtain a rich consistency.

Prep: 10 minutes **Bake:** 55 minutes
Stand: 10 minutes **Oven:** 375°F
Makes: 6 side-dish servings

3¼   **cups water**
1   **10¾-ounce can condensed cream of
      chicken and herbs, cream of
      chicken, or cream of celery soup**
1¼   **cups Arborio or medium-grain white
      rice**
⅓   **cup coarsely shredded carrot**
¼   **teaspoon salt**
¼   **teaspoon black pepper**

½   **cup fresh or thawed, frozen pea pods,
      bias-cut in halves**
½   **cup finely shredded Parmesan cheese
      (2 ounces)**
      **Shaved Parmesan cheese or finely
      shredded Parmesan cheese
      (optional)**

1. In an ungreased 2-quart casserole stir together water, soup, uncooked rice, carrot, salt, and pepper.

2. Bake risotto, covered, in a 375° oven for 55 to 60 minutes or until rice is tender, stirring twice during baking. Remove casserole from oven; gently stir in pea pods and the ¼ cup shredded Parmesan cheese. Let stand for 10 minutes before serving. If desired, garnish with shaved Parmesan cheese.

Nutrition Facts per serving: 163 cal., 4 g total fat (2 g sat. fat), 9 mg chol., 595 mg sodium, 27 g carbo., 1 g fiber, 6 g pro.
Daily Values: 21% vit. A, 1% vit. C, 10% calcium, 11% iron

Sour Cream Smashed Potatoes

For make-ahead ease, prepare potatoes as directed except place in a greased 1½-quart casserole before heating through. Cover and chill for up to 24 hours. When you want to serve it, bake, covered, in a 350°F oven for 55 minutes or until heated through. If desired, sprinkle with Parmesan cheese just before serving.

Prep: 20 minutes **Cook:** 20 minutes
Makes: 6 side-dish servings

4	medium baking potatoes (about 1⅓ pounds)
4	cloves garlic, peeled
½	cup dairy sour cream
2	to 3 tablespoons milk (optional)
	Salt and black pepper
1	tablespoon finely shredded Parmesan cheese (optional)

1. Peel potatoes, if desired. In a large saucepan cook potatoes and garlic, covered, in enough boiling water to cover for 20 to 25 minutes or until potatoes are tender; drain.

2. In a large bowl mash potatoes and garlic with a potato masher; add sour cream. If necessary, beat in enough milk to make mixture fluffy. Season to taste with salt and pepper. Return potatoes to pan and heat through. Transfer potatoes to a serving bowl. If desired, sprinkle with Parmesan cheese.

Nutrition Facts per serving: 112 cal., 3 g total fat (2 g sat. fat), 7 mg chol., 113 mg sodium, 18 g carbo., 2 g fiber, 3 g pro.
Daily Values: 2% vit. A, 28% vit. C, 4% calcium, 8% iron

Tortellini with Basil-Alfredo Sauce

A rather piquant herb, basil is often likened in flavor to licorice and cloves. Dried basil should not be substituted for fresh in this recipe, because the herb is used as one of the key ingredients rather than a complementary spice. In most supermarkets, fresh herbs are available year-round in the produce section.

Start to Finish: 20 minutes
Makes: 6 servings

2	9-ounce packages refrigerated meat- or cheese-filled tortellini
1	7-ounce jar roasted red sweet peppers
1	cup refrigerated light Alfredo sauce
1	cup shredded fresh basil
½	to ¾ teaspoon coarsely ground black pepper

1. Cook tortellini according to package directions; drain pasta thoroughly.

2. Meanwhile, drain sweet peppers and cut into 1/2-inch strips. In a large saucepan heat Alfredo sauce. Gently stir in the cooked and drained tortellini and the sweet peppers. Reduce heat. Simmer over low heat for 5 minutes, stirring often.

3. Stir in half of the basil. Sprinkle the remaining basil and the black pepper over the top. Serve immediately.

Nutrition Facts per serving: 355 cal., 10 g total fat (4 g sat. fat), 70 mg chol., 786 mg sodium, 48 g carbo., 1 g fiber, 18 g pro.
Daily Values: 17% vit. A, 116% vit. C, 8% calcium, 3% iron

Tortellini with Basil-Alfredo Sauce

Steak and Mushrooms

Consider treating your family to a wild mushroom medley heaped on the most tender of steak cuts. The smooth cream sauce is a delightful accompaniment.

Start to Finish: 30 minutes **Makes:** 8 servings

8	beef tenderloin steaks, cut 1-inch thickness (about 2 pounds)
1	teaspoon steak seasoning blend (such as Kansas City seasoning, blackened seasoning, or Montreal seasoning)
2	tablespoons olive oil
1	pound crimini, shiitake, baby portobello, and/or button mushrooms, sliced (6 cups)
½	cup beef broth seasoned with onion
¼	cup whipping cream
1	tablespoon Dijon-style mustard
	Salt and freshly ground black pepper

1. Season both sides of meat with steak seasoning. In a 12-inch skillet heat oil over medium-high heat until very hot. Add the steaks; reduce heat to medium and cook to desired doneness, turning once. Allow 7 to 9 minutes for medium-rare (145°F) or 10 to 13 minutes for medium (160°F). Remove steaks from skillet; cover with foil.

2. In the same skillet cook and stir mushrooms for 4 to 5 minutes or until tender. Stir in broth, whipping cream, and mustard. Heat to boiling; reduce heat and boil gently, uncovered, over medium heat for 2 to 3 minutes or until slightly thickened. Season to taste with salt and freshly ground black pepper. To serve, spoon mushroom mixture over steaks.

Nutrition Facts per serving: 271 cal., 18 g total fat (7 g sat. fat), 90 mg chol., 116 mg sodium, 2 g carbo., 0 g fiber, 26 g pro.
Daily Values: 5% vit. A, 2% calcium, 19% iron

Italian-Style Steak and Shrimp Skewers

Served together, steak and shrimp is a most rewarding pair. When presented next to Tortellini with Basil-Alfredo Sauce (page 149), your culinary talents will be the talk of the table.

Prep: 35 minutes **Broil:** 10 minutes
Chill: 30 minutes **Makes:** 6 servings

18	fresh or frozen peeled, deveined large shrimp with tails
2	tablespoons olive oil
¼	cup fine dry bread crumbs
1	teaspoon dried parsley
1	clove garlic, minced
⅛	teaspoon salt
⅛	teaspoon black pepper
1	pound beef tenderloin, cut into 1-inch cubes
4	teaspoons olive oil
1	teaspoon dried basil, oregano, and/or thyme, crushed
½	teaspoon salt
½	teaspoon black pepper

1. Thaw shrimp, if frozen. Rinse shrimp and pat dry with paper towels.

2. In a medium bowl toss the shrimp with the 2 tablespoons olive oil. In a small bowl combine bread crumbs, parsley, garlic, the ⅛ teaspoon salt, and the ⅛ teaspoon black pepper; add to shrimp. Toss to coat. Cover and chill for 30 minutes.

3. Meanwhile, in a medium bowl combine beef, the 4 teaspoons olive oil, basil, the ½ teaspoon salt, and the ½ teaspoon black pepper. Toss meat to coat.

4. On six 12-inch metal skewers thread shrimp and beef, leaving ¼ inch between pieces.

5. Place skewers on the unheated rack of a broiler pan. Broil 4 to 5 inches from the heat for 10 minutes or until shrimp turn opaque and meat is medium rare, turning once.

Nutrition Facts per serving: 258 cal., 14 g total fat (3 g sat. fat), 124 mg chol., 482 mg sodium, 4 g carbo., 0 g fiber, 28 g pro.
Daily Values: 2% vit. A, 2% vit. C, 5% calcium, 20% iron

Broiled Lobster Tails

Broiled Lobster Tails

Ring in the New Year with a special meal of lobster tail. Gone are the days of boiling live whole lobsters in a giant pot. Now all you need is the tail, some kitchen shears, and a broiler. In less than 20 minutes you can savor this buttery delicacy with your friends.

Prep: 10 minutes **Cook:** 9 minutes
Makes: 8 servings

   8   **5-ounce fresh or frozen lobster tails**
  ¼   **cup lemon juice**
   2   **tablespoons butter, melted**
  ¼   **cup sliced almonds**

1. Thaw lobster tails, if frozen. Butterfly* the lobster tails by cutting through the center of the hard top shells and meat. Spread the halves of the tails apart. Place lobster tails, meat side up, on unheated rack of a broiler pan.

2. In a small bowl combine lemon juice and butter. Brush mixture over lobster meat.

3. Broil 4 inches from the heat for 8 to 10 minutes or until nearly done. Sprinkle with almonds and broil 1 to 2 minutes more or until lobster meat is opaque and almonds are lightly toasted.

*Note: To butterfly the lobster, use kitchen shears or a sharp knife to cut the tail lengthwise through the center of the hard top shell. Cut to, but not through, the bottom shell. Use your fingers to gently spread the two halves apart.

Nutrition Facts per serving: 130 cal., 6 g total fat (2 g sat. fat), 89 mg chol., 273 mg sodium, 2 g carbo., 1 g fiber, 17 g pro.
Daily Values: 3% vit. A, 6% vit. C, 5% calcium, 2% iron

151

Linguine with Scallops and Capers

Full of tangy flavor that goes well with a variety of meats and sauces, capers are most commonly sold pickled and bottled. But what exactly is a caper? It's actually the tiny edible flower bud of a native Mediterranean bush.

Prep: 15 minutes **Cook:** 15 minutes
Makes: 6 servings

1	pound fresh or frozen scallops
12	ounces dried linguine
2	tablespoons butter
2	tablespoons olive oil
1	14-ounce can chicken broth
¾	cup dry vermouth or dry white wine
3	tablespoons lemon juice
¾	cup sliced green onion (6)
¾	cup snipped fresh parsley
2	tablespoons capers, drained
1	teaspoon dried dill
¼	teaspoon black pepper

1. Thaw scallops, if frozen. Cut any large scallops in half; set aside. Cook linguine according to package directions.

2. Meanwhile, in a 12-inch skillet heat butter and oil over medium-high heat. Add scallops; cook and stir about 2 minutes or until opaque. Remove scallops with a slotted spoon, reserving the juices in skillet.

3. Stir broth, vermouth, and lemon juice into juices in skillet. Bring to boiling. Reduce heat and simmer, uncovered, for 8 to 10 minutes or until liquid is reduced to about 1¼ cups. Stir in green onions, parsley, capers, dill, and pepper. Simmer, uncovered, for 1 minute more. Add scallops. Cook and stir just until heated through. Pour over linguine; toss gently to combine.

Nutrition Facts per serving: 398 cal., 10 g total fat (3 g sat. fat), 36 mg chol., 516 mg sodium, 47 g carbo., 2 g fiber, 21 g pro.
Daily Values: 19% vit. A, 30% vit. C, 6% calcium, 16% iron

Flavor Boost To maximize flavor from meats and sauces, try pan-searing meats to obtain a tasty crust, and then deglaze the pan to retrieve the tasty meat drippings left behind in the pan.

To pan-sear meat, heat a skillet over medium-high until drops of water sizzle on the surface. Butter will burn easily, so replace the amount called for in a recipe with oil, or use half oil and half butter. Add the fat to the hot pan and allow to heat slightly, then add meat (hold a lid slightly above the pan if oil spatters) and cook for 2 to 3 minutes on each side, or until the meat has a medium brown crust on it. Cook meat in small batches to prevent the pan and oil from cooling. If the internal temperature of the meat doesn't reach 165°F by the end of searing, it can be finished in the oven.

The brown crusty deposits left behind in the pan after searing are full of rich flavor which can enhance sauces and gravies dramatically (burned drippings will not impart desirable flavor). Deglaze the pan by adding liquid to the hot skillet once the meat is removed, and scrape the bottom of the pan when the liquid comes to a boil. Finish sauces as directed in recipe.

Veal Chops with Vegetables

If veal isn't a meat you care to try, this dish is also delicious with chicken. Just replace the loin chops with 4 pieces of breast meat and prepare the recipe as directed. Serve with rice or buttered noodles.

Start to Finish: 25 minutes
Makes: 4 servings

4	boneless veal top loin chops, cut ½ to ¾-inch thickness (1- to 1½-pounds total)
	Salt and black pepper
1	tablespoon butter or margarine
1	16-ounce package frozen broccoli, carrots, and water chestnuts
¾	cup chicken broth
1	clove garlic, minced, or ⅛ teaspoon bottled minced garlic
2	tablespoons Worcestershire sauce for chicken
2	teaspoons cornstarch

1. Trim fat from chops. Season chops lightly with salt and pepper. In a large skillet cook chops over medium heat in hot butter for 5 to 7 minutes or until veal is of desired doneness (160°F for medium), turning once. Transfer chops to a serving platter; cover with foil to keep warm.

2. Stir frozen vegetables, broth, and garlic into drippings in skillet. Bring to boiling; reduce heat. Cover and simmer for 5 minutes.

3. In a small bowl stir together Worcestershire sauce and cornstarch; stir into vegetable mixture in skillet. Cook and stir until thickened and bubbly. Cook and stir for 2 minutes more. Serve vegetable mixture with veal.

Nutrition Facts per serving: 209 cal., 7 g total fat (3 g sat. fat), 99 mg chol., 578 mg sodium, 10 g carbo., 3 g fiber, 25 g pro.
Daily Values: 57% vit. A, 35% vit. C, 2% calcium, 7% iron

Pork Diane

Searching for an elegant and incredibly simple dinner idea to serve your family on New Year's Eve? Look no further than this saucy pork delight. For an ultra simple side dish, toss boiled red potatoes in butter and snipped chives.

Start to Finish: 25 minutes
Makes: 4 servings

1	tablespoon water
1	tablespoon Worcestershire sauce for chicken
1	teaspoon lemon juice
1	teaspoon Dijon-style mustard
4	boneless pork top loin chops, cut ¾- to 1-inch thickness
1	teaspoon lemon-pepper seasoning
2	tablespoons butter or margarine
1	tablespoon snipped fresh chives or parsley (optional)

1. For sauce, in a small bowl stir together water, Worcestershire sauce, lemon juice, and mustard; set mixture aside.

2. Trim fat from pork. Sprinkle both sides of each chop with lemon-pepper seasoning. In a large skillet cook pork in hot butter over medium heat for 8 to

Pork Diane

12 minutes or until internal temperature reaches 160°F, turning once. Remove meat from skillet. Cover with foil. Remove skillet from heat.

3. Add sauce to skillet. Stir until well mixed. Pour sauce over meat; sprinkle with chives.

Nutrition Facts per serving: 216 cal., 11 g total fat (5 g sat. fat), 87 mg chol., 453 mg sodium, 1 g carbo., 0 g fiber, 25 g pro.
Daily Values: 4% vit. A, 2% vit. C, 3% calcium, 7% iron

Lemon Mousse Tarts

Elegant enough to be featured at a formal sit-down dinner, these mousse-filled tarts require no baking and minimum preparation. For a beautiful presentation, remove the foil pan from the tart shell before filling.

Start to Finish: 10 minutes **Makes:** 6 servings

- 1½ **cups whipping cream**
- 1 **cup prepared lemon curd**
- 6 **graham cracker tart shells**
  Kiwifruit slices and/or fresh raspberries

1. For filling, in a chilled medium mixing bowl beat whipping cream with an electric mixer on medium speed until soft peaks form (tips curl). Using a rubber spatula, fold in lemon curd just until combined. If desired, cover and refrigerate up to 2 hours until ready to serve.

2. To serve, spoon filling into tart shells. Top with kiwifruit and/or fresh raspberries.

Nutrition Facts per serving: 519 cal., 31 g total fat (16 g sat. fat), 122 mg chol., 213 mg sodium, 25 g carbo., 7 g fiber, 3 g pro.
Daily Values: 18% vit. A, 38% vit. C, 5% calcium, 3% iron

Partying with the Family New Year's Eve can be a family affair by including the children, grandchildren, and everyone else in party preparations and celebrations.

- Let the children make the invitations and select party gear and noise-makers.
- Give adult family members easy food preparation tasks and grocery shopping duty.
- Limit your menu by making more of fewer recipes.
- Plan activities for the children: Rent a movie, plan an art project, or set out board games.
- Make a few special treats for picky eaters. Miniature peanut butter and jelly or cheese sandwiches make them feel as if they're eating appetizers for adults.

Fruit-Filled Napoleons

Puff pastry is prepared by several steps of rolling and folding fat layers into pastry dough several times. The layers of fat produce steam during baking and cause the dough to puff to produce an attractive pastry. Once a very time-consuming task, puff pastry is now available frozen in most supermarkets.

Prep: 20 minutes **Bake:** 20 minutes **Oven:** 375°F
Makes: 8 servings

- ½ **of a 17.3-ounce package (1 sheet) puff pastry, thawed**
- 2 **cups pudding, fruit-flavored yogurt, or sweetened whipped cream**
- 2 **cups peeled and sliced kiwifruit, raspberries, and/or orange segments**
  Sifted powdered sugar (optional)

1. On a lightly floured surface, unfold thawed pastry. Using a small sharp knife, cut pastry into 8 rectangles (each the same size). Place pastry rectangles on an ungreased baking sheet. Bake in a 375° oven about 20 minutes or until puffed and golden. Cool on wire racks.

2. Just before serving, split each pastry rectangle in half horizontally. Spoon pudding into pastry bottoms. Top with fruit and pastry tops. If desired, sprinkle with powdered sugar and garnish with additional fruit. Serve immediately.

Nutrition Facts per serving: 218 cal., 11 g total fat (1 g sat. fat), 5 mg chol., 227 mg sodium, 27 g carbo., 1 g fiber, 4 g pro.
Daily Values: 3% vit. A, 35% vit. C, 8% calcium, 1% iron

Fruit-Filled Napoleons

Emergency Substitutions.

If you don't have:	Substitute:
Bacon, 1 slice, crisp-cooked, crumbled	1 tablespoon cooked bacon pieces
Baking powder, 1 teaspoon	1/2 teaspoon cream of tartar plus 1/4 teaspoon baking soda
Balsamic vinegar, 1 tablespoon	1 tablespoon cider vinegar or red wine vinegar plus 1/2 teaspoon sugar
Bread crumbs, fine dry, 1/4 cup	3/4 cup soft bread crumbs, or 1/4 cup cracker crumbs, or 1/4 cup cornflake crumbs
Broth, beef or chicken, 1 cup	1 teaspoon or 1 cube instant beef or chicken bouillon plus 1 cup hot water
Butter, 1 cup	1 cup shortening plus 1/4 teaspoon salt, if desired
Buttermilk, 1 cup	1 tablespoon lemon juice or vinegar plus enough milk to make 1 cup (let stand 5 minutes before using), or 1 cup plain yogurt
Chocolate, semisweet, 1 ounce	3 tablespoons semisweet chocolate pieces, or 1 ounce unsweetened chocolate plus 1 tablespoon granulated sugar, or 1 tablespoon unsweetened cocoa powder plus 2 teaspoons sugar and 2 teaspoons shortening
Chocolate, sweet baking, 4 ounces	1/4 cup unsweetened cocoa powder plus 1/3 cup granulated sugar and 3 tablespoons shortening
Chocolate, unsweetened, 1 ounce	3 tablespoons unsweetened cocoa powder plus 1 tablespoon cooking oil or shortening, melted
Cornstarch, 1 tablespoon (for thickening)	2 tablespoons all-purpose flour
Corn syrup (light), 1 cup	1 cup granulated sugar plus 1/4 cup water
Egg, 1 whole	2 egg whites, or 2 egg yolks, or 1/4 cup refrigerated or frozen egg product, thawed
Flour, cake, 1 cup	1 cup minus 2 tablespoons all-purpose flour
Flour, self-rising, 1 cup	1 cup all-purpose flour plus 1 teaspoon baking powder, 1/2 teaspoon salt, and 1/4 teaspoon baking soda
Garlic, 1 clove	1/2 teaspoon bottled minced garlic or 1/8 teaspoon garlic powder
Ginger, grated fresh, 1 teaspoon	1/4 teaspoon ground ginger
Half-and-half or light cream, 1 cup	1 tablespoon melted butter or margarine plus enough whole milk to make 1 cup
Molasses, 1 cup	1 cup honey
Mustard, dry, 1 teaspoon	1 tablespoon prepared mustard (in cooked mixtures)
Mustard, prepared, 1 tablespoon	1/2 teaspoon dry mustard plus 2 teaspoons vinegar
Onion, chopped, 1/2 cup	2 tablespoons dried minced onion or 1/2 teaspoon onion powder
Sour cream, dairy, 1 cup	1 cup plain yogurt
Sugar, brown, 1 cup packed	1 cup granulated sugar plus 2 tablespoons molasses
Sugar, granulated, 1 cup	1 cup packed brown sugar or 2 cups sifted powdered sugar
Tomato juice, 1 cup	1/2 cup tomato sauce plus 1/2 cup water
Tomato sauce, 2 cups	3/4 cup tomato paste plus 1 cup water
Vanilla bean, 1 whole	2 teaspoons vanilla
Wine, red, 1 cup	1 cup beef or chicken broth in savory recipes; cranberry juice in desserts
Wine, white, 1 cup	1 cup chicken broth in savory recipes; apple juice or white grape juice in desserts
Yeast, active dry, 1 package	about 2 1/4 teaspoons active dry yeast

Seasonings

Apple pie spice, 1 teaspoon	1/2 teaspoon ground cinnamon plus 1/4 teaspoon ground nutmeg, 1/8 teaspoon ground allspice, and dash ground cloves or ginger
Cajun seasoning, 1 tablespoon	1/2 teaspoon white pepper, 1/2 teaspoon garlic powder, 1/2 teaspoon onion powder, 1/2 teaspoon cayenne pepper, 1/2 teaspoon paprika, and 1/2 teaspoon black pepper
Herbs, snipped fresh, 1 tablespoon	1/2 to 1 teaspoon dried herb, crushed, or 1/2 teaspoon ground herb
Poultry seasoning, 1 teaspoon	3/4 teaspoon dried sage, crushed, plus 1/4 teaspoon dried thyme or marjoram, crushed
Pumpkin pie spice, 1 teaspoon	1/2 teaspoon ground cinnamon plus 1/4 teaspoon ground ginger, 1/4 teaspoon ground allspice, and 1/8 teaspoon ground nutmeg

INDEX

A

Almonds
Almond Broccoli, 25
Dutch Almond Cherry-Filled Braids, 78
health benefits from, 95
Prosciutto-Wrapped Dates, 42
Scandinavian Almond Bars, 95
Spicy-Savory Snack Mix, 30

Appetizers. See also Dips and spreads
Artichoke-Chèvre Pastry Bites, 40
Asparagus with Dijon-Horseradish Dip, 35
Blue Cheese–Pecan Phyllo Bites, 40
Brie en Croûte, 38
Holiday Nibblers, 30
last-minute, ideas for, 34
Oriental Shrimp Kabobs, 32
Pesto Brie, 38
Prosciutto-Wrapped Dates, 42
relish trays, ideas for, 37
Salami Cone Skewers, 42
Shrimp Crostini, 32
Shrimp Salad Toasts, 32
Spicy-Savory Snack Mix, 30
Spicy Spinach-Stuffed Mushrooms, 43
Stuffed Eggs, 142
Stuffed Jalapeños, 42

Apples
Apple-Spiced Sweet Potatoes, 106
No-Peel Apple Pie, 76
Plump Apple Dumplings with Caramel
    Sauce, 79
Slow-Cooked Apple Betty, 110
Spinach Salad with Apples and Pecans, 12

Apricots
Apricot, Spinach, and Couscous Dressing, 24
Apricot-Glazed Spiced Pork Roast, 17
Artichoke-Chèvre Pastry Bites, 40

Asparagus
Asparagus and Squash Soup, 10
Asparagus with Dijon-Horseradish Dip, 35
Lemony Asparagus and New Potatoes, 20
Roasted Asparagus, 147
Turkey-Asparagus Brunch Bake, 48

B

Bacon
Bacon-Cheddar Loaves, 59
Hash Brown Omelet, 47
Maple-Bacon Oven Pancake, 51

Bananas
Banana Pancakes, 51
Easy Banana-Nut Loaf, 120

Bar cookies
baking tips, 93
Candied Cherry Squares, 94
Chocolate Chip Cream Bars, 92
Double Chocolate Cream Bars, 92
Easy Gingerbread Bars, 94
Gift-Bag Fudgy Brownies, 125
Golden-Flecked Chocolate Bars, 92
Peanut Brittle Bars, 93
Scandinavian Almond Bars, 95
Surprise Cereal Bars, 120

Beans
Garlicky Green Beans, 146
Layered Black Bean Dip, 143
Split Pea and Tortellini Soup Mix, 128

Beef
Easy Shepherd's Pie, 135
Holiday Beef Tenderloin, 18
Italian-Style Steak and Shrimp Skewers, 150
One-Pot Pesto Pasta, 138
pan-searing, 152
Saucy Sloppy Joes, 132
Steak and Mushrooms, 150
Stroganoff-Sauced Beef Roast, 134

Berries. See also specific types
Berry Trifle Cake, 74
Mixed Berry Cobbler, 111

Birdhouse, Graham Cracker, 116

Biscuits
Buttermilk Biscuits, 60
Orange Biscuit Rolls, 65

Blueberries
Blueberry Breakfast Rolls, 63
Blueberry Crisp, 78
Mixed Berry Cobbler, 111

Breads. See also Coffee cakes; Tortillas
Bacon-Cheddar Loaves, 59
Blueberry Breakfast Rolls, 63
Buttermilk Biscuits, 60
Cheddar Spoon Bread, 58
Christmas Morning French Toast, 53
Cream Cheese–Filled French Toast, 52
Dried Cherry Scone Mix, 124
Easy Banana-Nut Loaf, 120
flavored butters for, 62
Fruit and Pecan Stuffing, 104
Gingerbread Scone Mix, 124
Lemon Tea Bread Mix, 126
Morning Fruit Bread, 66
Mostly Mushrooms Popovers, 59
Orange Biscuit Rolls, 65
Parmesan Rosettes, 60
Peppery Cheese Bread, 61
pita chips, easy ideas for, 143
Pumpkin Crescent Rolls, 66
Quick Bread Salad, 11
Sage Dressing, 105
Savory Holiday Bread, 62
Sweet Pretzel Snowflakes, 58
Toasted Pita Wedges, 143

Breakfast and brunch
Autumn Frittata, 46
Baked Denver Strata, 49
Baked Fruit Ambrosia, 54
Banana Pancakes, 51
Cheesy Ham Quiche, 49
Christmas Fruit Medley, 54
Christmas Morning French Toast, 53
Cream Cheese–Filled French Toast, 52
Dried Cherry Scone Mix, 124
Easy Cranberry-Orange Ring, 122
Gingerbread Pancakes, 50
Hash Brown Omelet, 47
Maple-Bacon Oven Pancake, 51
Oatmeal with Fruit and Nuts, 53
Tortilla Skillet, 46
Turkey-Asparagus Brunch Bake, 48

Broccoli, Almond, 25

Brownies, Gift-Bag Fudgy, 125
Brussels Sprouts and Onions, Maple-Glazed, 26
Butter, Maple-Nut, 124
Buttermilk Biscuits, 60
Butters, flavored, 62

C

Cakes. See also Cheesecakes; Coffee cakes
Berry Trifle Cake, 74
cake mixes, add-ins for, 74
Crunchy Pound Cake Slices, 73
Festive Red Velvet Cake, 72
Little Peppermint Cakes, 123
Nutmeg Cake with Lemon Sauce, 71
Triple Fruit Fruitcake Mix, 127
Triple-Nut Chocolate Torte, 72

Candies
Foolproof Fudge, 96
Fruitcake Candy Tarts, 98
Marbled Mint Candy, 97
P.B. and Chocolate Fudge, 96
Quick Toffee Delight, 97
Rocky Road Clusters, 98
Snack Truffles, 98
Sweet-and-Salty Peanut Rolls, 100
Tropical Snowballs, 99

Caramel Bubble Ring, 64

Carrots
Carrot Cake Cookies, 90
Ginger-Honey Glazed Carrots, 24
Sweet Baby Carrots, 106

Cashew, Chocolate, and Butterscotch
    Cookies, 87
Cauliflower-Crab Chowder, 10
Celery and Peas, Sautéed, 27
Cereal Bars, Surprise, 120

Cheddar
Bacon-Cheddar Loaves, 59
Cheddar Spoon Bread, 58
Cheesy Ham Quiche, 49
Hash Brown Omelet, 47
Maple-Bacon Oven Pancake, 51
Peppery Cheese Bread, 61

Cheese. See also Cheddar; Cream cheese
Alpine Cheese Soup, 144
Artichoke-Chèvre Pastry Bites, 40
Baked Denver Strata, 49
blue cheese, about, 40
Blue Cheese Ball, 37
Blue Cheese–Pecan Phyllo Bites, 40
Brie en Croûte, 38
Chile and Chorizo Cheese Dip, 39
Festive Cheesy Potatoes, 107
Feta-Walnut Dip, 36
Layered Black Bean Dip, 143
Monterey Jack Fondue, 36
Parmesan Rosettes, 60
Pasta with Three Cheeses, 147
Pesto Brie, 38
Quick Chile Con Queso Dip, 37
Salami Cone Skewers, 42
Savory Holiday Bread, 62
Southwest Cheese Fondue, 35
Tortellini with Basil-Alfredo Sauce, 149
Tortilla Skillet, 46
Volcano Potatoes, 146
Walnut-Sage Potatoes, 22

Cheesecakes
Chocolate-Macaroon Cheesecake, 70

157

Index

Chocolate-Mocha Cheesecake, 70
store-bought cheesecake, embellishing, 70

Cherries
Candied Cherry Squares, 94
Cherried Pork Roast, 108
Dried Cherry Scone Mix, 124
Dutch Almond Cherry-Filled Braids, 78

Chicken
Chicken Tacos, 132
Chicken Teriyaki, 137
Easy Sweet-and-Sour Chicken, 136
Tortilla Skillet, 46

Chips, pita and tortilla, 143

Chocolate
Cashew, Chocolate, and Butterscotch Cookies, 87
Chocolate Cappuccino Cookies, 91
Chocolate Chip Cream Bars, 92
Chocolate-Dipped Eggnog Spritz Sticks, 121
Chocolate-Macaroon Cheesecake, 70
Chocolate-Mocha Cheesecake, 70
Chocolate-Pecan Chess Pie, 76
Chocolate-Peppermint Malts, 80
Chocolate-Sauced Pears, 81
Crunchy Pound Cake Slices, 73
Double Chocolate Cream Bars, 92
Festive Red Velvet Cake, 72
Foolproof Fudge, 96
Gift-Bag Fudgy Brownies, 125
Golden-Flecked Chocolate Bars, 92
Heavenly Hot Fudge Sauce, 128
Marbled Mint Candy, 97
Mocha Fondue, 80
P.B. and Chocolate Fudge, 96
Peanut Brittle Bars, 93
Peppermint-Stick Pie, 75
Peppermint Thins, 91
Quick Toffee Delight, 97
Rocky Road Clusters, 98
Triple-Nut Chocolate Torte, 72

Chowder
Caraway Potato Chowder, 134
Cauliflower-Crab Chowder, 10

Chutney, Christmas, 12

Coconut
Chewy Coconut Macaroons, 87
Christmas Macaroon Mix, 126
Coconut Shrimp with Mango-Ginger Dip, 34
Snack Truffles, 98
Tropical Snowballs, 99

Coffee
Chocolate Cappuccino Cookies, 91
Chocolate-Mocha Cheesecake, 70
Frozen Tiramisu Squares, 74
Mocha Fondue, 80

Coffee cakes
Caramel Bubble Ring, 64
Easy Cranberry-Orange Ring, 122
Pecan Streusel Coffee Cake, 62

Coleslaw, On-the-Side, 139

Cookies. See also Bar cookies
Angel Kisses, 100
Browned Butter Cookies, 84
Candy Cane Shortbread, 86
Carrot Cake Cookies, 90
Cashew, Chocolate, and Butterscotch Cookies, 87
Chewy Coconut Macaroons, 87
Chocolate Cappuccino Cookies, 91

Chocolate-Dipped Eggnog Spritz Sticks, 121
Christmas Macaroon Mix, 126
Crackled Sugar Cookies, 84
Fairy Dust Cookies, 85
Little Lemon Snowbites, 90
Maple-Cinnamon Wedges, 88
Orange-Iced Fruitcake Cookies, 88
Peppermint Thins, 91
Strawberry Meringue Stars, 101
Super-Simple Sugar Cookies, 88
Thumbprint Sugar Plum Pies, 89

Corn, Scalloped, 27
Countdown, Christmas, 14
Couscous, Apricot, and Spinach Dressing, 24
Crab-Cauliflower Chowder, 10

Cranberries
Christmas Chutney, 12
Cranberry-Pear Sauce, 13
Easy Cranberry-Orange Ring, 122
Holiday Nibblers, 30

Cream cheese. See also Cheesecakes
Chocolate Chip Cream Bars, 92
Cream Cheese–Filled French Toast, 52
Double Chocolate Cream Bars, 92
Stuffed Jalapeños, 42
Tropical Snowballs, 99

Crostini, Shrimp, 32

D

Dates
Orange-Iced Fruitcake Cookies, 88
Prosciutto-Wrapped Dates, 42
Snack Truffles, 98

Desserts. See also Cakes; Candies; Cookies; Pies
Blueberry Crisp, 78
Chocolate-Peppermint Malts, 80
Chocolate-Sauced Pears, 81
Dutch Almond Cherry-Filled Braids, 78
Frozen Tiramisu Squares, 74
Fruit-Filled Napoleons, 154
Heavenly Hot Fudge Sauce, 128
Lemon Mousse Tarts, 154
Mixed Berry Cobbler, 111
Mocha Fondue, 80
Old-Fashioned Rice Pudding, 110
Plump Apple Dumplings with Caramel Sauce, 79
Pretty Pear Gingerbread Tart, 80
Slow-Cooked Apple Betty, 110

Dips and spreads
Asian Shrimp Dip, 34
Asparagus with Dijon-Horseradish Dip, 35
Blue Cheese Ball, 37
Chile and Chorizo Cheese Dip, 39
Coconut Shrimp with Mango-Ginger Dip, 34
Feta-Walnut Dip, 36
Garlic and Spinach Dip with Pita Wedges, 142
Layered Black Bean Dip, 143
Mocha Fondue, 80
Monterey Jack Fondue, 36
Quick Chile Con Queso Dip, 37
Roasted Red Pepper Spread, 128
Southwest Cheese Fondue, 35

Dressings and stuffings
Apricot, Spinach, and Couscous Dressing, 24
Fruit and Pecan Stuffing, 104

Sage Dressing, 105

Drinks
Chocolate-Peppermint Malts, 80
Easy Eggnog Fix-Ups, 31
Fruity Holiday Punch, 31
Tomato Sipper, 31

E

Eggnog, Easy, Fix-Ups, 31

Eggs
Autumn Frittata, 46
Baked Denver Strata, 49
Cheesy Ham Quiche, 49
egg dishes, names for, 48
Hash Brown Omelet, 47
Stuffed Eggs, 142
Tortilla Skillet, 46
Turkey-Asparagus Brunch Bake, 48

F

Fennel
Autumn Frittata, 46
buying and preparing, 46

Feta-Walnut Dip, 36

Figs
Christmas Chutney, 12
Golden Fruit Holiday Salad, 11

First courses
Alpine Cheese Soup, 144
Asparagus and Squash Soup, 10
Cauliflower-Crab Chowder, 10
Creamy Wild Rice, Mushroom, and Spinach Soup, 8
Golden Fruit Holiday Salad, 11
Mushroom and Leek Soup, 144
Potato and Leek Soup, 8
Quick Bread Salad, 11
Solid Gold Squash Soup, 145
Spinach Salad with Apples and Pecans, 12

Fish. See Tuna

Fondue
Mocha Fondue, 80
Southwest Cheese Fondue, 35

French toast
Christmas Morning French Toast, 53
Cream Cheese–Filled French Toast, 52
origins of, 52

Frittata, Autumn, 46

Fruits. See also specific types
Baked Fruit Ambrosia, 54
Christmas Fruit Medley, 54
Easy Gingerbread Bars, 94
Fruit and Pecan Stuffing, 104
Fruitcake Candy Tarts, 98
Fruit-Filled Napoleons, 154
Fruity Holiday Punch, 31
Golden Fruit Holiday Salad, 11
Morning Fruit Bread, 66
Oatmeal with Fruit and Nuts, 53
Orange-Iced Fruitcake Cookies, 88
Triple Fruit Fruitcake Mix, 127
Tropical Snowballs, 99

Fudge
Foolproof Fudge, 96
P.B. and Chocolate Fudge, 96

G

Garlic and Spinach Dip with Pita Wedges, 142
Garlicky Green Beans, 146

Gift foods
Chocolate-Dipped Eggnog Spritz Sticks, 121
Christmas Macaroon Mix, 126
Dried Cherry Scone Mix, 124
Easy Banana-Nut Loaf, 120
Easy Cranberry-Orange Ring, 122
Gift-Bag Fudgy Brownies, 125
Gingerbread Scone Mix, 124
Heavenly Hot Fudge Sauce, 128
Lemon Tea Bread Mix, 126
Little Peppermint Cakes, 123
Maple-Pecan Pie in a Jar, 123
Roasted Red Pepper Spread, 128
Split Pea and Tortellini Soup Mix, 128
Surprise Cereal Bars, 120
Triple Fruit Fruitcake Mix, 127
Gingerbread Bars, Easy, 94
Gingerbread Houses, 114–17
Gingerbread Pancakes, 50
Gingerbread Scone Mix, 124
Ginger-Honey Glazed Carrots, 24
Graham Cracker Birdhouse, 116
Gravy, Herb, 13
Green Beans, Garlicky, 146

H
Ham
Baked Denver Strata, 49
Caraway Potato Chowder, 134
Cheesy Ham Quiche, 49
Fruited Baked Ham, 18
Prosciutto-Wrapped Dates, 42
Tortilla Skillet, 46
Herb Gravy, 13

I
Ice cream desserts
Chocolate-Peppermint Malts, 80
Frozen Tiramisu Squares, 74
Peppermint-Stick Pie, 75
Ingredients, pantry, 136

L
Lamb, Roast Leg of, Dijon-Rosemary, 16
Leftovers, transforming, 139
Lemons
juice and zest yields, 71
Lemon Mousse Tarts, 154
Lemon Tea Bread Mix, 126
Little Lemon Snowbites, 90
Nutmeg Cake with Lemon Sauce, 71
Linguine with Scallops and Capers, 152
Lobster Tails, Broiled, 151
Log Cabin, Rustic Pretzel, 114

M
Macaroons
Chewy Coconut Macaroons, 87
Chocolate-Macaroon Cheesecake, 70
Christmas Macaroon Mix, 126
Main dishes
Apricot-Glazed Spiced Pork Roast, 17
Broiled Lobster Tails, 151
Caraway Potato Chowder, 134
Cherried Pork Roast, 108
Chicken Tacos, 132
Chicken Teriyaki, 137
Creamy Tuna Mac, 136
Dijon-Rosemary Roast Leg of Lamb, 16

Easy Shepherd's Pie, 135
Easy Sweet-and-Sour Chicken, 136
Fruited Baked Ham, 18
Holiday Beef Tenderloin, 18
Italian-Style Steak and Shrimp Skewers, 150
Linguine with Scallops and Capers, 152
One-Pot Pesto Pasta, 138
Pasta with Three Cheeses, 147
Pork Diane, 153
Saucy Sloppy Joes, 132
Speedy Turkey Wraps, 132
Spicy Glazed Turkey Breast, 16
Steak and Mushrooms, 150
Stroganoff-Sauced Beef Roast, 134
Tortellini with Basil-Alfredo Sauce, 149
Tuna Salad with a Twist, 133
Turkey Roast Chablis, 108
Turkey with Raspberry Sauce, 14
Two-Tomato Pasta, 138
Veal Chops with Vegetables, 152
Maple syrup
Maple-Bacon Oven Pancake, 51
Maple-Cinnamon Wedges, 88
Maple-Glazed Brussels Sprouts
and Onions, 26
Maple-Nut Butter, 124
Maple-Pecan Pie in a Jar, 123
Mushrooms
Creamy Wild Rice, Mushroom, and Spinach
Soup, 8
Mostly Mushroom Popovers, 59
Mushroom and Leek Soup, 144
Spicy Spinach-Stuffed Mushrooms, 43
Steak and Mushrooms, 150
Stroganoff-Sauced Beef Roast, 134
Wild Rice and Spinach Skillet, 22

N
Nutmeg Cake with Lemon Sauce, 71
**Nuts. See also Almonds; Peanuts; Pecans;
Walnuts**
Cashew, Chocolate, and Butterscotch
Cookies, 87
Crunchy Pound Cake Slices, 73
Holiday Nibblers, 30
Oatmeal with Fruit and Nuts, 53
Triple-Nut Chocolate Torte, 72

O
Oats
Cashew, Chocolate, and Butterscotch
Cookies, 87
Oatmeal with Fruit and Nuts, 53
Omelet, Hash Brown, 47
Onions
Caramelized Onions and Potatoes, 105
Maple-Glazed Brussels Sprouts and
Onions, 26
Sweet Baby Carrots, 106
Oranges
Baked Fruit Ambrosia, 54
Easy Cranberry-Orange Ring, 122
juice and zest yields, 71
Orange Biscuit Rolls, 65
Orange-Iced Fruitcake Cookies, 88

P
Pancakes
Banana Pancakes, 51

Gingerbread Pancakes, 50
Maple-Bacon Oven Pancake, 51
Parmesan Rosettes, 60
Parsley-Herb Rice, 21
Pasta
Creamy Tuna Mac, 136
Linguine with Scallops and Capers, 152
One-Pot Pesto Pasta, 138
Pasta with Three Cheeses, 147
Split Pea and Tortellini Soup Mix, 128
Tortellini with Basil-Alfredo Sauce, 149
Two-Tomato Pasta, 138
Peanut butter
P.B. and Chocolate Fudge, 96
Rocky Road Clusters, 98
Surprise Cereal Bars, 120
Peanuts
P.B. and Chocolate Fudge, 96
Peanut Brittle Bars, 93
Rocky Road Clusters, 98
Sweet-and-Salty Peanut Rolls, 100
Pears
Chocolate-Sauced Pears, 81
Cranberry-Pear Sauce, 13
Pretty Pear Gingerbread Tart, 80
Peas and Celery, Sautéed, 27
Pecans
Blue Cheese–Pecan Phyllo Bites, 40
Caramel Bubble Ring, 64
Chocolate-Pecan Chess Pie, 76
Easy Gingerbread Bars, 94
Fruit and Pecan Stuffing, 104
Maple-Nut Butter, 124
Maple-Pecan Pie in a Jar, 123
Pecan Streusel Coffee Cake, 62
Quick Toffee Delight, 97
Spicy-Savory Snack Mix, 30
Spinach Salad with Apples and Pecans, 12
Peppermint
Candy Cane Shortbread, 86
Chocolate-Peppermint Malts, 80
Little Peppermint Cakes, 123
Marbled Mint Candy, 97
Peppermint-Stick Pie, 75
Peppermint Thins, 91
Peppers
Baked Denver Strata, 49
Chile and Chorizo Cheese Dip, 39
Easy Sweet-and-Sour Chicken, 136
Quick Chile Con Queso Dip, 37
Roasted Red Pepper Spread, 128
Stuffed Jalapeños, 42
Tortellini with Basil-Alfredo Sauce, 149
Pies
Chocolate-Pecan Chess Pie, 76
easy ideas for, 77
Maple-Pecan Pie in a Jar, 123
No-Peel Apple Pie, 76
Peppermint-Stick Pie, 75
Pineapple
Baked Fruit Ambrosia, 54
Easy Sweet-and-Sour Chicken, 136
Fruity Holiday Punch, 31
Orange-Iced Fruitcake Cookies, 88
Pita chips, easy ideas for, 143
Pita Wedges, Toasted, 143
Popovers, Mostly Mushroom, 59
Pork. See also Bacon; Ham; Sausages
Apricot-Glazed Spiced Pork Roast, 17

Cherried Pork Roast, 108
Pork Diane, 153
Potatoes. See also Sweet potatoes
Caramelized Onions and Potatoes, 105
Caraway Potato Chowder, 134
Easy Roasted Potatoes, 21
Easy Shepherd's Pie, 135
Festive Cheesy Potatoes, 107
Hash Brown Omelet, 47
Lemony Asparagus and New Potatoes, 20
Potato and Leek Soup, 8
Savory Mashed Potatoes, 20
Sour Cream Smashed Potatoes, 149
varieties of, 23
Volcano Potatoes, 146
Walnut-Sage Potatoes, 22
Pretzels
Holiday Nibblers, 30
Rustic Pretzel Log Cabin, 114
Spicy-Savory Snack Mix, 30
Prosciutto-Wrapped Dates, 42
Pudding, Rice, Old-Fashioned, 110
Pumpkin Crescent Rolls, 66

Q

Quiche, Cheesy Ham, 49

R

Rice
Baked Risotto, 148
Creamy Wild Rice, Mushroom, and Spinach Soup, 8
Old-Fashioned Rice Pudding, 110
Parsley-Herb Rice, 21
Wild Rice and Spinach Skillet, 22
Wild Rice Pilaf with Squash, 107
Risotto, Baked, 148
Rolls
Blueberry Breakfast Rolls, 63
Orange Biscuit Rolls, 65
Parmesan Rosettes, 60
Pumpkin Crescent Rolls, 66

S

Sage Dressing, 105
Salads
deli, add-ins for, 134
Golden Fruit Holiday Salad, 11
On-the-Side Coleslaw, 139
Quick Bread Salad, 11
Spinach Salad with Apples and Pecans, 12
Tuna Salad with a Twist, 133
Salami Cone Skewers, 42
Sandwiches
Saucy Sloppy Joes, 132
Speedy Turkey Wraps, 132
Tuna Salad with a Twist, 133
Sauces
Cranberry-Pear Sauce, 13
Heavenly Hot Fudge Sauce, 128
Herb Gravy, 13
pan sauces, preparing, 152
Sausages
Chile and Chorizo Cheese Dip, 39
One-Pot Pesto Pasta, 138
Spicy Spinach-Stuffed Mushrooms, 43
Scallops and Capers, Linguine with, 152
Scones
Dried Cherry Scone Mix, 124

Gingerbread Scone Mix, 124
Shellfish. See also Shrimp
Broiled Lobster Tails, 151
Cauliflower-Crab Chowder, 10
Linguine with Scallops and Capers, 152
Shepherd's Pie, Easy, 135
Shortbread, Candy Cane, 86
Shrimp
Asian Shrimp Dip, 34
Coconut Shrimp with Mango-Ginger Dip, 34
Italian-Style Steak and Shrimp Skewers, 150
Oriental Shrimp Kabobs, 32
Shrimp Crostini, 32
Shrimp Salad Toasts, 32
Side dishes
Almond Broccoli, 25
Apple-Spiced Sweet Potatoes, 106
Apricot, Spinach, and Couscous Dressing, 24
Baked Risotto, 148
Caramelized Onions and Potatoes, 105
Easy Roasted Potatoes, 21
Festive Cheesy Potatoes, 107
Fruit and Pecan Stuffing, 104
Garlicky Green Beans, 146
Ginger-Honey Glazed Carrots, 24
Glazed Sweet Potatoes, 19
Lemony Asparagus and New Potatoes, 20
Maple-Glazed Brussels Sprouts and Onions, 26
On-the-Side Coleslaw, 139
Parsley-Herb Rice, 21
Roasted Asparagus, 147
Sage Dressing, 105
Sautéed Peas and Celery, 27
Savory Mashed Potatoes, 20
Scalloped Corn, 27
Sour Cream Smashed Potatoes, 149
Sweet Baby Carrots, 106
Volcano Potatoes, 146
Walnut-Sage Potatoes, 22
Wild Rice and Spinach Skillet, 22
Wild Rice Pilaf with Squash, 107
Slow cooker dishes
Apple-Spiced Sweet Potatoes, 106
Caramelized Onions and Potatoes, 105
Cherried Pork Roast, 108
Festive Cheesy Potatoes, 107
Fruit and Pecan Stuffing, 104
Mixed Berry Cobbler, 111
Old-Fashioned Rice Pudding, 110
Sage Dressing, 105
Slow-Cooked Apple Betty, 110
Sweet Baby Carrots, 106
Tomato Sipper, 31
Turkey Roast Chablis, 108
Wild Rice Pilaf with Squash, 107
Soups
Alpine Cheese Soup, 144
Asparagus and Squash Soup, 10
Caraway Potato Chowder, 134
Cauliflower-Crab Chowder, 10
Creamy Wild Rice, Mushroom, and Spinach Soup, 8
healthful thickeners for, 8
Mushroom and Leek Soup, 144
Potato and Leek Soup, 8
Solid Gold Squash Soup, 145
Split Pea and Tortellini Soup Mix, 128

Spinach
Apricot, Spinach, and Couscous Dressing, 24
Creamy Wild Rice, Mushroom, and Spinach Soup, 8
Garlic and Spinach Dip with Pita Wedges, 142
Spicy Spinach-Stuffed Mushrooms, 43
Spinach Salad with Apples and Pecans, 12
Wild Rice and Spinach Skillet, 22
Split Pea and Tortellini Soup Mix, 128
Squash
Asparagus and Squash Soup, 10
Pumpkin Crescent Rolls, 66
Solid Gold Squash Soup, 145
Wild Rice Pilaf with Squash, 107
Strata, Baked Denver, 49
Strawberry Meringue Stars, 101
Stroganoff-Sauced Beef Roast, 134
Sweet potatoes
Apple-Spiced Sweet Potatoes, 106
Autumn Frittata, 46
Glazed Sweet Potatoes, 19
Potato and Leek Soup, 8

T

Tacos, Chicken, 132
Tarts
Lemon Mousse Tarts, 154
Pretty Pear Gingerbread Tart, 80
Toffee Delight, Quick, 97
Tomatoes
Tomato Sipper, 31
Two-Tomato Pasta, 138
Tortillas
Chicken Tacos, 132
Speedy Turkey Wraps, 132
Tortilla Skillet, 46
Truffles, Snack, 98
Tuna
Creamy Tuna Mac, 136
Tuna Salad with a Twist, 133
Turkey
frozen, thawing, 16
Speedy Turkey Wraps, 132
Spicy Glazed Turkey Breast, 16
Turkey-Asparagus Brunch Bake, 48
Turkey Roast Chablis, 108
Turkey with Raspberry Sauce, 14

V

Veal Chops with Vegetables, 152

W

Walnuts
Blue Cheese Ball, 37
Easy Banana-Nut Loaf, 120
Feta-Walnut Dip, 36
Snack Truffles, 98
Walnut-Sage Potatoes, 22
Wild rice
Creamy Wild Rice, Mushroom, and Spinach Soup, 8
Wild Rice and Spinach Skillet, 22
Wild Rice Pilaf with Squash, 107